Black Christology and the Quest for Authenticity

Philosophy of Race

Series Editor: George Yancy, Emory University

Editorial Board: Sybol Anderson, Barbara Applebaum, Alison Bailey, Chike Jeffers, Janine Jones, David Kim, Emily S. Lee, Zeus Leonardo, Falguni A. Sheth, Grant Silva

The Philosophy of Race book series publishes interdisciplinary projects that center upon the concept of race, a concept that continues to have very profound contemporary implications. Philosophers and other scholars, more generally, are strongly encouraged to submit book projects that seriously address race and the process of racialization as a deeply embodied, existential, political, social, and historical phenomenon. The series is open to examine monographs, edited collections, and revised dissertations that critically engage the concept of race from multiple perspectives: sociopolitical, feminist, existential, phenomenological, theological, and historical.

Titles in the Series

Black Christology and the Quest for Authenticity: A Philosophical Appraisal, by John H. McClendon III
Buddhism and Whiteness, edited by George Yancy and Emily McRae
For Equals Only: Race, Equality, and the Equal Protection Clause, by Tina Fernandes Botts
Politics and Affect in Black Women's Fiction, by Kathy Glass
The Habits of Racism: A Phenomenology of Racism and Racialized Embodiment, by Helen Ngo
Philosophy and the Mixed Race Experience, edited by Tina Fernandes Botts
The Post-Racial Limits of Memorialization: Toward a Political Sense of Mourning, by Alfred Frankowski
White Self-Criticality beyond Anti-Racism: How Does It Feel to Be a White Problem?, edited by George Yancy

Black Christology and the Quest for Authenticity

A Philosophical Appraisal

John H. McClendon III

LEXINGTON BOOKS
Lanham • Boulder • New York • London

Published by Lexington Books
An imprint of The Rowman & Littlefield Publishing Group, Inc.
4501 Forbes Boulevard, Suite 200, Lanham, Maryland 20706
www.rowman.com

6 Tinworth Street, London SE11 5AL, United Kingdom

Copyright © 2019 by The Rowman & Littlefield Publishing Group, Inc.

All rights reserved. No part of this book may be reproduced in any form or by any electronic or mechanical means, including information storage and retrieval systems, without written permission from the publisher, except by a reviewer who may quote passages in a review.

British Library Cataloguing in Publication Information Available

Library of Congress Cataloging-in-Publication Data
Names: McClendon, John H., author.
Title: Black Christology and the quest for authenticity : a philosophical appraisal / John H. McClendon III.
Description: Lanham : Lexington Books, 2019. | Series: Philosophy of race | Includes bibliographical references and index.
Identifiers: LCCN 2019006379 (print) | LCCN 2019012333 (ebook) | ISBN 9781498585361 (electronic) | ISBN 9781498585354 (cloth) | ISBN 9781498585378 (pbk.) Subjects: LCSH: Black theology. | Jesus Christ--African American interpretations. | Race. Classification: LCC BT82.7 (ebook) | LCC BT82.7 .M388 2019 (print) | DDC 232.089/96--dc23 LC record available at https://lccn.loc.gov/2019006379

Contents

Acknowledgments		vii
Introduction		1
1	The African American Quest for the Historical Jesus and the Problem of Black Christology: Who Was Jesus and What Is His Relationship to Christianity?	9
2	Black Theology and Christianity: The Philosophical Problem of Definition	27
3	The Critique of Black Theology: Richard I. McKinney on the Fundamental Elements of Christianity	59
4	Black Messiah as the Authentic Christ: Alternative Biblical Myth or Real History?	83
5	Whiteness and Christology: Why Does the Racial Identity of Jesus Theologically Matter?	115
6	The Color of God and Jesus's Divinity: A Philosophical Assessment	153
Bibliography		191
Index		205
About the Author		209

Acknowledgments

My exploration into the topic of Black Christology encompasses the combination of extensive study, critical reflection, sustained research, and most importantly the unconditional support of a host of family members, friends, colleagues, along with having very fine student research assistants. In the aftermath of an unexpected family calamity, the resolute commitment of the fine professionals at Lexington Books ensured the publication of my manuscript. Special thanks to Dr. George Yancy, editor of the Philosophy of Race book series; Ms. Jana Hodges-Kluck, senior acquisitions editor, Mr. Trevor Crowell, assistant editor, and Ms. Brianna Westervelt, assistant production editor, who went the extra mile by assisting in the completion of the final proofs. I greatly appreciate your understanding of my personal circumstances and confidence in this project. George Yancy is a colleague with whom I have fruitfully shared, on many occasions, the ideas that not only inform this work but also broader considerations on the philosophy of race and the history of African American philosophy.

Drs. Malik Simba and Stephen C. Ferguson II both not only read the entire manuscript but also offered insightful advice and timely criticism that vastly improved the outcome. Dr. Simba took time out from writing his own book to constantly encourage me to push ahead with my writing. Dr. Ferguson's contribution to this manuscript goes beyond just his superb intellectual insights that considerably enhanced the final product. Without his technical expertise and assiduous concern in assisting with important details on formatting and the like, this project would not have come to fruition. Furthermore, my comrade Dr. Terry Day presented me with his personal insight on Rev. Albert Cleage that sharpened my understanding of Cleage's notions on Black Christology. All of you have steadfastly buttressed my efforts at every turn, and saying thank you does not fully convey my gratitude.

Among family, friends, and colleagues who gave support at various stages, I must acknowledge my late parents Garnet M. McClendon and John McClendon Jr., the late William R. Jones, my late mentor Francis A. Thomas, my late brother in-law LaMonte Carter, Deborah McClendon, Malik Simba, Stephen Ferguson, the late Terry Day, John Mendez, Brittany O'Neal, George Yancy, Clanton C. W. Dawson, Ike Iyioke, Kerry Maloney, George Carter, Keith Parker, James Roper, Musa Foster, Dianna Reese, Kimberly Harris, Andrew Woodson, Renee McClendon, Roger

McClendon, Suzanne McClendon, Pia McClendon, Jeffrey Edwards, Dwayne Freeman, Percy Jones, Robert Bass, Wilson Jones, and Henry Foster. Over the years, each person made distinctively rich contributions to my philosophical views on Christianity. Notably, the thought-provoking discussions I have had with Deja, Maya, Marquis, Jordan, and Shawntre recurrently serves as the catalyst for deeper reflections on the substance of my work. Perhaps without them knowing so, they are persistently the intellectual sparks that ignite my deepest philosophical thinking.

Student research assistance from Ramon Wright, Nanfeng Li, Brittany O'Neal, Lorenzo Buchanan, Andrew Woodson, Kimberly Harris, Dwayne Freeman, Ayanna Spencer, and D'Antae Gooden—all have been an invaluable resource. Of special note, my student Tamara Porter assumed the crucial task of indexing. In part, funding from the Undergraduate Research Initiative (URI) of the College of Arts and Letters at Michigan State University provided some of the student research support. Student research assistance constitutes an immeasurable component expediting the successful completion of my tasks. Dr. Lydia Tang, archivist with MSU Libraries, facilitated both the student researchers and my own queries about vital reference materials. With a dedicated team of MSU librarians, Dr. Tang and Ms. Amy McDonald, assistant university archivist at Duke University, provided extensive support on matters of copyright obligations. Your due diligence (beyond the call of duty) is most appreciated. Additionally, the chair of the Department of Philosophy at MSU, Dr. Matt McKeon, supported my request for sabbatical leave during the spring semester of 2018. I thank you for that opportunity and your consistent demonstration of collegiality over the years.

Lastly, *Black Christology and the Quest for Authenticity: A Philosophical Appraisal* is dedicated to two very significant influences on my personal sojourn across the sea of life and struggle, my wife Deborah L. McClendon and my sister Renee L. McClendon. Without hesitation, they have maintained profound respect and astute appreciation regarding my philosophical (dialectical) materialist viewpoint on religion. I love both of you and indeed your resolute determination and unfaltering courage in our collective struggle persistently illuminates the path that the next generation of our family assuredly must follow. Although I am indebted to many of my family, friends, and colleagues, I maintain solitary responsibility for any mistakes in this book.

Introduction

Comprising a vital component of Black Liberation Theology, Black Christology has formally existed for over some fifty years. Although, we should note that the general public remained essentially unaware of Black Christology, until Barack Obama's initial candidacy for president of the United States in 2008. At that time, it was disclosed that Black Theology advocate Rev. Jeremiah Wright was the spiritual mentor of then Senator Obama. Obama was a member of Wright's Trinity United Church of Christ in Chicago, when the general public was abruptly and sensationally introduced to Black Liberation Theology and its ancillary Black Christology.[1]

During interviews with the media, Wright cited Dr. James H. Cone—one of the pioneering figures in Black Liberation Theology—as his reference point on crucial principles of theological merit. The very idea of Black Liberation Theology immediately raised significant questions about race and religion that astonished many in the white listening audience. As Daniel José Camacho observes,

> While Cone proceeded to reimagine theology and American Christianity, many Christians ignored him or rejected his work. The national spotlight brought upon Cone's black liberation theology in 2008 by the Jeremiah Wright-Obama controversy led to some sympathetic hearings but also sparked Christian accusations of "Marxist victimology." Conservative Christians have consistently ignored or rejected Cone—and liberation theologies—as heretical, unbiblical, reverse-racist class-warfare.... Even when he is not vehemently repudiated, I believe that Cone is largely misunderstood.[2]

Even though Obama ultimately terminated his association with Wright, nevertheless, Wright had the opportunity to expound on the basic tenets of Black Theology before the mass media. The footage of Wright's critique of racism in the United States set forth the alarm that Christianity in its secular import extended beyond the parameters of the white evangelical right. In March 2008, NPR's Barbara Bradley Hagerty interviewed several African American theologians. Summary comments from Dr. Linda Thomas were quite informative respecting the chasm between African American Christians and their white counterparts. Barbara Bradley Hagerty notes that Thomas conveyed, "Black liberation preaching can be a loud, passionate, physical affair. Linda Thomas, who teaches at the Lutheran School of Theology in Chicago, says the whole point of it is to challenge the powerful and to raise questions for society to think about. Thomas says if white people are surprised by the rhetoric, it's because most have never visited a black church."[3]

Lurking in the background was a decidedly Black viewpoint on Christianity that considerably differed from how Christianity is conventionally conveyed in the message associated with African American clergy such as Dr. Martin Luther King Jr. For instance, the conventional treatment of King's March on Washington speech ("I Have A Dream") is often presented as an acceptable form of Christianity, which—on the secular plane—appeals to liberal democratic principles. Yet, King's position on the Vietnam War and his criticism of U.S. imperialism and capitalist exploitation are often relegated to marginal concerns within the broader framework of his philosophy of nonviolence.[4]

In contrast, Wright's Black Liberation Theology, in the snippets provided by the mass media, appeared as significantly unpatriotic, radical in orientation, and ostensibly militant in the tone of its criticism about racism and the sociopolitical implications respecting U.S. governmental policy and practices. When this particular image of Black Theology gained public view—as a form of Christianity—we discern it gave more pronounced attention to Black discontentment with the racist status quo.

Despite the fact that Wright published his ideas on Black Liberation Theology as well as preached and lectured widely around the country, for most observers, however, the media spin on his views gained the most attention. Although there was considerable outcry regarding Wright's pronouncements on Black Theology and his critique of racism, the fact remains that the scholarly examination of Black Theology and its associated Black Christology primarily continues as restricted to the works undertaken by Black Theologians. Mainstream scholars of theology and the philosophy of religion, for the most part, have not considered this corpus of scholarship with due diligence.[5]

Accordingly, this text, *Black Christology and the Quest for Authenticity: A Philosophical Appraisal*, encompasses our philosophical inquiry on Black Theology and its attendant Christology.[6] Explicitly, this philosophical examination tackles how Black Theology conceptually maps its quest for establishing authentic Christology. In synopsis, we critically expound on the methodologies and arguments that guide how Black Theology specifically affirms Black Christology as the definitive paradigm for authentic Christianity. Wherein, it is presumed, authenticity is intimately allied with the historic liberatory tradition in Black Christian thought. The primary value of this quest for authenticity precisely resides in the associated presumption about the liberatory dimension of African American Christianity contra the oppressive stance of white Christianity.

Of special note, we contend that the descriptor Black—in Black Theology—has specified theological import. Given this theological import, the reader should be aware that the racialized character of theology immediately sets this discourse within the context of philosophy of race. How racial designations transpire—in theological manner—as overdetermining categories set the course for philosophy of race; namely, how philosophy of race substantially influences the interpretive contours, respecting the philosophy of religion as mode of inquiry.

Transparently, the overlay of such conceptual matters immediately places our work on philosophy of religion within the orbit of the philosophy of race. In this way, *Black Christology and the Quest for Authenticity: A Philosophical Appraisal* stands as a unique contribution to philosophy of race. This distinctive body of literature—philosophy of race—in its scope is continually expanding. Subsequently, African American philosophy of religion, we submit, considerably enriches its content.

In a nutshell, the racial formation of theology encompasses more than offering a racial description of the given participants within this dichotomous context relating to Christianity. The specification "Black Theology" in its meaning signifies how racial categories infuse determinate theological meaning and value. As signifier, "Black" indicates an authentic and liberatory Christology, while "white"—points to inauthentic and oppressive religious practices that in effect attempt at impersonating real Christian ideals.[7]

At the heart of the matter, we have an essential point of contention regarding how definitive theological meaning is affixed to racial nomenclature. Black Theology vis-à-vis its white counterpart epitomizes opposing conceptualizations of Christian theology. Hereafter, our philosophical assessment of theological claims concurrently embodies projects regarding philosophy of race as well as the philosophy of religion. Our presumptive context incorporates how the philosophy of race is intricately connected to the theological methods employed, which successively develops as the subject matter under philosophical examination. Our critical review of Black Christology must take into consideration how this approach renders the significance of race. Wherein racial categories are indispensably adjoined to the very meaning of Christian theology and explicitly Christology.

Sequentially, Black Christologists argue, white Christianity—foundationally—represents what amounts to racist theology, which stands as an impediment to Black liberation. Black Christologists also claim, this putative Christianity—irrefutably racist theology—was historically manifested in slavery, colonialism, and segregation. Moreover, this so-called Christianity endures today in white racist churches, along with civil religion, which we also find in contemporary society at-large. Wherein, the hegemonic civil religion presumes the United States is essentially the prototype for the racially framed cultural designation of "white Christian nation."[8]

Likewise, it is argued that its subsidiary Christology is correspondingly racist, remaining no more than an inauthentic form of Christianity.

Black Theology similarly claims, we can incontrovertibly state, genuine Christianity is far from the infamous white man's religion. Considering such realities—according to Black Theology—what is before us is not authentic Christianity. Consequently, Black Theology argues that African Americans should not reject Christianity, that is, base their dismissal on the false conception that the white man's religion is indistinguishable from Christianity. Proponents of Black Theology think that this conflation—authentic Christianity with the prevailing white religion—results in throwing the baby out with the bathwater. Summarily, the white man's religion is not a genuine form of Christianity. Therefore, we must seek "true" Christianity from behind the veil of racism, by embracing the historic Black Christian experience.

African American theologian Joseph Washington perceptively comments on the sociopolitical ramifications of this historic Black Christian experience. The critical outlook embodied in this Black religious tradition brings the issue of race and religion to the forefront. Thus, Black Christian thought, as derived from the masses of African Americans, ushers forth a critique that centers on the authenticity of Christianity. Washington declares, "The only radical human challenge to white folk religion and its social-cultural establishment is the Negro. The element of reconciliation has been primary in the religion of the Negro folk. They have joined it with the democratic creed. Both have been at the heart of the Negro folk; they have accepted the *authentic declarations* of these religious and secular creeds"[9] [Italics added]. Washington further suggests,

> Freedom and equality with and for all are for the Negro folk both an affirmation of mainstream religion and the creed of democracy as well as a protest against their repudiation in white folk religion. The heart of Negro folk religion is the heart of mainstream religion which, however, has been perverted by the white pre-consciousness. This perversion has repressed the heart of the religion and democracy, initiated by the "chosen people" and set forth in the Old Testament. . . . Freedom and equality with and for all—Negro folk religion—is the genius of the Negro folk.[10]

Equally, we must note that this text—in many ways—is a continuation of an earlier work, namely *Philosophy of Religion and the African American Experience: Conversations with My Christian Friends*. During the writing of *Conversations*, it became apparent that there was a pressing need to expand on several questions encountered along the way toward completion. However, at that juncture, the space and time available required more focused attention on the direct problems at hand.[11]

Additionally, given the immediate conceptual link to *Conversations*, it stands to reason that this text is de facto the second part of a two-part series addressing the philosophy of religion and the primary matter of race as a conceptualization on theology within the African American experience. Nevertheless, the reader need not have read *Conversations* to understand and appreciate the thesis, method, and purpose of *Black Christology and the Quest for Authenticity: A Philosophical Appraisal*.

Given this is a work in the philosophy of religion respecting African Americans—as with *Conversations*—*Black Christology* sets out as a corrective to the general omission of African American theological and religious thinkers from the corpus of the discipline. Most works in the mainstream of philosophy of religion simply ignore the important contributions of Black thinkers and scholars.[12] Let us now explore how *Conversations* forms the backdrop for *Black Christology and the Quest for Authenticity*.

The aim of *Conversations with My Christian Friends* was engagement in a conversation about Christianity, wherein Christianity was viewed as a specified belief system situated around core beliefs. For *Conversations*, the Christian core beliefs such as God, prayer, and biblical Scriptures were the primary objects of inquiry. These core beliefs, in a conceptual manner, stand intimately positioned with important presumptions concerning Christian theology.

In *Conversations*, we argued that the key presumptions of Christian theology remain: God is a personal God and the supernatural entity that created the universe; Christians must believe in the word of God and Christ, and it follows that the Bible is the inspired manifestation of the sacred word of God and Jesus Christ; Christ is the Son of God, and his resurrection offers the possibility of human salvation from sin; sin is the primary condition for the spiritual and moral context of human existence on earth, and Christian ethics are based on absolute morals as outlined in biblical Scripture and in accordance with church doctrines, creeds, and traditions.[13]

Key questions guided our discussion—case in point, "What is the value of Christianity respecting the African American community?" This entails such value in all its manifestations as belief system and worldview in dynamic interplay—that is, over the course of African American history in the United States. For example, going all the way back in history to African American enslavement, the Bible was the anchor on which African American Christians viewed Christianity as a viable belief system. Over the years, the common African American Christian viewpoint on ancient history was considerably shaped by biblical references.[14]

For many of our African American Christian friends today, biblical Scripture constitutes the sacred text that can assist exclusively in making intelligible their spiritual experiences and secular encounters. With devotional study as the primary method of investigation, the Bible—for many Black Christians—operates not only as a source of spiritual enlightenment but also as a practical guidebook on life. However, in *Conversations*, we explained and demonstrated what the limits to devotional study of the Bible were.

This was done specifically by contrasting the devotional approach with the methods of academic biblical study. Notably, one limitation is the fact that when the Bible is rendered as sacred text, it is removed from its social (human) background. Although human hands were manifestly involved in the actual writing of biblical texts, it—the Bible—remains for Christian devotees the inspired word of God and Jesus. From the Christian theological perspective, the elevation of the Bible to sacred text is unalterable. Consequently, any form of academic extraction gives the immediate appearance that with secular evaluations—such as philosophical appraisal—we have a devaluation of the status of the Bible.

Yet, from a philosophical perspective, what takes place, indeed, is a secular *reevaluation* of biblical texts. The secular *reevaluation* demands the reintegration of such texts into their social and historical milieu. The Bible becomes a worldly document as with other texts with sacred self-importance and earthly moorings—that is, religious books such as the Koran and Tanakh. The reintegration of biblical texts into their social and historical circumstances, for instance, is greatly facilitated by philosophical methods such as we find with the philosophy of religion.

In concrete terms, with respect to method of investigation, the philosophy of religion is not encumbered by Christian articles of faith as its starting point. Consequently, while the object of our investigation is substantively theological in character, our *method of investigation* via philosophical inquiry, critically applies rational methods based on secular principles. While this text, *Black Christology and the Quest for Authenticity: A Philosophical Appraisal*, tackles the formidable problem of theological subject matter, nonetheless, the reader must be aware that this is *not* a work executed methodologically in any theological manner, inclusive of Christian theology.[15]

As with *Conversations*, while this book is a scholarly endeavor, it is primarily written for a general audience. The idea of writing a book for the general reader on the philosophy of religion and the African American experience, undoubtedly, has an immediate impact respecting our method of presentation. While there are numerous endnotes to the relevant sources that inform this work, there is not an extensive treatment regarding commentary on the attendant secondary literature. Correspondingly, more technical points—when discussed—are rendered as annotations within the endnotes rather than in the body of the text. The reader can consult these referenced sources for additional comprehensions, but as a work of engaged scholarship, with a general reading audience in mind, the aim is to be scholarly without a great amount of technical challenges.

In their unique way, each chapter of *Black Christology* faces the intellectual challenge of wrestling with the questions in this introduction. Certainly, such problems and questions form the conceptual adhesive linking the following chapters. Consecutively the chapters are: chapter 1,

"The African American Quest for the Historical Jesus and the Problem of Black Christology: Who Was Jesus and What Is His Relationship to Christianity?"; chapter 2, "Black Theology and Christianity: The Philosophical Problem of Definition"; chapter 3, "The Critique of Black Theology: Richard I. McKinney on the Fundamental Elements of Christianity"; chapter 4, "Black Messiah as the Authentic Christ: Alternative Biblical Myth or Real History?"; chapter 5, "Whiteness and Christology: Why Does the Racial Identity of Jesus Theologically Matter?"; chapter 6, "The Color of God and Jesus's Divinity: A Philosophical Assessment."

A NOTE TO THE READER

The word, "Black" is capitalized when making reference to Black Africans and people of African descent. As a proper noun, "Black" is capitalized such as found with *Negro* or *African American*. Over a number of generations, there was a consistent fight to capitalize the word "Negro" as a way of establishing racial respect and dignity. Since the word "Black" has now come to replace "Negro" as the contemporary convention, this text follows in that tradition with the capitalization of "Black." As Robert S. Wachal observes: "The failure to capitalize Black when it is synonymous with African American is a matter of unintended racism, to put the best possible face on it."[16] Now let us move forward to our critical review of Black Christology in our first chapter. Our immediate topic becomes "The African American Quest for the Historical Jesus and the Problem of Black Christology: Who Was Jesus and What Is His Relationship to Christianity?"

NOTES

1. For a comprehensive and scholarly account of the events surrounding Wright and Obama debate consult, Carl A. Grant and Shelby J. Grant, *The Moment: Barack Obama, Jeremiah Wright, and the Firestorm at Trinity United Church of Christ* (New York: Rowman & Littlefield, 2013).

2. Daniel José Camacho, "Why James H. Cone's Liberation Theology Matters More Than Ever," *Religious Dispatches* (June 2, 2015), religiondispatches.org/why-james-h-cones-liberation-theology-matters-more-than-ever/.

3. Unlike most of the mass media outlets, Nation Public Radio did several in-depth treatments on Black Liberation Theology. Consult NPR Radio host, Barbara Bradley Hagerty, "A Closer Look at Black Liberation Theology," *NPR*, https://www.npr.org/templates/story/story.php?storyId=89236116.

4. Stephen C. Ferguson II, "King as Philosopher: An Examination of the Influences of Hegelian Dialectics on King's Political Thought and Practice," in Robert E. Birt, ed., *The Liberatory Thought of Martin Luther King Jr.: Critical Essays on the Philosopher King* (Lanham, MD: Lexington Books, 2012). John H McClendon III, "Is Our Belief That Martin Luther King Jr. Is a Black Philosopher Justified?" in Robert E. Birt, ed., *The Liberatory Thought of Martin Luther King Jr.: Critical Essays on the Philosopher King* (Lanham, MD: Lexington Books, 2012).

5. See Jeremiah A. Wright Jr. and Colleen Birchett, *Africans Who Shaped Our Faith* (Chicago: Urban Ministries Inc., 1995), and Jeremiah A. Wright, Jr., *A Sankofa Moment* (Dallas: St. Paul Press, 2010).

6. The capitalization of "Black Theology" as well as "Black Theologians" amplifies the notion that this trend is a distinctive school of thought and not merely racially descriptive of the given authors and practitioners.

7. Brittany L. O'Neal, *Apologia for Black Liberation: The Concept of God in James H. Cone's Black Liberation Theology and William R. Jones' Humanocentric Theism* (Doctoral Dissertation, Michigan State University, 2015).

8. Robert P. Jones, *The End of White Christian America* (New York: Simon & Schuster, 2016). Read especially chapter 5, "Race: Desegregating White Christian America." Furthermore Wuthnow states, "Although it is not an established religion, Christianity is the nation's majority religion, and its leaders and followers have often claimed it had special, if not unique, access to divine truth." Consult Robert Wuthnow, *America and the Challenges of Religious Diversity* (Princeton, NJ: Princeton University, Press, 2007), 9. Daniel B. Lee, "The Great Racial Commission: Religion and the Construction of White America," in Henry Goldschmidt and Elizabeth McAlister, eds., *Race, Nation, and Religion in the Americas* (New York: Oxford University Press, 2004). Carol M. Swain, *The New White Nationalism in America: Its Challenge to Integration* (New York: Cambridge University Press, 2002). Consult chapter 3, "Racial Holy War! The Beliefs and Goals of the Radical Racist Right."

9. Joseph R. Washington Jr., *The Politics of God* (Boston: Beacon Press, 1969), 154–55.

10. Joseph Washington continues his argument, "Develop not out of an elite breakthrough of its minority but the suffering of its majority, it parallels the genius of religion and democracy rooted in biblical faith." See note 9 for cited reference.

11. John H. McClendon III, *Philosophy of Religion and the African American Experience: Conversations with My Christian Friends* (Leiden: Brill Academic Publishers, 2017).

12. Representative works include: Louis P. Pojman, ed., *Philosophy of Religion: An Anthology* (Belmont, CA: Wadsworth, 2003), and Allen Stairs and Christian Bernard, eds., *A Thinker's Guide to the Philosophy of Religion* (New York: Pearson Longman, 2007).

13. Katie Cannon, Emilie Townes, and Angela Sims, eds., *Womanist Theological Ethics: A Reader* (Louisville, KY: Westminster John Knox Press, 2011). Cheryl Sanders, "Christian Ethics and Theology in Womanist Perspective," *Journal of Feminist Studies in Religion* 59(2) (1989): 83–112. J. Deotis Roberts, "Black Theological Ethics: A Bibliographical Essay," *The Journal of Religious Ethics* 3(1) (1975): 69–109. George D. Kelsey, "The Nature of Christian Ethic," *The Journal of Religious Thought* 2(1) (Autumn–Winter, 1945): 7–19. Riggins R. Earl, *Toward a Black Christian Ethic: A Study of Alexander Crummell and Albert Cleage* (Nashville: Vanderbilt University, 1978). William A. Banner, "Christian Ethics and the Moral Life," *The Journal of Religious Thought* 14(1) (1956–1957): 7–16.

14. Dwight Hopkins, *Down, Up and Over: Slave Religion and Black Theology* (Minneapolis: Fortress Press, 2000). Charles B. Copher, *Black Biblical Studies: Biblical and Theological Issues on the Black Presence in the Bible* (Chicago: Black Light Fellowship, 1993). Vincent L. Wimbush, *The Bible and African Americans: A Brief History* (Minneapolis: Fortress Press, 2003).

15. For a work in introductory Christian theology, read Howard W. Stone and James O. Duke, *How to Think Theologically* (Minneapolis: Fortress Press, 1996).

16. Robert S. Wachal, "The Capitalization of Black and Native American," *American Speech* 75(4) (2000): 365. For a further discussion of this issue, see John H. McClendon III, "Black/Blackness: Philosophical Considerations," in *Encyclopedia of the African Diaspora: Origins, Experiences, and Culture*, volume 3, edited by Carol Boyce Davies (Santa Barbara, CA: ABC-CLIO, 2008), 198–203.

ONE

The African American Quest for the Historical Jesus and the Problem of Black Christology

Who Was Jesus and What Is His Relationship to Christianity?

Christian theology is the theoretical framework for the analysis pertaining to the being, attributes, and works of God which chiefly emanate from his holy bond with Jesus Christ. Consecutively, this divine ensemble has a uniquely spiritual connection to human reality. Accordingly, God's very being—along with Jesus Christ's historic worldly appearance—is assumed to be divinely linked to human existence. Therefore, Christian theology is principally engaged in offering not only a definition of God but also an explanation of God and Jesus Christ's sacred relation to humans. For Black Christologists this sacred connection is preeminently involved with matters about race and racism.[1]

Crucial to the aims of Christian theology is the matter of faith. Articles of faith sustain the Christian believer's allegiance to God and Jesus Christ in their divine supremacy. However, the philosophy of religion does not begin with articles of faith nor presume such a divine relationship, rather it investigates such theological claims offered by Christian theologians. The reasoned assessment of Christological assumptions and claims guide us along the path of critical inquiry.

This chapter, "The African American Quest for the Historical Jesus and the Problem of Black Christology: Who Was Jesus and What Is His Relationship to Christianity?" takes us to the center of the subject matter respecting the authenticity of Black Christology. Most Christians are committed to an ensemble of articles of faith. Wherein, their principle article of faith involves Jesus as Christ (or Messiah). Sequentially, this infallible article of faith originates as the keystone of Christianity, the anchor for Christians regarding their religious belief system.

Black Christology is a specification on this cardinal belief. For Black Christologists, this core belief is considerably enriched by the notion that Jesus was precisely and thus authentically Black. Wherein, the authentic Jesus—manifested in Black terms—is fundamentally rooted in the history of Christianity. Subsequently, Christology immediately fastens onto the historical circumstances of African American life via the ascendency of the Black Christ-concept.

Indeed, it follows that the very authenticity of Christianity is significantly connected to presuppositions about race and racism. The authentic version of Christianity resides in the affirmation of the Black Christ. Correspondingly, white racism and consecutively white Christology stand as distortions on the basic articles of Christian faith. Black Theologian Joseph A. Johnson in no uncertain terms states, "The tragedy of the interpretations of Jesus by white American theologians during the last three hundred years is that Jesus has been too often identified with the oppressive structures and forces of the prevailing society. His teachings have been used to justify wars, exploitation of the poor and oppressed peoples of the world."[2]

Black Christology foregrounds the matter of race, and we discover that race evolves as the most decisive element in Christian theology. Theological categories, in turn, cannot be removed from race as an overriding concern, especially when constructing definitive Christological formulations. Accordingly, from a conceptual standpoint, the philosophy of race turns out to be foundational, regarding theological conceptualizations about Christology.[3] Black Theologian Major J. Jones affirmatively states the following:

> Black Christology is not a mere writing of another life of Christ; it is, rather, a liberating reflection upon an interpretation of the Black religious experience. It aims to lead the believer to encounter the risen Redeemer who is the Liberator of both the oppressor and the oppressed. Black Christology fuses the "Jesus of history" together with the "Christ of faith" into a third, new man—the Black Messiah of liberation.[4]

It stands to reason, Black Christologists generally presume that the historical person of Jesus—as Black person—is one and the same as the Christ of faith. Hence, the fact that Jesus as Christ is Black is more than a social designation on race, moreover, it is a theological assumption of prime importance. The conversion of race as social category into a substantively theological designation effectively merges the philosophy of race with the immediate subject matter of theology and the philosophy of religion. The concept of Blackness prevails in terms of molding the very essence of Christological commitment.

In sequence, this racialization of Christian theology becomes the pivotal factor in comprehending how its theological import encompasses the circumstances of present-day African American life. The Black Christ is believed to offer a living principle that sustains the spiritual existence—if not practically confronting the material conditions—of Black Christians. Moreover, the notion of Black Christ comes to be an essential component of authentic Christianity.

Therefore, the Black Christian Theology School contends that in a very fundamental sense, white Christology misses the mark regarding the actual legacy of Jesus Christ and the import of the real meaning affixed to his salvation (liberation?) message. This notion about the authentic Christian meaning of salvation (soteriology) substantially rides on the view, Jesus is chiefly—if not exclusively—the Savior of the Black oppressed. Concomitantly, the theologically genuine Jesus stands on the side of the Black oppressed and not racism nor white supremacy. Black salvation of necessity points to a specified form of racialized theology as authentic Christianity. This is explicitly manifested in terms of Black Theology and its associated Christology.[5]

Hence, Black Theologians in their critical inspection of white theology and Christology yield false Christianity. In its quest for authenticity, Black Christology seeks to deliver the necessary corrective as well as alternative to perceived racist difficulties related to Christology and whiteness. Black Christology, therefore, becomes an integral component of the Black Theology School, especially regarding its mission of confronting white theology in its Christological expression.[6] Black Theologian William L. Eichelberger argues,

> When one moves studiously into the realm of Black Christology, there is an important follow-up action which must be taken. One must initiate immediately an analysis of that which stands in dialectical opposition to the discipline he is articulating; therefore, any person beginning a study of Black Christology must surely deal with White Christology. One has to do an analysis of it. The analysis will divulge the fact there is a form of misanthropy in certain aspects of white Christology. There is a kind of corruptiveness in white Christology.[7]

Of course, the assumption "There is a kind of corruptiveness in white Christology" must be rationally demonstrated, thus based on the notion of—compared with—a differing kind of (antiwhite) Christology, which is established as authentic in character and free of oppressive ideology. Without historical proof of authenticity then what we can gather is that Eichelberger merely asserts what must be proven. It could very well be that instead of white Christology as the culprit, the real perpetrator of these tribulations was Christianity pure and simple. What is at stake is the presumption that authentic Christianity remains pristine and removed from oppressive attribution.[8]

The legitimacy of the authenticity claim must stand the test of critical review, specifically relating to Christianity's essential makeup as nonoppressive. Precisely with Eichelberger's claim, we unearth that it emerges from an a priori Christological viewpoint. Hence, Eichelberger's stance is not founded on an investigation into the historical formation of Christianity—that is, how in historical terms Christianity can be seen apart from the transgressions of putatively white Christology. In fact, Biblical texts contradict the substance of this distinction. Later, we examine how J. Leonard Farmer and Howard Thurman both approach the historical dimension of race, in the formative period of Christianity's development.[9]

Nonetheless, Black Christology is an approach that seeks to clarify the core meaning attached to Christology in the broadest sense of definitional categorization. What then is meant by Christology? By Christology, we mean, "[T]hat part of Christian doctrine concerned with the revelation of God in Jesus Christ. Traditionally, this has been expressed in the doctrine of incarnation, the doctrine of the union divine and human natures and the one person."[10]

This Christological doctrine—the revelation of God in Jesus Christ—centers primarily on matters of Christian *faith* rather than historical research and examination; wherein Jesus of the past is removed from the historical viewpoint affixed to methods such as empirical inquiry and verification. This latter approach—empirical research into the historical past about Jesus—is generally referenced, in the scholarly literature, as the quest for *the historical Jesus*.[11]

Theologians and biblical scholars alike have debated whether (or not) the quest for the historical Jesus is a separate concern from the Jesus Christ of faith, which is directly adjoined to Christology. For several Black Theologians, Christology along with the quest for the historical Jesus mutually comprise the same project. Thus, it is presumed that Black Christology—the Jesus of faith—ultimately facilitates the African American pursuit of the historical Jesus. James H. Cone's following statement is highly representative of the Black Theology School. He states,

> It should be made clear that this essay is being written on the assumption that there is no radical distinction between the Jesus of history and the Jesus of faith. . . . The key, therefore, to the baptism incident (and with others reported in the Gospels) for our purposes is not only "Did it really happen?" but rather "What is the theological meaning embedded in it?"[12]

Hence, Black Christology surfaces both as a matter of history as well as faith. Since Black Christology is a vital feature of Black Theology, then the meaning of Black Theology is crucially related to the perceived tasks of

Black Christology. At root, what we have before us is the philosophical problem of definition. Specifically, how we define Black Theology is overtly applicable to concretely associated Christological questions and problems.[13]

Consistently, we must also explore—in some depth—the questions, Who was Jesus and What is his relationship to Christianity? Furthermore, how is this relationship linked to the Black experience? Therefore, how would Black Christology enter the theological picture? Such considerations mandate that we ask, Does making Christian theology Black (in its orientation) successively engender Black Christology? This crucial supposition resides in the very meaning of Black orientation. Nevertheless, it is believed, if a Black orientation enables Black Christology, then we have made a step forward toward recovering the Jesus of Christian faith and therein the historical Jesus. This viewpoint on Black Christology precipitates some challenging questions for our consideration.

How do we determine whether Jesus is Black rather than white? Can it be historically confirmed that Jesus was a Black Messiah? Or is this Christological concept—Black Messiah—the product of faith commitments and theological construction? Moreover, why does the racial identity of Jesus Christ theologically matter? Do we have an anachronistic reading when race is inserted into the question of Jesus's identity? When such adjectives as Black and white come into play, thus signifying racial categories, are we speaking metaphorically or literally?[14]

Were the Jews a race, not to mention "Black" in racial makeup? Are we referencing an ethnic group or an association of strictly religious affiliation? For some Black Christologists, the idea of Blackness signifies a condition of nationhood. Therein, we confront the thesis that Black people in the United States are a Black nation just as Jews were in the time when Jesus lived. Thus, the theological substance of Black Christology is based on the commonality of national oppression and the ensuing pursuit of Black liberation.

For instance, Rev. Albert Cleage makes the argument that Jews were a Black nation, while Rome was a "white" nation with its attendant nationally oppressive and racist political structure. Subsequently, the theological meaning attached to racial identification is based on the historical precedent that Jesus actually belonged to a Black nation under white oppression. For Cleage, Jesus was literally Black and subject to white oppression. The Black Messiah was a revolutionary affiliated with the Zealots who militantly challenged Roman (white) authority and power.[15]

Nevertheless, how can we determine if the ancient Jews formed a Black nation? What is the criteria for judgments about Jews constituting a Black nation? Additionally, if the ancient Jews were a Black nation, does that necessarily imply that the Roman Empire was a "white" political structure? As a result, does the historic relationship between ancient Jews with their Roman counterparts subsequently emerge as a matter of race/

national relations, comparable to how we observe such practices respecting contemporary standards in the United States?[16]

Finally, how can we establish that Black Christology (as an expression of Black Christian Theology) is authentically Christian? Accordingly, can it be biblically confirmed—however that may be conceived—that white Christianity is not authentically Christian? What is the criteria for judgments about the inauthenticity or authenticity for judging various forms of Christianity? These are some of the questions about Black Christology that become fodder for philosophical appraisal.

This compilation of questions clearly demonstrates how the philosophy of race becomes vitally important to our deliberations on Black Christology. The racialized nature of Black Christology poses thought-provoking questions for scholars and students engaged in the discourse concerning philosophy of race. The historical location of racial categories—within the orbit of Christianity—is a rather complex issue necessitating rigorous philosophical analysis.

Nonetheless, many in the Black Theology camp presume, without question, that their theological position is not only authentic Christianity but also in practical terms that the liberation of Black people is a central facet of Christology. Major J. Jones argues, "In Black theology, we seek to make God's relation to Jesus more personal and particular. Black Christology particularizes God's redemptive act and relates it to the struggle of Black people. The human depth of the 'Word was made flesh' in Jesus Christ that Black people clearly see in self-identification with an oppressed people's struggle and aspirations."[17]

The advocates for Black Christology all agree that Black Theology and its associated Christology is authentically Christian. However, they do not all agree on the precise content and substance of Black Theology as well as what establishes the elements that forge Black Christology. In their broad consensus, what instantaneously becomes apparent is that white theology is not genuine Christian theology. Hence, we not only have the *displacement* of white Christian theology but also its necessary theological *replacement* with Black Christology. It is believed that this necessity—this urgency for replacement—becomes compulsory due to the continual religious oppression of Black people at the hands of those advocating white Christology. Therefore, with this push for replacement we have the equivalent arguments for Black Liberation Theology.[18]

This effort toward mapping out an authentic Christianity, that is, Black Theology—with its ancillary Christology—faces some provocative questions. Foremost, we have the question, "Who was Jesus and what is his relationship to Christianity?" Thus, the critical imperative of identifying Jesus and his concrete relation to what is defined—in Black Theological terms—as authentic Christianity. This problem converts into the subject matter behind our object of investigation. Explicitly, we must explore "The African American Quest for the Historical Jesus and the Problem of Black Christology."[19]

In substance, we're exploring the meaning of the declaration that Jesus is both an actual historical figure and the Christ of Christian faith. The implications of the historical quest—an empirically based venture—become far reaching respecting the formulations associated with Christology as a faith-based (theological) project. For that reason, we ask, is the historical Jesus the same as the Christ of faith?

THE AFRICAN AMERICAN QUEST FOR THE HISTORICAL JESUS: THE PROBLEM OF BLACK CHRISTOLOGY

The quest for the historical Jesus requires straightforwardly that we evaluate documentary sources, while the notion of Jesus as *the Christ* or *Messiah* has profound theological implications resting on biblical interpretation. What is expected of the Christ? Was he to liberate Jews of his time or instead save the entire world? Does the Messiah/Christ perform miracles or serve as the leader of a social and spiritual movement? How does the New Testament depict Christ? Is there a singular or multiple depictions? Does he have divine status? Is he a deity on par with God?

Such questions are the subject matter of Christology. In fact, it is an academic inquiry with substantial research in the form of books and scholarly articles. Nonetheless, for many Christians the quest for the historical Jesus and theological answers to questions on Christology are directly a matter of simply consulting the New Testament and particularly the Gospel texts.[20] Quite a few Christians believe the Bible is a history book that documents that Jesus is the Christ and thus Savior of the world. From this perusal of the New Testament, it is believed that we can ascertain not only the identity of Jesus but also the meaning of Christianity as religious worldview.

Now we shall address these two statements that highlight this matter, "The African American Quest for the Historical Jesus and the Problem of Black Christology." Our examination of these two propositions entails offering dissimilar views on the topic—the historical Jesus and his racial identification—from very distinguished African American religious scholars, Drs. J. Leonard Farmer and Howard Thurman. Among several designations, James Leonard Farmer Sr. was an Old and New Testament scholar, educator, social scientist, philosopher, and theologian as well as ordained minister. In turn, Howard Thurman wore many hats such as educator, spiritual advisor, creative writer, religious philosopher, theologian, and ordained minister. Thus, both men are well prepared academically to tackle our question about the historical Jesus and its connection to varied formulations on Christology.[21] Now let us review the respective propositions. From J. Leonard Farmer, we find he affirmatively states,

As the Son of God and the Son of Man interpreting God to men and adjusting men to God, there was a practical need for his [Jesus's] critical attitude toward Old Testament Scriptures. . . . He spoke not merely with documentary authority. . . . He created as well as related Scripture. Through his influence he founded a new "school" of religious thought. In some respects his school complemented, and in other respects contrasted, the old school. The Old Testament was concerned with *a racial God*."[22] [Italics added]

While Howard Thurman argues,

It is impossible for Jesus to be understood outside of the sense of community which Israel held with God. This does not take anything away from him; rather does it heighten the challenge which his life presents, for such reflection reveals him as the product of the constant working of the creative mind of God upon the life, thought, the character *of a race of men*.[23] [Italics added]

We witness that Farmer's position does not venture far from the orthodox Christological idea. In Farmer's Christology, Jesus was not merely a mortal man among humanity on earth. We observe that Jesus was a divine mediator and spokesperson for God concerning humans on earth. Moreover, Farmer informs us that Jesus had a "critical attitude toward Old Testament Scriptures." This critical attitude is reflected in the fact that the Old Testament was "not merely with documentary authority." It follows that Jesus did not approach the Old Testament/Hebrew Bible as a "closed book."[24] Consequently, Jesus "created as well as related Scripture."

We can assume that this created Scripture is a new form of Holy Writ. Now, this last point is something we must carefully examine. What Scripture did Jesus create? Are we to assume that the New Testament is what Jesus created or at least created what we know as the canonical Gospel texts? This is far from a trivial question. It is compelling since it is crucially attached to the problem of Christology. Did Jesus view himself as the Christ such as we discover with the Book of John or what the fourth-century church established as its creed? Where did Jesus document his viewpoint on such matters? Is our only recourse what we uncover in the canonical Gospel texts?

Most New Testament scholars know that Jesus left no written documents, not even a diary of his day-to-day life. So how did Jesus create Scripture? In his book, *John and Jesus in Their Day and Ours*, Farmer does not offer an answer to this question. However, in an earlier work, Farmer informs us that Jesus left no manuscripts of any sort. This disclosure appears in Farmer's book review (1944) of Clarence T. Craig's *The Beginning of Christianity*. In the pages of the Howard University School of Religion scholarly periodical—*The Journal of Religious Thought*—Farmer penned the following statement: "The unstated premise from which the study proceeds, a supposition now freely affirmed by all competent New Testament scholars that much of the teaching ascribed to Jesus in the Gospels did not come from him, but arose out of the experiences of the church up to the time when these Gospels were written."[25]

How then did Jesus create Scripture? Where can we find it? Why does Farmer maintain that Jesus created such literature, when there is no apparent body of works? If the entirety of the Gospels did not come from Jesus, then how can we determine their source? The answers to all these questions we will not give at this time, rather they will serve as a conceptual link or continuous thread tying together the forthcoming chapters of this text. What we can state at this point is that the answers to these questions do not rely exclusively on articles of faith. Instead, it is a pressing issue that critical examination of biblical texts must provide.[26]

It is clear that Farmer's insistence that Jesus created a new body of works allows for claiming that we have a fracture or discontinuity between Judaism and the teachings of Jesus. Yet, it becomes transparent the absence of actual works which in reality can document such a break significantly weakens his argument. Undeniably, we can observe that Farmer betrays his formerly well-established scholarly opinion. Thus, Farmer's retraction facilitates his alignment with conventional Christian thinking about the importance of the relationship between the New and the Old Testaments. Without well-founded scholarly grounds, Farmer elects the conventional approach to biblical texts, popularly espoused with the devotional method of study. We alternatively submit that the historical critical method is more suitable in this instance.[27]

The critical examination of biblical texts, consequently, is not grounded on the devotional approach to the Biblical Scriptures. We cannot assume there are self-evident truths affixed to the Bible and the portrayal of Jesus and his life. In fact, biblical texts have conflicting accounts on the life and message of Jesus. Not to mention, they have differing theological orientations that draw heavily from mythic presumptions.[28]

Now that we have covered Farmer, let us proceed to an analysis of Thurman's argument. If it "is impossible for Jesus to be understood outside of the sense of community which Israel held with God," then it appears Thurman's take on the Hebrew Bible could very well be quite different from Farmer's. Since the identity of Jesus rests on the foundations of his Jewish communal ties to God; therefore, it becomes most evident that this accent on the primacy of the Jewish community gives a humanist tint to the person of Jesus.

Consequently, we ask, Must we explore the Hebrew Bible to better understand who Jesus was? Is there something in the New Testament that might take us away from this understanding? After all there is much in the New Testament that is outright anti-Jewish. The very death of Jesus falls heavily in the laps of Jews, especially if the New Testament and particularly when the Gospel text of John becomes our source for the life and death of Jesus.

No matter how we may answer the above questions, one thing we can be sure about, namely that both Farmer and Thurman (in their respective interpretations) end on a note about race and Jews. Additionally, there are comments about Jewish theology that are specifically concerned with the racial notion of God. This stands as particularly important since as theologians they precede the emergence of the Black Theology School in Christian thought. (In fact, this subject of Black Theology and Christianity becomes the immediate topic of our next chapter.) As Christian theologians—coming before the advent of the Black Theology School—there is a tendency toward the impression that both men viewed Jesus in nonracialized language. Neither talked in terms about a Black Messiah or Black Christology.

Therefore, we must query, How does race play out for both men? It appears they jointly apprehend Jewish identity as racial in nature. Jews are understood to be not just people who share in a common religion but also persons with collective racial identity. Hence, we have Farmer's statement: "The Old Testament was concerned with *a racial God*" and then from Thurman, "for such reflection reveals him [Jesus] as the product of the constant working of the creative mind of God upon the life, thought, the character of a *race of men*" [Italics added].

We will begin with Farmer's viewpoint. Implicit in Farmer's idea of a "racial God," we have a racialized theology exhibited in the Old Testament/Hebrew Bible that contrasted with what Jesus taught about God. There are two options available for the interpretation regarding the Jewish God. One view is the idea expressed by the early Christian theologian Marcion, who argued that there were two different Gods. The God of the Hebrew Bible is not the same God whom Jesus talks about and claims as his father. Hence, we can discard the Hebrew Bible in its entirety. The rejection of the Jewish God results from the dismissal of all aspects of this God, including the racial element affixed to Yahweh. It follows that the affirmation of a new Christian God requires a completely new body of Scripture. Based in part on Paul's letters, Marcion of Sinope, in fact, was the first person to write a Christian Bible.[29]

We can presume with warrant that Marcion's belief in dual Gods is not Farmer's notion about Christian theism. Although Farmer's new school of religious thought necessitates Jesus bringing forth a new Scripture, this new Scripture both *contrasted* as well as *complemented* the old school of thought—Hebrew Bible. Having components that complemented each other would mean there was a line of continuity which persisted through the old to the new school of religious thought. Correspondingly, the *contrasted* elements pertain to the discontinuous components, which make creating new Scripture an imperative for Jesus.

Where we notice a contrasted relationship, we can assume it is specifically about the Old Testament and the adjoining theological view about a racial God. Farmer conveys that with the coming of Jesus—and his new religious school of thought—the true understanding of God is no longer bound by race. God is no longer a Jewish deity. With Jesus's proclamations, we ascertain that God subsequently becomes nonracial and universal. What is rejected is not the God affixed to the old school of religion. Rather we discover it is this wrong racial conception—false consciousness—respecting the nature of God.

Farmer's theological view is monotheism, and therefore it persists that there is one God and that God is absent of racial characteristics. In concert with this monotheistic conclusion about a nonracial God, successively, Jesus's Jewish identity—as racial appellation—has no significant theological meaning. For if Jesus is the Son of God and God is nonracial, then the same principle applies to Jesus regarding his divinely influenced status versus his human existence as the Son of Man.

In divergence from Farmer, we discover, in Thurman's view, the very "character of a race of men" is of no small historical matter. Expressly, if we are to understand who Jesus was, then his racial identity—as Jew—has upmost significance. While Farmer conveys that Judaism was a body of religious thought, which Jesus ultimately surpasses, in contrast Thurman recaptures the very life, thought, and character of Jesus within Jewish circumstances. Unlike Farmer, Thurman argues there is no contrast between an old and new religious school of thought. Thurman makes abundantly clear: Jesus's racial identity remains essentially communal. Importantly, this identity is based on the Jewish community, graphically depicted in the Old Testament/Hebrew Bible. Thurman argues that Jews are collectively a race of men, under the influence of God. Therefore, Jesus's racial identity emerges as pivotal for comprehending who Jesus was. Importantly, Jesus's racial identity—along with viewing God in *racial terms*—appear as sustaining factors in our remaining discussion.

WHO WAS JESUS AND WHAT IS HIS RELATIONSHIP TO CHRISTIANITY?

Our inquiry on the matter of Jesus and his relationship to Christianity is a progression on the African American quest for the historical Jesus and the problem of Christology. In the background of Christology and historical Jesus studies, we have the problem of what is the meaning of Christianity when functioning as the historical circumstance for identifying Jesus as the Christ or Messiah. Consequently, such works in the quest for the historical Jesus and Christology that structure theological inquiry require answering the question: "Who was Jesus and what is his relationship to Christianity?" With this as an introductory remark of clarification, we will start first with J. Leonard Farmer's penetrating statement:

> From the beginning of Christianity and for several centuries after Saint John the historical situation with suppression, oppression and persecution vetoed the hope of a gradual and progressive development of the Kingdom of God on the earth. When Christians could do next to nothing about saving human societies, they gave up the world as totally lost, and only waited impatiently for its sudden and certain destruction. . . . Still the idea prevailed among some that if the Kingdom of God should ever be established on earth, Christ must return in person and establish it.[30]

Farmer's statement "*From the beginning of Christianity* and for several centuries after Saint John the historical situation with suppression, oppression and persecution vetoed the hope of a gradual and progressive development of the Kingdom of God on the earth," implies that Jesus—albeit a gradualist social reformer instead of revolutionary—nevertheless, must have initially set out to establish the kingdom of God on earth. Therefore, the followers of Jesus were at first—when under his direct guidance—not in pursuit of a heavenly kingdom, and thus Jesus's religion was not otherworldly. For Jesus and his followers, the kingdom of God required social change and the end of oppression. In Farmer's account, Jesus assumes the position of liberation theologian, fighting for reforms on this side of Jordan.

On our closer analysis of Farmer's statement and his notion about "From the beginning of Christianity," we can infer that the *religion of Jesus* preceded *the beginning* of Christianity. After starting with the teachings of Jesus, what becomes known as Christianity increasingly evolves into accepting the status quo of suppression, oppression, and persecution. If this is the case, what occurred prior to the beginning of Christianity was the idea that the kingdom of God on earth was an immediate goal that was realizable in some near future—and Jesus was to lead the way into the kingdom of God on earth. Furthermore, since Jesus was the only one who could lead this movement—as the Christ or Messiah—then, after his death, some of his followers concluded that only his return from heaven could bring about the necessary social change.

In effect, Farmer characterizes the evolution of Christianity as growing into a distinctively historic religion, which drastically transforms from what it was under the earthly guidance of Jesus. Instead of fighting for freedom from oppression and persecution, there is the acceptance on the part of Christianity to wait for the coming apocalypse. If Farmer's apocalyptic conception points to authentic Christianity, it follows that Christianity is far from a liberation theology. Even the Blackening of Christianity cannot change this fact. The disjunction of Jesus (the historical Jesus as Christ) from Christianity—as such—is most apparent in

Farmer's view. Furthermore, since Jesus is committed to a nonracialized theology, then Black Christology has no meaningful value.

Thus, Jesus does not have the same goals in mind that ultimately appear as the substance of Christianity. The relation of Jesus to Christianity then becomes one of a drastic hiatus—a discontinuity and break from a worldly religion to a heavenly one. Sequentially, we think this conclusion about the discontinuity between the teachings of Jesus—the worldly kingdom—and Christianity—the heavenly kingdom—is explicitly stated in Farmer's proposition.

While Farmer explicitly states that there is a substantial divide between Jesus and emergent Christianity, Thurman is even more explicit about this estrangement and disconnect. This separation turns on a fundamental demarcation respecting the function of Christian theology as an oppressive instrument of Roman hegemony over Jews. Thurman highlights that Jesus was a cardinal leader in the Jewish struggle against Roman ideological hegemony. Therefore, we have Thurman's contrasting argument:

> I make a careful distinction between Christianity and the religion of Jesus.... From my investigation and study, the religion of Jesus projected a creative solution to the pressing problems of survival for the minority of which he was a part in the Greco-Roman world. Christianity became an imperial and world religion, it marched under banners other than the teacher and the prophet of Galilee.[31]

Thurman boldly states that there is a line of demarcation between Christianity and the religion of Jesus. However, it is not simply a matter of this-worldly focus contrasted to a heavenly one. Rather it is a concern about how a different group of people participated in laying claim to Jesus and his teachings via the formal mantle of Christianity. Wherein, Christianity in its very makeup is an imperial religion—the oppressor's religion—which is removed from its Jewish roots. Thurman supplies us with considerable substance with respect to the sociopolitical content for the expanse between the teachings of Jesus and Christianity.

Thurman highlights what are the Jewish roots of Jesus's religion. Moreover, such roots are located among an oppressed Jewish minority. Christianity develops into the official religion of the Greco-Roman world, the imperial religion that claimed universal scope. The considerable expanse between the religion of Jesus and Christianity effectively becomes the matter of an actual theological separation between Judaism and Christianity. In Thurman's estimation, the idea of some form of continuity between an old and new school of religion, which we found with Farmer, obscures the efforts to uncover what is the authentic religion of Jesus. This authentic religion, according to Thurman, was a survival religion aimed at the Jewish minority surrounded by the Greco-Roman Empire.

The creative solution to problems faced by this Jewish minority becomes the substance of the religion of Jesus. In stark contrast, Christianity not only fails to offer a solution but in fact it is the main problem. The problem affixed to how the Roman oppressors laid claim to Christianity as a weapon against the Jewish minority that were supporters of Jesus. It follows that the quest for authentic Christianity embarks on a different road quite distinct from the authentic religion of Jesus. Hence, Thurman tells us, Christianity had nothing to do with the religion of Jesus insofar as it became the very religious ideology that facilitated Roman oppression. Hereafter, Thurman concludes, "Christianity became an imperial and world religion, it marched under banners other than the teacher and the prophet of Galilee."

If we take this conclusion in conjunction with Thurman's first statement, namely that racially Jesus was a Jew, then logically he cannot be the Black Messiah as depicted in Christian theology. At best, in racial terms, he was a *Jewish* Messiah. Furthermore, given that Christianity is antithetical to the religion of Jesus, we can surmise that in Thurman's assessment then the Blackening of Christianity fails to advance an authentic Christology or at least it falls short of recovering the historical Jesus. At best, the Blackening of Christianity can only replicate in Black form what Christianity sustains by its essential makeup, explicitly operating as an oppressive rather than a liberation theology. Thus, in Thurman's view, Black Christology is not a viable option.[32]

In Thurman's considered opinion, the historical Jesus was a Jew and his Jewishness stamps his *racial identity*. Additionally, Jesus's Jewish racial identity has historical and theological importance. This importance is manifested in the special relationship that the Jewish community had with God. It goes without saying that Jesus was a key part of this relation, hence, the theological import of his Jewish identity. On this matter, Thurman departs from Farmer's conclusion. Where they do agree is that the authentic religion of Jesus is not found in Christianity as such. What became Christianity was not the religion of Jesus.

Undoubtedly, Farmer and Thurman both have given us much food for thought concerning the affiliation of Jesus to Christianity. While differing in their analysis, the same conclusion is evident—namely, there is a vast difference between Jesus's teachings and what we know to be Christianity as embodied by a definitive religious outlook. It should be self-evident to the reader, the selection of Farmer and Thurman for our initial commentary is not fortuitous. Although not committed to Black Christology, they openly confront how race is related to our comprehension of Christology and the historical Jesus.

In this confrontation, both theologians are not in alignment with the Black Christology premise that race is essentially linked to Christianity based on racial distinctions, where the Black versus white nexus is the key point of departure. For both, Jesus is neither Black nor white, they are not caught in the trap of an anachronistic reading. Contemporary racial categories fail to highlight the fact that Jesus was a Jew. On this presumption (about Jesus as Jew) they conclude how race is a relevant concern.

For Farmer, Jesus departs from Jewish racialized theology. Race has no theological meaning, since Jesus has a religious message that reflects on God's nonracial status. While Thurman concludes that race remains crucial for comprehending the historical Jesus and his theological message. The import of Jesus as Jew sequentially has determinate theological meaning. After all, Judaism as religious worldview has its own theological stance, which is rooted in how Jews (specifically as a race) relate to God.

As African American theologians, Farmer and Thurman have been long ignored in the main body of work with respect to the philosophy of religion. Significantly, although not generally considered by scholars as belonging to the ranks of Black Liberation Theology, Farmer and Thurman—as theologians of African American descent—provide us with an important set of background assumptions.[33]

This background no doubt illuminates how we can consider the prime question, "Who was Jesus and what is his relationship to Christianity?" Concurrently, two vital questions arose: first, how does this relationship illuminate issues about racial identity during the time of Jesus?; second, did racial identity have any theological repercussions? Our conceptual scheme made this most transparent, because the concern with recapturing the authenticity of Christianity (along with its ancillary Christology) was at the center of our examination on racial identity. Particularly with respect to Jesus and religion, the complexity of how racial categories are infused with theological content does not—in any manner—present the kind of evidence for reaching an easy consensus.

In due course, such considerations expedite our addressing specific questions: Can it be historically confirmed that Jesus was a Black Messiah? Moreover, why does the racial identity of Jesus theologically matter? These and other questions raised at the start of the chapter are directly related to the tasks before us in *Black Christology and the Quest for Authenticity*. With this chapter serving as our foundation, now let us move on to our next chapter, "Black Theology and Christianity: The Philosophical Problem of Definition."

NOTES

1. For works on Black systematic theology, consult Major J. Jones, *The Color of God* (Macon, GA: Mercer University Press, 1990). James Evans, *We Have Been Believers: An African-American Systematic Theology* (Minneapolis: Fortress Press, 2012).

2. Joseph A. Johnson Jr., "Jesus, The Liberator," in James H. Cone and Gayraud S. Wilmore, eds., *Black Theology: A Documentary History, Volume One, 1966–1979* (Ossining, NY: Orbis Books, 1993), 208.

3. Diana Hayes, "Christology in African American Theology," in Katie G. Cannon and Anthony B. Pinn, eds., *The Oxford Handbook of African American Theology* (New York: Oxford University Press, 2014). Kelly Brown Douglas, *The Black Christ* (Ossining, NY: Orbis Books, 1994).

4. Major J. Jones, *The Color of God*, 88.

5. James T. Murphy, Jr., *Defining Salvation in the Context of Black Theology* (Bloomington, IN: Xlibris Corporation, 2012).

6. George Yancy, ed., *Christology and Whiteness: What Would Jesus Do?* (New York: Routledge, 2012).

7. William L. Eichelberger, "A Mytho-Historical Approach to the Black Messiah," *The Journal of Religious Thought* 33(1) (April 1976): 64–65. Also, read Joseph A. Johnson Jr., "The Need for a Black Christian Theology," *The Journal of Interdenominational Theological Center* 2(1) (Fall 1974).

8. Hector Avalos, *Fighting Words: The Origins of Religious Violence* (Amherst, NY: Prometheus Books, 2005).

9. Hector Avalos, *Slavery, Abolitionism, and the Ethics of Biblical Scholarship* (Sheffield, UK: Sheffield Phoenix Press, 2013).

10. Van A. Harvey, *A Handbook of Theological Terms* (New York: Simon & Schuster, 1992), 48.

11. Albert Schweitzer and William Montgomery (trans.), *The Quest of the Historical Jesus: A Critical Study of Its Progress from Reimarus to Wrede* (New York: Macmillan, 1968). Helmut Koester, *From Jesus to the Gospels: Interpreting the New Testament in Its Context* (Minneapolis: Fortress Press, 2007). Howard Thurman, *Jesus and the Disinherited* (Boston: Beacon Press, 1996). Howard Thurman, "The Significance of Jesus I: Jesus the Man of Insight" (September 12, 1937), in Howard Thurman and Walter E. Fluker, *The Papers of Howard Washington Thurman* (Columbia: University of South Carolina Press, 2009). David Friedrich Strauss, *The Life of Jesus, Critically Examined* (Philadelphia: Fortress Press, 1973). J. Leonard Farmer, *John and Jesus in Their Day and Ours: Social Studies in the Gospels* (New York: Psycho–Medical Library, Incorporated, 1956).

12. James H. Cone, "Biblical Revelation and Social Existence," in James H. Cone and Gayraud Wilmore, ed., *Black Theology: A Documentary History* (Ossining, NY: Orbis, 1993), 175.

13. For a helpful introduction centering on Black Theology and Christology, consult Dwight N. Hopkins, *Introducing Black Theology of Liberation* (Ossining, NY: Orbis Books, 2014). Also consult, Frederick L. Ware, *Methodologies of Black Theology* (Eugene, OR: Wipf and Stock, 2012). Noel Leo Erskine, *Black Theology and Pedagogy* (New York: Palgrave Macmillan, 2008). Calvin E. Bruce and William R. Jones, eds., *Black Theology II: Essays on the Formation and Outreach of Contemporary Black Theology* (Lewisburg, PA: Bucknell University Press, 1978).

14. For a literal reading that Jesus was Black and the Jews (Ancient Israelites) were a Black nation see Albert Cleage, *The Black Messiah* (New York: Sheed and Ward, 1968). For a metaphorical interpretation consult James H. Cone, *Black Theology and Black Power* (New York: Seabury Press, 1969), and Gayraud S. Wilmore, "Black Messiah: Revising the Color Symbolism of Western Christology," *The Journal of the Interdenominational Theological Center* 2(1) (Fall 1974).

15. Consult Cleage, *The Black Messiah*, 3–4.

16. For critical historical studies on race and ethnicity in the Roman Empire, read Lloyd A. Thompson, *Romans and Blacks* (New York: Routledge, 2015). Geoffrey Dunn and Wendy Mayer, eds., *Christians Shaping Identity from the Roman Empire to Byzantium* (Leiden: Brill, 2015). Hayim Lapin, "The Law of Moses and the Jews: Rabbis, Ethnic Marking, and Romanization," in Natalie B. Dohrmann and Annette Yoshiko Reed, eds., *Jews, Christians, and the Roman Empire* (Philadelphia: University of Pennsylvania Press, 2013).

17. Major J. Jones, *The Color of God*, 97.

18. Joseph A. Johnson Jr., "The Need for a Black Christian Theology."

19. Edward J. Plum and Paul Harvey, *The Color of Christ: The Son of God the Saga of Race in America* (Chapel Hill: The University of North Carolina Press, 2012). Douglas, *The Black Christ*. Jacquelyn Grant, "Womanist Theology: Black Women's Experience as a Source for Doing Theology, with Special Reference to Christology," *The Journal of the Interdenominational Theological Center* 13(2) (Spring 1986), 195–212.

20. Hayes, "Christology in African American Theology." Raymond E. Brown, *An Introduction to New Testament Christology* (New York: Paulist Press, 1994). Bart D. Ehrman, *How Jesus Became God: The Exaltation of a Jewish Preacher from Galilee* (New York: HarperCollins, 2014). Jacquelyn Grant, *White Women's Christ and Black Women's Jesus: Feminist Christology and Womanist Response* (Atlanta: Scholars Press, 1989).

21. The son of former slaves, Farmer was born in 1886. After attending Cookman Institute in Daytona Beach, Florida, where he was a straight-A student, he earned a scholarship to Boston University in 1909. Lacking money for transportation, Farmer walked all the way from Florida to Boston. At Boston, he earned his bachelor's degree in 1913, his Bachelor of Sacred Theology in 1916, and his PhD in 1918. His doctoral dissertation was *The Origin and Development of Messianic Hope in Israel with Special References to Analogous Beliefs among Other People*. Farmer died in 1961. For important biographical material on Farmer, read Gail K. Beil, "James Leonard Farmer: Texas' First African American PhD," *East Texas Historical Journal* 36(1) Article 7 (March 1998). Also consult the African American Registry at http://www.aaregistry.org/historic_events/view/james-farmer-sr-born [accessed June 12, 2016]. The grandson of a former slave (his maternal grandmother) Thurman was born in 1899. Thurman attended the Florida Baptist Academy in Jacksonville, Florida, before admission to Morehouse College. He graduated at the head of his class in 1923. As with Farmer, Thurman was a brilliant scholar and graduated from Rochester Theological Seminary as valedictorian of his class. Thurman died in 1981. In *Conversations with My Christian Friends*, there is a chapter devoted to Howard Thurman. See "Howard Thurman as Historical Investigator: On Jesus—the Man—as Jew and the Meaning of Christianity," which is chapter 3 of the text. For more biographical information on Thurman consult his autobiography, Howard Thurman, *With Head and Heart* (New York: Harcourt Brace & Company, 1979). Both Farmer and Thurman were at Howard University School of Religion in the early 1940s.

22. J. Leonard Farmer, *John and Jesus in Their Day and Ours* (New York: Psycho-Medical Library, 1956), 64.

23. Howard Thurman, *Jesus and the Disinherited* (Boston: Beacon Press, 1996), 17–18.

24. Farmer's full statement is, "He spoke not merely with documentary authority, as if the revelation of God had been a closed book" (*John and Jesus in Their Day and Ours*, 64).

25. J. Leonard Farmer, "Review," *The Journal of Religious Thought* 1(2) (Spring–Summer, 1944), 164.

26. Van A. Harvey, *The Historian and the Believer: The Morality of Historical Knowledge and Christian Belief* (Urbana: University of Illinois Press, 1996).

27. Helmut Koester, *From Jesus to the Gospels*. Edgar Krentz, *The Historical-Critical Method* (Eugene, OR: Wipf and Stock, 2002).

28. John M. Allegro, *Dead Sea Scrolls and the Christian Myth* (Amherst, NY: Prometheus Books, 1992). Burton Mack, *Who Wrote the New Testament?: The Making of the Christian Myth* (San Francisco: HarperCollins, 1995).

29. Marcion of Sinope (James Hamlyn Hill [trans.]), *The Gospel of the Lord* (New York: AMS Press, 1980). Robert Smith Wilson, *Marcion* (New York: AMS Press, 1980). Markus Vinzent, *Marcion and the Dating of the Synoptic Gospels* (Walpole: Peeters, 2014). Bruce Metzger, *The Canon of the New Testament* (Oxford: Clarendon Press, 1987).

30. Farmer, *John and Jesus in Their Day and Ours*, 25.

31. Thurman, *With Head and Heart*, 113.

32. For Thurman's assessment of Black theology, consult his book review of J. Deotis Roberts's *Liberation and Reconciliation: A Black Theology* in Book Reviews, *Religious Education* 66(6) (November/December 1971): 465–66.

33. Read Justin C. West, "Mysticism and Liberation: An Exploration into the Relationship between Howard Thurman's Spirituality and Black Theology," *Black Theology* 11(1) (2013): 31–57.

TWO

Black Theology and Christianity

The Philosophical Problem of Definition

The topic of this chapter, "Black Theology and Christianity: The Philosophical Problem of Definition," further explores the racialized meanings affixed to Christianity. This requires particular attention to how Black Theology forms the basic contours of our inquiry on Christianity. The attempt to define Black Theology, at core, is a philosophical endeavor. It follows that our method of investigation centers on the philosophical assessment of claims, which are associated with the very formulations that definitively function to establish Black Theology as Christian project. While not all advocates of Black Theology are Christians, Christianity is in fact the dominant religious orientation. Hence, the term—Black Theology—is synonymously used throughout this work with Black Christian Theology, strictly as a matter of consistent and convenient expression.[1]

Why call upon philosophy for our discussion on Black Theology and Christianity? It would stand to reason; Black theologians would have as their subject matter—none other than Black Theology. It seems there's nothing philosophically complex here. On the face of it, Black Theology is whatever Black theologians do. Nonetheless, we do have before us the proposal for philosophical inquiry. The answer to "What is Black Theology?"—our initial philosophical question—arises from how the conventional definition for Black Theology commands historical description. Case in point, we often encounter reports on how Black Theology developed in the late 1960s, particularly in the wake of the Black Power movement.[2]

This fact prompts the rudimentary (historical) question, What were Black theologians doing before this time? Are we to assume, during this earlier period, Black theologians were not engaged in Black Theology?

Therefore, what does it mean to be a Black theologian, if Black Theology is not the subject matter at hand? What initially appears as a clear and basic statement, namely, Black theologians engage in Black Theology, becomes rather multifaceted—and, as we shall uncover, thus fastened to a host of philosophical questions.

African American theologian Frank T. Wilson perceptively argues that the declaration for Black Theology is essentially directed toward the call for Black theologians. He states,

> Clarification and a historically informed perspective are mandatory as this theme [Black Theology] is pursued. There is a sense in which the call is for *Black theologians* and *not for a genetically unique Black Theology*. This is predicated, rightfully, upon the assumption that the *only authentic interpretation* of the very "core of existence" and "structure of faith" by which a people have been sustained and renewed will come from those who have lived the life and known the faith.[3] [Italics added]

Our study in this chapter will demonstrate whether Wilson's presumption about Black Theology and theologians is true. We contend, this idea—*genetically unique Black Theology*—is not as far-fetched as Wilson believes. Along with the claim of returning to authentic Christianity, Black Theology jointly assumed the garb of 1960s "Black Revolution" rhetoric. Certainly, we unearth that Black Theology made bold (if not revolutionary) declarations about its new—*genetically unique?*—approach to Christian theology. On what basis was something new in the offering? Why declare Black Theology is something different and innovative in African American Christian thought? Did a revolution really take place in African American theology? We cannot overlook the context of African American theological culture and history, precisely when answering our previous questions about Black Theology.

There are certain assumptions affixed to the idea that the appearance of Black Theology amounted to "revolution" within African American Christian thought. For illustration, a revolutionary departure assumes a fundamental break from the past, which occurs in terms of acute measures toward progressive transformation. With revolutionary thought, the old ways of thinking are rendered as obsolete and moribund. Accordingly, can it be affirmed that Black Theology was a revolutionary development within African American Christian theology?

At the same time, how should we then characterize the work of previous African American theologians? Was it an outmoded approach to Christian theology? What was lacking in (or antiquated about) the efforts of prior African American theologians? Does the answer point to Black identity? If this is the case, why must the "Blackness" of earlier theologians come under question? In what way are they not suitably "Black" theologians? Moreover, how do we define "Blackness" in this context? Lastly, what is the motivation for decidedly proclaiming that African

American theological inquiry now embodies this new viewpoint—*Black Theology*? This last question, subsequently, takes us back to the relevant historical developments of the late 1960s.

In many ways, Black Theology sought to become the religious arm of the Black power movement. Hence, the impetus for this distinctively "Black" Theology was based on reclaiming Christianity for the Black power movement and the banner of Black Revolution—therefore, we observe, the ensuing adoption of a Black nationalist predisposition toward Christian theology. This predisposition arises because Black nationalism was the ideological foundation of the Black power movement and its revolutionary rhetoric.[4]

In summary, the alignment of the Black Theology School with the Black power movement fundamentally meant an ideological commitment to Black nationalism. Significantly, the prior school of African American Christian thought was not generally inclined toward Black nationalist ideology and its subsidiary antiwhiteness rhetoric. Working harmoniously with whites was the key objective of the earlier school, and this objective was viewed as consistent with Christian doctrines. The clue for the improvement of race relations corresponded with Christian fellowship extending beyond racial boundaries. Integration—rather than Black nationalism—was the chief tenet of this school. On integration, theologian Benjamin E. Mays argues,

> Integration, therefore, is a spiritual quality which must be achieved through love of and respect for peoples of all races, religions, nationalities, and cultures. To speak of a new social order when integrated is like speaking of a society which has achieved in reality the Fatherhood of God and the Brotherhood of Man. When society becomes truly integrated we will be approaching the Kingdom of God on earth.[5]

A significant number of Black power nationalists rejected Mays's notion of racial integration as well as Christianity, which were viewed as equivalent with the white man's religion. Black Theology sought to demonstrate it was white theology rather than Christianity that failed Black people. Respectively, Black Theology pursued an oppositional position to "white" theology as an authentic representation of Christianity. In advocating "The Need for a Black Christian Theology," theologian Joseph A. Johnson Jr. declares,

> Black theology emerged *as a reaction* against the so-called classical [white] theologies which have been unable to realistically and *authentically relate* to the theological implications of the black experience; *it is a reaction to the refusal of white theologians* to come to grips with the theology of the disadvantaged, the disenfranchised and of the oppressed. Black theology, in essence, affirms the centrality of the Scriptures. In this affirmation it calls for reinterpretation of the Scriptures, whereby they can be seen not only as *supporting the struggles for justice, freedom,*

and human dignity in times past, but also as a norm for the same endeavors in times present and for all times to come.[6] [Italics added]

Given Johnson's argument for Black Theology, we reveal there are two aspects of important repercussions: first, we have the relationship of Black Theology to its white counterpart; and second, Black Theology and its connection to previous African American theology. If Black Theology is merely a reaction to white theology—based on this assumption—then Black Theology in its meaning and very existence is dependent on the meaning and very existence of white theology. The autonomy of Black Theology is effectively undermined when viewed simply as a reactive project. We thus need to ask, Did the prior forms of African American theology persist as a reaction to white theology? Or did this preceding African American theology maintain some measure of autonomy in its pursuit of Christian theology?

Additionally, Johnson informs us, this Black (reactive) Theology centers on the interpretation of Scriptures. While it is transparent Johnson presumes a failure on the part of white theology, however, can we say the former African American theologians failed to interpret Scriptures respecting the norm consistent with "supporting the struggles for justice, freedom, and human dignity?" Any alternative claim that asserts the absence of this norm demands providing documentation in support for such a claim.

For illustration, how should we place a work like Howard Thurman's (1949) *Jesus and the Disinherited* respecting "the struggles for justice, freedom, and human dignity?" We ask because these principles were the centerpiece of Thurman's seminal work. In fact, they were present—in Thurman's corpus of scholarship—long before the emergence of the "Black" Theology School and Liberation Theology was in vogue. With respect to Johnson's criteria, are we subsequently permitted to correctly identify Howard Thurman exactly in terms of Black Liberation Theology?

About Thurman belonging to the ranks of Liberation Theology, Sean Chabot argues, "Inspired by his meeting with Gandhi in 1936, this 'liberation theology frame' expresses of the basic insights of the Gandhian repertoire in familiar Christian language."[7] In contrast, Vincent Harding is quite instructive. In his foreword to the Beacon Press edition of Howard Thurman's *Jesus and the Disinherited*, Harding states:

> For although it is possible to glean elements of a liberation theology from its pages, this richly endowed, seminal work can be more accurately and helpfully described as a profound quest for a liberating spirituality, a way of exploring and experiencing those crucial life points where personal and societal transformation are creatively joined.[8]

What is clear from Chabot's and Harding's observations, although Thurman is not closely aligned with the Black Theology School, he is far distant from Johnson's characterization of white theology. This raises the more general question, How did preceding African American theologians—not aligned with the Black Theology School—respond to the declarations of Black Theology? This question comes to light as especially significant. It is significant because this presumption—concerning the revolutionary nature of Black Theology—entails not only Christian thought in general, but also, more specifically, preceding forms of African American theology.

Did a "Black" revolution actually occur in African American theology? Or was African American theology facing what amounted to conflicting paradigms about the very definition of Christianity and its association to Blackness? Given its commitment to integration and Christian universality, the earlier school of African American theology was primarily critical of the Black Theology School. In summation, instead of revolution in thought, we have what are conflicting paradigms concerning the universality of the Christian message as related to the particularity of Blackness. What should not be missed is that this critical reception to Black Theology had substantial impact on the resultant definitional forms.

For us to grasp the big picture, we must be cognizant that the birth of the Black Theology School was a dialectical encounter of contending forces. These contending (dialectical) forces—within African American Christian thought—meant the definition of Black Theology resulted from more than an easily achieved broad consensus, wherein consensus was based on shared background assumptions. Truly, the lack of shared background assumptions—on the general principles of Christianity—was the major source of tension and the basis for critique.

In a substantial manner, the critique of Black Theology exposed fundamental theological differences. Indeed the critical response—on the part of fellow African American theologians—was crucially influential in the developmental process of Black Theology. Despite the importance of this earlier assessment, considerable segments of this critical rejoinder remained marginalized in the subsequent literature on Black Theology.[9]

Seldom do we find scholarly discussions on what African American theologians—Benjamin E. Mays, Howard Thurman, Richard I. McKinney, George D. Kelsey, Frank T. Wilson, and Leon E. Wright, among others—said about Black Theology as a school of thought. Although not members of the Black Theology School, the previously mentioned theologians were not silently awaiting its arrival—in the late 1960s—to make their mark. Long before, they made their own theological pronouncements on African American religious life and more pointedly the subject of Christian theology and white racism. If we would hazard to think otherwise, it would amount to viewing the emergence of Black Theology in a historical vacuum.[10]

In this philosophical inquiry, on the definition of Black Theology, our major emphasis and focus are consequently directed on the early development of—and parallel critical responses to—Black Theology. What should not be underestimated (by the reader) is precisely that this African American critical response noticeably materialized as a serious factor in the initial development of Black Theology. Hence, comprehending the nature of this historic critique tremendously facilitates our understanding of how Black Theology was eventually defined. Furthermore, the sustained body of previously conceived theological thought—by African American theologians—weighs heavily on the landscape of African American Christian intellectual culture. Its influence—even today—is of no small measure, particularly respecting the dominant (practical) theology found in many Black churches and religious communities.[11]

Therefore, we ask, What kind of theology did African American theologians pursue before the late 1960s? How should we define this theology? We could conclude that they—earlier African American theologians—studied and espoused some form of white (classical) theology, with the view it was pertinent to the Black community. The idea that Black Theology occurred in the late 1960s seems to imply as much. Does it follow that previous African American religious thought must be deemed as white theology, if it is not "Black Theology?"

The twofold differentiation of Black versus white gives us little room for any other choice. Yet, paradoxically, the very definition of Black Theology seems to be more a reaction that hinges on the description and definition of white theology. Joseph A. Johnson further explains,

> White theology has not presented blacks with good theological reasons why they should not speak out against this gross perversion of the Christian faith. White theology has not been able to re-shape the life of the white church so as to cleanse it of its racism and to liberate it from the iron claws of the white racist establishment of this nation. White theology has presented the blacks a religion of contentment in the state of life in which they find themselves[12]

We observe Johnson's distinction between Black and white theologies thus poses the question, What do we mean by Black Theology contra its white counterpart? This question becomes especially important if white theology is presumed to be racist on the very basis of its whiteness. Johnson claims white theology is a "gross perversion of the Christian faith" and that reciprocally Black Theology fundamentally comprises a reaction to white theology. Given this claim, we must query, Does Black Theology remain essentially an antiwhiteness theology? Furthermore, since Johnson thinks white theology is a perversion of Christianity, it stands to reason that this view presumes some idea of authentic Christian faith. Perhaps, it is the Black form of Christianity which is removed from whiteness.

At the very least, Johnson deduces that Black Christian Theology is the path to authentic Christian faith, a path paved by "the centrality of the Scriptures," wherein given what we know about white theology, the reinterpretation of the Scriptures is set against white theological interpretation. Therefore, considering the assumption that white theology is a perversion of Christian faith, is whiteness innately sinful and oppressive thus mandating an antiwhiteness posture from Black Theology? Can we surmise—from Johnson's argument—that the prior group of African American theologians did not comprehend need for critically examining biblical Scripture? Did they neglect the "whiteness problem?" Why, therefore, does whiteness appear concerning our subject matter, presumably suitable for critique as inauthentic Christianity?

The African American philosopher George Yancy offers significant insights into whiteness, respecting its status as our primary theological concern on Christianity. We should note, Yancy does not explicitly present any precise notions about Black Theology. However, his comments on whiteness are quite relevant for our deliberation. Yancy states,

> I think about how whiteness would have been nominated as a problem, as something that needs to be militated against, as a something that is both a deeply embodied problem and a form of structural sin. As it is a form of structural sin . . . [it] will have raised the distinction between those who are oppressors and those who are oppressed.[13]

Yancy continues,

> I argue that through a certain hermeneutic lens Christian theology and whiteness—that is whiteness as a historical process that continues to express its hegemony and privilege through various cultural, political, interpersonal, and institutional practices, and forces bodies of color to the margins and politically and ontologically position them as sub-persons—are incompatible. Given this understanding of whiteness, I agree with James Cone where he says succinctly, "Love is the refusal to accept whiteness."[14]

Hence, if we follow Yancy's logic—with an eye toward its application to Black Theology—if whiteness is a form of structural sin and correspondingly oppressive, then the justification for the antiwhiteness makeup of Black Theology is seemingly—in Christian theological terms—justified. At the very least, we unearth that Christian theology and whiteness are incompatible. In sequence, we can conclude that to the extent that Black Theology is Christian theology, it is incompatible with whiteness.

In response to Yancy, however, we think when whiteness is rendered as synonymous with white racism, therein lies the real danger. For whiteness is not necessarily racism. The claim that all white people are racist is rooted in the assumption that whiteness is equated with white racism. The conflation of whiteness with white (anti-Black) racism amounts to a category mistake. This category mistake is the upshot of binary logic, an either/or dilemma. The binary logic of Blackness versus whiteness is very restrictive and offers few credible alternatives.[15]

Despite this dilemma, can we fathom some other option besides Black and white theology? How are we to view African American theologians and their subject matter before the advent of "Black" Theology? Perhaps there is a middle ground (possibly Negro Theology?) between Black and white theologies. Where the idea of "Negro Theology" denotes—if not a different subject matter—then at least a peculiarly dissimilar orientation toward the subject of Christian theology and whiteness. Could it be that Black Theology's posture is antiwhiteness, while this putatively "Negro" theology is not? We must ask, Does this term "Negro" theology truly capture the substance of what preceded the emergence of "Black" Theology in the African American intellectual and Christian community? We will later, in this chapter, make the case that "Negro" contra Black theologian is an unsatisfactory rendering.[16]

AFRICAN AMERICAN CHRISTIAN THEOLOGY: THE LEGACY BEFORE THE BLACK THEOLOGY SCHOOL

Before the occurrence of "Black" Theology in the late 1960s, where did the great number of theologians—of African American descent—published their ideas? What would a content analysis uncover? By locating such sources, the empirical basis for our answers would render less speculation. One such source was *The Journal of Religious Thought*. If we were to peruse the pages of *The Journal of Religious Thought*—founded by Dr. William Stuart Nelson at Howard University in 1943—what would best describe its contents (for nearly twenty-five years) before the debut of late 1960s "Black" Theology?[17]

Certainly, we would discover discussions on the critique of racism, alternative Christian means to improved race relations, and commentary on the utility of the philosophy of nonviolence for social change, among other themes relevant to Christian theology and ethics. For illustration, in 1945, Nelson published an article, "Religion and Racial Tension in America Today," and white theologian Buell Gallagher's article, in the same year, was on "Conscience and Caste: Racism in the Light of the Christian Ethic." Furthermore, in an editorial (Autumn–Winter, 1945) entitled "Invitation to Imperialism," *The Journal* took a strong anti-imperialist stance by pronouncing,

> On this question [imperialism] the religious community needs, first, to come swiftly to an unequivocal conviction. It is inconceivable that such a conviction—soberly, thoughtfully, prayerfully arrived at—will be other than a profound distrust of any imperialistic designs. Having made its decision the religious community should concertedly and systematically oppose its influence to any movement to make us a nation

of international exploiters. This opposition should include the most complete cooperation possible with those so-called secular forces in the nation which are now so persistently calling attention to the evils of imperialism.[18]

In the same issue of the *Journal*, a second editorial spoke to "The Christian Imperative in Race Relations." Noteworthy was its editorial statement on the radical character of the "genuine Christian tradition." Almost twenty-five years before the Black Theology School's declarations on the radicalism of authentic Christianity, we have the following:

> A second Christian imperative is that action in the area of race relations partake of *the radical quality inherent in the Christian gospel*. The most serious influence of secularism (defined as the spirit of deliberate self-interest) upon religion has not been its opposition to spiritual values but its power subtly to neutralize them. The secular spirited confronted with need for social change is timid, tentative, ameliorative in character. The religious spirit in the *genuine Christian tradition is bold, definite, radical*.[19] [Italics added]

In 1946, Howard University philosopher and theologian, Dr. William A. Banner wrote an article on "The Transmission of Our Religious Heritage: Christian Ideas of Human Equality and Social Justice," and in 1956–1957, Dr. George D. Kelsey pens "Churches and Freedom." In this essay, Kelsey introduces the idea of racism as sin, manifested in the form of idolatry. In 1959, we have theologian and church historian Charles B. Ashanin's "Afro-American Christianity: Challenge and Significance." By the latter 1960s, increased Black activism generated more articles on the African American protest movement. Consequently, we have articles from (Black philosophers) Richard I. McKinney, "Existentialist Ethics and Protest Movement" (1965/1966), and Everett F. S. Davies, "Negro Protest Movement: The Religious Way" in 1967/1968.[20]

Not limited to Christian theology, Nelson and *The Journal of Religious Thought* approached other regions of religious thought including Buddhism, Hinduism, and African religions. The notions of world community and human rights were not absent from *The Journal*. Gandhi's notion of Satyagraha was introduced as a pertinent theological concept for African American consideration. However, what we would not find are calls for Black Theology, a distinctively particularistic theological orientation departing from the universal principles of Christianity—whatever they may be.[21]

Yet, we can still ask, How do such topics relate to the themes that are prominent in Black Theology? Can it be said that since it did not espouse a genetically unique form of Black Theology that *The Journal of Religious Thought*—for twenty-five years—was caught in the quagmire of white theology? Only a narrow Black nationalist interpretation—on African American theology—would allow for such a conclusion. However, this conclusion has persisted throughout, and this is why we have the ancillary (conventional) historical description affixed to Black Theology. Successively, it was argued that African American theology—before the advent of the Black Theology School—was not authentically "Black." Subsequently, given its Black nationalist orientation, the Black Theology School publicly claimed sole possession of authentic "Blackness."[22]

In the wake, the Black Theology movement assumed the veneer of a revolutionary awakening, while prior African American theological trends were proclaimed relics of the past. The decisive factor for this "revolutionary awakening" was the adoption of "authentic" Blackness. Consequently, we have the following comments from J. Deotis Roberts on George D. Kelsey: "Kelsey's work makes a solid case for the theological basis for racial concern and presents one of the finest statements on Christian anthropology by a black scholar so far. This is true even if Kelsey was not 'thinking black.'"[23]

Here we have a Black philosopher/theologian presenting a vast and profound contribution to the Christian anthropology on race. However, Roberts finds it necessary to employ the caveat—Kelsey is not "thinking Black." Why is this contribution—arguably the best for its time—a matter of not thinking Black? Is this a code phrase for lacking the Black nationalist viewpoint in theology? Code for adhering to the principle of universalism—rather than Black particularism—as basic to the Christian world-outlook? In short, do we have the failure to express an ideological disposition in the form of Black (nationalist) consciousness? We think that Black nationalist—religious—ideology functions as the overriding principle behind Roberts's judgment on Kelsey.[24]

From this perspective, thus *being* Black and *thinking* Black are not in accord. In other words, although Kelsey is Black, he fails to think according to what is conceived as the true meaning of Blackness. Roberts's declaration amounts to a prescriptive judgment—that is, given Kelsey is Black, he ought to think in a particular manner. This assumption entails that Kelsey lacks the requisite—authentic form of—Black consciousness. Of course, we must ask, Why is Kelsey not thinking Black? We do know that Kelsey limits his critique to white racism, and the expanse between the anti-whiteness of Black Theology and Kelsey's opposition to white racism is not a short stretch.[25]

Does the idea of thinking Black theologically mandate an antiwhite posture? Why is this important? What impact did Kelsey's not thinking "Black" have on his contribution? Did he lack something in his analysis—by not thinking "Black"—or in reality did he just have a different point of view on racism and white Christianity than what we find within the Black Theology School? If the latter is the case, then the whole matter about not thinking Black is an ideological ruse, a misdirected presupposition, which fosters a deceptive outlook on how to define Black Theology.

How we designate who belongs in the ranks of "Black" theologians should not be gauged by the narrow prism of Black nationalist ideology.

The notions of sufficient (or insufficient) Blackness dictates some kind of "authentic" Blackness by which we can judge. On this account, why must we conclude that the previous African American theologians were not thinking "Black?" How do we recover authentic Blackness? Where is it located in space and time, respecting the intellectual horizon? When does *being* Black transform into *thinking* Black, that is, "authentic Blackness"? Uncovering the answers to these questions requires our critical inspection on the very notion—authentic Blackness.

On closer scrutiny, it seems the very idea of "authentic Blackness" derives from the presumptions surrounding the Black nationalist posture in theology, which is no more than the binary logic of Black versus white. In view of this logic, we think resorting to the appellation of Negro—to describe the African American theologians of the pre-Black power era—fails to address the chief pitfall with this delineation. Namely, the supposition there actually exists an authentic form of Blackness. At best, authentic Blackness, we submit, is a subjective determination without material (objective) grounds.[26]

Alice Echols correctly points out, "When Stokely Carmichael called on blacks to develop an 'ideology that speaks to our blackness' he, like other black nationalists, suggested that there was somehow an essential and authentic 'blackness.'" Following Echols's claim, if we substitute *theology* for *ideology* in the above, then we capture the direction and cardinal principle taken by the Black Theology School.[27]

Whether Kelsey becomes "Negro" theologian or Black theologian that fails to think "Black," the result becomes that both designations rest on the presumptive context of some kind of "authentic" Blackness. Yet, we unequivocally know that the notion of "authentic" Blackness solidly stands on ideological—Black nationalist—grounds rather than an actual (racial) description of the given subjects. Here, ideological bias constitutes the presumptive context. If one disagrees with the tenets of the Black Theology School, this should not signify that such an individual is not thinking Black or that she/he holds the status of "Negro" theologian. The concern with delegating "authenticity" is perilously conflict-ridden and contentious. The supposition of authentic Blackness ultimately reduces to the Blacker-than-thou principle. Yet, this debate over authentic Blackness is no minor concern respecting the historical process, which ultimately established the conventional definition for Black Theology.

From the Black Theology School's standpoint, it meaningfully follows that the *authentic form of Christianity* must subsist on the idea of authentic "Blackness." At the heart of the matter about Blackness, we are witnessing a polemic on the very foundations of authentic Christianity. It is imperative we not lose sight of this foundational concern—what's at stake is the very definition of Christianity itself. What cannot be overlooked is that authentic Blackness is a core notion of Black Theology. Concertedly, this element of Blackness is the catalyst for the line of demarcation regarding Christian authenticity vis-a-vis whiteness and white Christian theology. Hence, Black Theology—strictly on the basis of Blackness—claimed the right as successor to authentic Christianity.

It should be most evident that our interrogations on Blackness pointedly complicate arriving at a sound definition of Black Theology. For such a definition exceeds the mundane description of the authors/practitioners engaged in African American Christian theology. In short, the background assumptions affixed to authentic Blackness create a disruptively ideological wedge within the very process of defining African American theology as "Black."

BLACK THEOLOGY: THE PROBLEM OF "AUTHENTIC" BLACKNESS AND CHRISTIANITY

There is a certain degree of complexity to our efforts at defining Black Theology. It is this conceptual complexity which dictates that we confront and address an assortment of philosophical problems and questions that adjoined to the process. For example: how does the concept of "Black"—in Black Theology—prevail as its defining feature? We could conclude it is an identification regarding the race of the author (practitioner) or likewise the description of the theological subject matter under review. It could possibly involve certain kinds of theological theories or methods. If Black Theology is a direct reaction to whiteness and Christology, the chief outcome of this project boils down to the suggestion for instituting efforts at the "Blackening" of Christianity. Perhaps, instead, Black Theology is the result of personal involvement with the unique character of the Black experience.[28]

One of the pioneering architects of Black Theology, Dr. James H. Cone states, "[B]lack theology located the theological starting point in the black experience and not the particularity of the western theological tradition. We did not feel ourselves accountable to Aquinas, Luther, or Calvin but to David Walker, Daniel Payne, and W. E. B. Du Bois."[29]

It appears that Cone thinks that Black Theology makes a significant departure from the past African American intellectual discourse and culture. Can it be argued that African American theologians—before the advent of the Black Theology School—held themselves accountable to Aquinas, Luther, or Calvin—that is, accountable to putatively white theology? What kind of theological message did they bring before the Black community? Did it involve various forms of African American struggle? Or were these African American theologians beholding to white theology and theologians? Consequently, were they effectively removed from the interests of the Black community? What does a content analysis of their research tell us?

Now, we ask, did Nelson and others discuss the works of white theologians? Surely they did and with erudite acumen and critical insights. They were not averse to examining various and diverse theological positions and consistently from a global context. Yet, from our previous analysis of *The Journal of Religious Thought*, the prior generation was far from worshipping at the altar of Aquinas, Luther, or Calvin. In the pages of *The Journal of Religious Thought*, Eugene G. Prater published, in fact, an article (1957/1958) on Daniel Payne—"Bishop Payne of African Methodism."[30]

The founder of *The Journal*, William Stuart Nelson, published his text *The Christian Way in Race Relations* (1948), along with the article "Satyagraha: Gandhian Principles of Non-Violent Non-Cooperation" (1957/1958). Rather than confirming the legitimacy of white theology, Nelson's publications directly focused on the movement for civil rights. Besides, Nelson mentored Martin Luther King Jr. on the philosophy of nonviolence, with a view toward shaping this philosophy into a practical tool for the struggle. In addition to conducting workshops for King and fellow civil rights activists, Nelson actually shared with King the previously referenced article on Satyagraha. In his correspondence with Nelson, King noted, "one of the best and most balanced analyses of the Gandhian principles of nonviolent, noncooperation that I have read."[31]

Nelson not only engaged in the U.S. civil rights struggles but also collaborated with Gandhi, Nehru, and others in the international peace movement. Furthermore, William Stuart Nelson, in point of fact, participated in non-violent marches with Gandhi in India. Prior to Nelson's engagement with the peace movement, he worked with Dr. W. E. B. Du Bois in the burgeoning Pan African movement. More than just acknowledging Du Bois—respecting some kind of intellectual accountability to the Black experience—Nelson actually joined forces with Du Bois in the concrete struggle. After working with Du Bois, we discover, Nelson traveled throughout the African continent espousing the philosophy of nonviolence as crucial to the aim of African emancipation. Far from worshipping at the altar of "white" theology, Nelson embodies the Black experience of resistance associated with David Walker, Daniel Payne, and W. E. B. Du Bois.[32]

Moreover, it is necessary to point out if engagement in the Black experience is the litmus test, we must be mindful of the fact that before the arrival of Black Theology, as a school of thought, African American theologians largely lived the Black experience and theologically were engaged within the Black community and its struggles. They were even involved in movements at the international level. Dennis Dickerson points out,

On black campuses where they taught and delivered addresses, these intellectuals trained preministerial and seminary students. Many of them, including James Farmer of the Congress of Racial Equality and Martin Luther King, Jr. of the Southern Christian Leadership Conference, became major leaders in the civil rights movement. [Mordecai] Johnson, [Benjamin] Mays, [Howard] Thurman, and [George] Kelsey also preached regularly in black churches in the North and South. Their sermons stressed the same themes that they conveyed in their campus chapels and classrooms. Segregation was immoral, it was un-Biblical, and moral methods could be used to undermine it. Additionally, they traveled abroad to say the same things at ecumenical gatherings and other worldwide religious meetings.[33]

William Stuart Nelson's *Bases of World Understanding, An Inquiry into the Means of Resolving Racial, Religious, Class, and National Misapprehensions and Conflicts* — published by Calcutta Press (1949) — is just one example of the global dimension to his theology and Nelson's direct participation in movements for social change. Nelson was far from the exception to the rule. Many other African American theologians — of the pre–Black power era — were scholar-activists.[34]

As Frank T. Wilson earlier remarked, they — African American theologians — were "those who have lived the life and known the faith." Under the conditions of segregation — de jure and de facto — the Black experience became an inescapable fact of their lives. For example, African American theologians often and typically worked and spoke at Black venues such as churches and college campuses. Few African American theologians were located with positions teaching in white institutions, including divinity schools or seminaries before the 1960s.[35]

Not to mention, *The Journal of Religious Thought* along with others such as the *A. M. E. Church Review*, *The A.M.E. Zion Quarterly Review*, and *The Negro Journal of Religion* were produced by Black institutions that existed in the African American community. Prior to the Black Theology School, African American theologians were intimately linked, if not entirely locked, in the Black community and its experiences. To that end, we must locate Black Theology — according to its definitive features — outside of solely the Black experience. Hence, the line of separation originates in shifting from its *theological* rather than *physical* location.[36]

What we previously unearthed is that the Black nationalist orientation in theology becomes the chief defining feature of the Black Theology School vis-à-vis earlier African American theological thought. The prior school of thought was committed to racial integration and the universality of the Christian message. With the Black Theology School, at root, a qualitatively different theological paradigm was introduced into African American Christian intellectual culture.[37]

This shift in theological paradigms to various forms of Black religious nationalism has several ramifications with accompanying questions. In concert with such definitive nationalist features, can we assume that God and Jesus in some manner become Black? According to Black Theology, do they—God and Jesus—act to serve Black interests at the expense of whites and other non-Black groups? In sum, is God pro-Black?[38]

In turn, we noted the concept of "Black" functions as a particular kind of ideological—Black nationalist—*orientation* directed toward the subject matter of Christian theology. The earlier school in its conception of Christianity eschewed race as a defining feature of Christianity; meanwhile, the Black Theology School found that race and thus Blackness was decisive. Hence, what is the meaning of Black ideology or Blackness, specifically in relation to Christian theology and whiteness?[39] Theologian Leon E. Wright keenly suggests,

> That Christian theology creatively conceived as an open-ended corpus stands in need of contemporary and constant reappraisal is painfully clear. It would be hazardous to insist, however, that one has made a case for a uniquely oriented worldview—"Black Theology"—whose posture consists essentially in judgment and protest of "White Christianity" and/or "racist" society. Though such judgment can be shown to be supremely righteous and just and the protest be seen to stem from deep prophetic depths, there is involved in all this no distinctive alternative to the traditional approaches to "God talk" and man's self-understanding.[40]

This leads us to ask, How does fostering the Black nationalist religious orientation shape the very character and substance of Christian theology? If authentic Christian theology is essentially a manifestation of Black Theology, how can Black Theology be differentiated from the core beliefs of white and other non-Black forms of Christian theology? Must authentic Christianity be encumbered by racially informed theologies? Proponent of Black Theology, Gayraud Wilmore insightfully argues,

> The problem of the whitenized black churches today is how to recover their own self-respect by demythologizing the white cultural bag through which the faith was transmitted to them and in which they have curled themselves up so comfortably. In doing so they may discover that the essence of the Christian faith not only transcends ultimately the ethnocentric culture of the white man, but that of the black man as well; that this Christ, in whom there is neither Jew nor Greek, bond nor free, is also neither black nor white.[41]

As a result, if ethnocentrism is problematic, what makes differing racial theologies—all inclusively—Christian in principle? Among any of them—given the problem of ethnocentrism—can we select what is authentically Christianity? Accordingly, can Black Theology essentially determine or define what is meant by the authentic form of Christianity? In defining Black Theology, some advocates concluded that Black Theology captures what is authentic about Christian theology. They argued Black

Theology in "Blackening" Christianity facilitates in arriving at its authentic form. Yet, from Wilmore's previous remarks, it appears that some in the Black Theology School do not reject the idea that eventually Christianity can obtain some form of universality—that is, stand without racial monikers.

Wilmore seems to think that through the function of demythologizing white theology, it is still possible to arrive at authentic Christianity as universal. Wilmore's terminal point—universality—is actually the starting point for many theologians that are not in accord with the Black Theology School. With the problem of Black ethnocentrism in mind, Frank T. Wilson counsels, "One of the major errors of these times is the attempt to draw circles around certain culturally induced modes of expression and to treat these as 'life forms' or 'thought forms' devoid of elements of universality." [42]

In concert with Wilson's observation, Howard Thurman brings into bold relief the chief problem associated with Black Theology.

> The central problem of Black theology is not unlike the central issue of any theology—is the totality of life grounded in a spiritual reality which not only bottoms existence but also, at the same time, infuses and informs life with a divine dimension? More directly, are the God of life and the God of religion one and the same? If they are, then the Black experience cannot be separated from the totality of experience and the sense of being cut off or isolated, despite the intensity of the reality, has no ultimate significance and justification. [43]

Thurman's warning is quite explicit. Clearly, "the Black experience cannot be separated from the totality of experience and the sense of being cut off or isolated, despite the intensity of the reality, has no ultimate significance and justification." The ultimate significance and justification of Black Theology is a matter of having links to the totality (universality?) of experience. We contend that without such links Black Theology stumbles into the abyss of ethnocentrism. Hence, the ethnocentric elements within Black Theology could very well reproduce the essential problems associated with white racist theology.

For it stands that it is ethnocentricity as Eurocentrism—with its ancillary racism—which prevails as most problematic with white Christianity rather than whiteness as such. We should not think that Black ethnocentricity—in the guise of demythologizing white theology—could even persist as a plausible short-term solution. Instead of reaching a solution, the problem of ethnocentricity morphs into a compounded predicament. African American theologian Leon E. Wright warns:

> [I]t should not be supposed that one advances the cause of a "Black Theology" merely by painting faces black or partisanly juggling spiritual preferences before God, respecting persons or groups. Whatever the case for Black Theology may turn out to be, let us not cavalierly

create a set of mythological assumptions whose credibility deserves only to be "de-mythologized" at the same instant. If racism is bad, it cannot achieve respectability by masquerading within any preferred ethnic or racial stock.[44]

Yet, this specific process on how Black Theology came to be defined—via Black nationalist orientation—thus grants to it a certain elevated status—one of primacy—regarding views on Christian theology. It follows that in substance, it [the Black nationalist orientation] is qualitatively different from white theology. Such substantial differences entail that Christianity—in some universal sense—cannot serve as common ground or standard bearer. Thus, a comparative approach for theological authenticity becomes an impossibility.

Nevertheless, without a universal (objective) measure for authenticity, white theology fails precisely because it is not Black and nothing more. The whiteness of white Christianity—instead of racism—comes to light as the problem. In this case, rather than judged on its Christian merits, white theology fails and becomes inauthentic Christianity because Black Theology functions as the standard bearer of authentic Christianity.

This is a crucial issue for Black Theology and the legitimacy of its critique on white theology. Any claim to authenticity requires more than an expression of self-assertion; for self-assertion is anchored in subjectivism—that is, it goes without presenting any kind of rational (objective) justification open to public scrutiny and consensus. For instance, the determination for uncovering counterfeit currency is not based on arbitrary criteria. If arbitrary criteria were in play, then the very notion of counterfeit currency would not make any sense. We would have no line of demarcation separating what is counterfeit from what is authentic currency. Authentic currency derives from criteria that are established on an objective measure, which allows for wide-ranging agreement that is beyond reasonable doubt.

Just as we cannot print our own money and declare it authentic, we cannot deduce the nature of authentic Christianity without requisite criteria. Given "authentic" Blackness encompasses what amounts to a subjective accounting, then authentic Blackness cannot function as the stand-in for authentic Christianity. Indeed, we have pointed out why the very idea of "authentic" Blackness—in itself—is a subjective (ideological) determination. Authentic Christianity—if there is such an entity—must be rationally demonstrated and not merely asserted. Sequentially, the criteria for authenticity must be all-inclusive, universally comprehensive, and not haphazard and randomly selective. In short, it demands the recognition of a complete standard bearer by which we can measure the claim of authenticity.

Prior to the formation of the 1960s Black Theology School, the issue of the authenticity of racist theology had several Black critics. Rather than a blanket rejection of "white" Christianity, we realize the focus was on racism and its embodiment in varied institutional arrangements, including slavery. There was a clear distinction between white Christians and racist Christianity. Such clarity is often missing when the Black Theology School advances its criticism of whiteness and Christian theology. Hence, let's turn to one of the most stringent critics of racist Christianity, Frederick Douglass. In the nineteenth century, Frederick Douglass categorically pronounced,

> What I have said respecting and against religion, I mean strictly to apply to the slaveholding religion of this land, and with no possible reference to Christianity proper; for, between the Christianity of this land, and the Christianity of Christ, I recognize the widest possible difference—so wide, that to receive the one is good, pure, and holy, is of necessity to reject the other as bad, corrupt, and wicked.... I love the pure, peaceable, and impartial Christianity of Christ: I therefore hate the corrupt, slaveholding, women-whipping, credo-plundering, partial and hypocritical Christianity of this land. I can see no reason but the most deceitful one, for calling the religion of this land Christianity.[45]

In Douglass's view, the Christianity adjoined to slaveholding was inauthentic. Hence, he seeks to find authentic Christianity in "the pure, peaceable, and impartial Christianity of Christ." What is salient is that his claim does not rest on a particularistic Black Theology. The "Christianity of Christ" has no racial blinders. Rather its impartiality stands as good, pure, and holy. Douglass's position is not a Black versus the white claim to Christian authenticity.

Yet, definitively—in this chapter—we are concerned with the Black claim to Christian authenticity. If Black nationalist religious orientation shapes the character and substance of Christian theology, then the concept of "Black" orientation arises as conclusive for defining Christianity. The ontological framework (perspective on reality) that molds the Christian ideal is the particularity of Blackness and not the ideal of universality, which—therein—serves as the grounds for God as ultimate reality.

With Black Theology, it stands to reason, the very meaning of "Ultimate Reality" or God is founded on Blackness. Unlike Douglass's viewpoint, with Black Theology in its quest for authenticity, we uncover that the centerpiece of Christian theology becomes the matter of Blackness vis-à-vis whiteness. Where the particularity of Blackness calls into question the universality of (white?) Christianity. Therein, the very idea of universality is conceived in terms of the false (white?) conception. Successively, this false—white—conception renders a gross distortion of Christian faith and theology.

This particular notion of false conception necessitates placing the particularity of Blackness at front and center. Herein lies the philosophical puzzle concerning the appropriate categories of Black Theology as authentic Christianity. Does the critique of racist theology entail Black Theology's embracing an antiwhiteness position? Consecutively, does this antiwhiteness worldview direct us to conclude that Black Theology remains as the singular (authentic) form of Christianity?

Moreover, is authentic Christianity essentially an antiwhiteness worldview? If it's the case, what evidence do we have that the particularity of Black Theology fits the bill for authenticity? Or has Wilmore given us the arrow that hits the target—namely, "the essence of the Christian faith not only transcends ultimately the ethnocentric culture of the white man, but that of the black man as well"?

If this holds true then the particularity of "authentic" Blackness—and hence Black Theology—cannot deliver authentic Christian theology, that is, in any universal sense. We are simply caught in the web of ethnocentrism, along with its associated pitfalls. The theological ramifications of such pitfalls loom large; this is especially so when we explore the implications surrounding the classical Christian idea of God.

CONE'S NOTION OF BLACKNESS AS ULTIMATE REALITY VERSUS HIS FORMAL GOD-CONCEPT

The centrality and particularity of Blackness—contra whiteness—is a cardinal motif of Black Theology. The pivotal nature of this motif cannot be underestimated or understated in terms of its theological worth. Accordingly, how does Blackness fit into the theological equation? Forerunner of Black Theology, James H. Cone argues,

> The fact that I am black is my ultimate reality. My identity with blackness [a term for one who is oppressed], and what it means for millions living in a white world controls the investigation. It is impossible for me to surrender this basic reality for a "higher, more universal" reality. Therefore, if a higher, Ultimate Reality is to have meaning, it must relate to the very essence of blackness.[46]

Let us review Cone's statement, "The fact that I am black is my ultimate reality." It seems he means that Blackness overrides the idea of "God talk" as ultimate reality. This extrapolation is due to the fact that when many theologians speak of ultimate reality, it becomes synonymous with the classical expression of "God" in Christian theology. Most who are aware of the theological lexicon are mindful of this shift in terminology. This shift—from the nomenclature of God to the notion of Ultimate Reality—was a direct response to critical arguments challenging formal proofs for God's existence.[47] For example, Robinson states,

> God is, by definition, ultimate reality. And one cannot argue whether ultimate reality exists. One can only ask what ultimate reality is like— whether, for instance, in the last analysis what lies at the heart of things

and governed their working is to be described in personal or impersonal categories. Thus, the fundamental theological question consists not in the "existence" of God as a separate entity but in pressing through in ultimate concern to what Tillich calls "the ground of our being."[48]

With John A. T. Robinson's explanation of ultimate reality, it logically follows that for Cone, Blackness is more than racial signifier and transforms into his *key* theological category. Wherefore, the theological consequences of Blackness are enormous. From the traditional Christian perspective, Cone's ontological presumption—what grounds reality—emerges as problematic. As his main theological category, Blackness—in its ontological function—becomes primary. God talk converts into a deliberation on Blackness as "ultimate reality." Surreptitiously, Cone's proposition takes Black Theology outside of conventional Christian theological discourse. Herein, let's not overlook Leon E. Wright's previous remarks,

> It would be hazardous to insist, however, that one has made a case for a uniquely oriented worldview—"Black Theology"—whose posture consists essentially in judgment and protest of "White Christianity" and/or "racist" society. Though such judgment can be shown to be supremely righteous and just and the protest be seen to stem from deep prophetic depths, there is involved in all this *no distinctive alternative to the traditional approaches to "God talk."*[49] [Italics added]

Contrary to Wright's claim, we discover what Cone's Black Theology tenders is precisely a distinctive alternative about the traditional approaches to "God talk." As ultimate reality, Blackness assumes divinely conceived eminence, the status usually reserved for the Christian deity. Furthermore, this ultimate reality—Blackness—must give meaning to the "higher, more universal" ultimate reality. However, given its prescribed status, which rests on describing ultimate reality, this latter concept must also be deemed as Cone's God-concept. Consequently, we ask, What becomes the theological locus for this latter God-concept contra Blackness?

Let's judiciously review Cone's methodology. On the one hand, he substitutes Blackness for the conventional (Christian) God-concept, on the other, Cone conveys there is still room for believing in God as the higher more universal ultimate reality. Although, quite significantly, the former—Blackness—prevails as justification for holding this belief regarding the latter. Cone's compounded proposition—on ultimate reality—plainly lacks theoretical clarity. Given that Cone's Black Theology is ostensibly presented as authentic Christianity, one can only surmise that theoretical confusion abounds at this point.

This becomes manifest, when we return to what Robinson expounded—namely, *ultimate reality* serves as theological surrogate for the traditional Christian God-concept. How Cone's respective qualifications fastened onto *ultimate reality* fundamentally disrupt any manner of intelligible rendering of *ultimate reality*/God. In view of Cone's adherence to monotheism—along with his attendant claim to authentic Christianity—his bifurcation of ultimate reality becomes theologically dubious. If Blackness is ultimate reality, how can we decipher the true meaning adjoined to Cone's God-concept?

Of course, Cone understands that Christian monotheism does not allow for more than one God. Yet, Cone's specifications on ultimate reality designate that we have conceptually different categories. The corresponding descriptor, in fact, changes the relevant meaning of ultimate reality. If the notion of *ultimate reality*—however defined—functionally translates into the traditional Christian God-concept, then Cone faces an intractable contradiction. Since, for Christian believers, there is only one God, then why suggest two different conceptions of ultimate reality?

This contradiction rests on a significant conflation, expressly the conflation of "ultimate reality" with Blackness. This conflation effectively transforms Christian "God talk" into "Black talk." Since Cone affirms Blackness—as ultimate reality—then this category (Blackness) actually functions in terms of the highest universal reality. The descriptor of "higher, more universal," in fact, does not change the applicable meaning of ultimate reality. We cannot disregard a very important issue of semantics, there is *no superlative for ultimate*. Therefore, we note that conventionally, the God-concept is rendered—ultimate reality.

The theological inference is clear: ultimate reality is the apex of reality—the reason why we earlier noted the contradictory use of theological terminology. In as much as ontological distinctions prove necessary, then Cone's respective qualifier radically seeks to transform the logic surrounding the idea of God as ultimate reality. Logically speaking, what is the higher, more universal ultimate reality, if it is not ultimate reality as such?

Since Blackness emerges as ultimate reality, why even broach this idea—higher, more universal ultimate reality? Why resort to these ambiguous conceptions on ultimate reality? Notice, Cone does not explicitly state that his God-concept is founded on Blackness. The actual terminology denoting "God" becomes lost to equivocation and qualifications on ultimate reality. The singular conception of ultimate reality rapidly fades into chaos and confusion.

In truth, Cone's bifurcated conception of ultimate reality conceals an important fact. Namely, his deliberations not only nominally change from "God" to "ultimate reality," but also ontologically relocate the Christian God-concept. This develops into Cone's chief theological predicament—how to recover the God-concept in accordance with Christian theology? Since Cone *essentially* relinquishes Christian conventional God-talk, he must recover it—the God-concept—in formal terms. Now we can readily make the deduction: the "higher, more universal ultimate reality" transpires as Cone's "formal" God-concept.

Even though ultimate reality gains priority as Blackness, the notion of ultimate reality—as such—is not entirely relinquished. We still have some semblance of ultimate reality via the "higher, more universal" form. Obviously, this reference, "higher, more universal ultimate reality," remains no more than a makeshift effort, Cone's feeble attempt at constructing the approximate synonym for the Christian (conventional) God-concept. Now it cannot be said that the needed surrogate for the God-concept fails to reside within the fold of Cone's Black Theology. For without this surrogate pertaining to the "formal" God-concept, Cone's Black Theology runs the risk of appearing as inauthentic Christianity.

However, Cone's formal God-concept becomes trapped within the snare of ontological difficulties. Despite the theological formality of the God-surrogate (higher, more universal ultimate reality), Blackness continues as the de facto pinnacle of Cone's theological ordering. The translation from ultimate reality "talk" to "God-talk" makes this fact most apparent.

With Cone's thesis, the conventional idea of the Christian God is *conditionally situated* on the theological principle—Blackness. Sequentially, any notion about an entity possessing *derived meaning* entails a relation of conditional dependence. In Christian theology, inhabiting the ontological position of highest ultimate reality denotes absolute being. According to Cone's argument, *theological* Blackness is primary or basic ultimate reality, hence the Christian God cannot have absolute being; and we should add along with the subsidiary attribution of complete ontological independence.[50]

The logical implication of Cone's thesis—in terms of ontological hierarchy—is that it permits Blackness to replace the Christian God-concept. Although Cone could argue that this is not his intention, the logical meaning—how Blackness is theologically positioned—is inconvertible. Cone's formal placement of the God-concept vis-à-vis the essential (primary) ontological character of Blackness can only stand by theologically disguising the concept—higher, more universal ultimate reality—via the employment of this surrogate God-talk. The reader must assume that "higher, more universal ultimate reality" in some manner points to Cone's God-concept, while, at the same time, Cone argues, Blackness is the most essential (theological) category.

Plainly, we have conceptual confusion on display, which results from ontologically locating Blackness vis-à-vis the classical (Christian) placement of God. With Blackness now occupying the theological space usually afforded to the (Christian) God-idea, then Cone's God-concept must, in turn, be relocated. We can surmise that the "higher, more universal" reality (or more precisely, Cone's formal God-concept) continues as ontologically dependent upon theological Blackness. In this case, particularity—Blackness—supersedes the universality affixed to Ultimate Reality or the traditional Christian notion of God. Thus, for Cone, universal Ultimate Reality—the formal concept of God—is futile without a concrete association with and more importantly the dependent relationship on Blackness.

In other words, Cone argues, Blackness ontologically anchors his formal God-concept, albeit its categorical expression remains under the guise of universal ultimate reality. Given that ontological primacy resides in Blackness, then the formal God-concept continues in a perpetual state of *dependency*. In terms of Christian authenticity, the theological import of this proposition is seismic. If the God-concept (formal or otherwise) is dependent on Blackness, why should Black people maintain their dependency on God? Could it be that God needs the help of Black people? What sense can we make of this notion, namely that universal ultimate reality is conditional or ontologically dependent?[51]

We reply: if universal ultimate reality is conditional or ontologically dependent—in any fashion—then the idea of "higher universal ultimacy" actually fails to have any substantive theological meaning. The substantive meaning of "higher universal ultimacy" connotes that it has ontological priority over all other entities including Blackness. Without this ontological priority, then the notion of "higher universal ultimacy" becomes empty and meaningless.

When he argues that Blackness becomes his basic/ultimate reality, Cone thus renders the idea of "higher universal ultimacy" as hollow and pointless. For the very meaning of universality—affixed to this ultimate reality—gives way to the particularity of Blackness as basic/ultimate reality. In effect, the universality of ultimate reality—the formal notion of God—is only an appearance, for its essence resides in Blackness. In sum, what appears as the universal God in Christian theology, Cone's Black Theology proclaims is essentially based on the Black experience of oppression.

We must remember that Cone says Blackness is "a term for one who is oppressed" in a white-dominated world. Given that the term "Blackness" is the generic category for the oppressed, it is not clear if Cone means those who are white and oppressed are symbolically Black. Given Cone's presumptive logic on Black/white dichotomy, it is more likely that he believes that all whites are oppressors. Thus, "white" and "oppressed" [Blackness] are mutually exclusive categories. Furthermore, this Black categorization could include other oppressed non-Black people of color and they are in some sense—symbolically—"Black" people. Cone's conflated and thus generic idea (oppressed/Blackness) is ambiguously presented, serving no more than as a catch-all term for the myriad of possible social categories and relations.

Cone's whole account of oppression hinges on his myopic Black/white dichotomy. Whatever Cone's intent, the identification of the oppressed with the singular label of Blackness is a reductionist move of theological and social consequences. As with whiteness, Blackness is conventionally used as the category designating human social (racial) groupings of a *particular* type. With Cone, the God-concept necessarily reduces to Blackness and subsequently Blackness becomes not only a social designation but also his pivotal theological category. Successively, Blackness arises as foundational to the whole theological project. Thus, Cone's theology is founded on a philosophy of race that offers Blackness both as a theological and social category with significant ontological implications. Reality itself is grounded on Blackness and this involves its theological dimension.

Now we must ask, Why render such a formulation on Blackness as social category in theological terms? Indeed, there is a practical dimension to this exercise. Expressly, Cone's formal God-concept seeks to demonstrate that God is on the side of the Black oppressed. More significantly, the white oppressors of Black people shape the ontological foundation launching—his formal—God-concept. Hence, Cone commits an important theological inversion regarding the fundamental tenets of conventional Christian theology. Blackness develops into the centerpiece for Christian theology.

Cone's notion of Blackness thus serves as both theological as well as social category. It speaks to God's nature, and it also describes how Black people exist in the white (oppressive) world. Unceasingly, Cone's ontology generates a theological inversion in Christian thought, wherein the social conditions surrounding Blackness have theological primacy. On that account—pertaining to the dual function of Blackness—not only does a theological inversion take place, but also we unquestionably have an act of racial chauvinism, at the social level.

We submit racial chauvinism because this reduction imposes Blackness onto the identity of all who are oppressed in the white world. The claim is offered without regard to actually designating specification on racial (social) identity. In Cone's viewpoint, given the state of white oppression in the world, then anyone who is oppressed is subsequently considered Black. What is transparent—with Cone's claim—is that Blackness becomes a symbolic term, which reverses the racist stigma of Blackness as a negative social identity. Cone's symbolic Blackness is a catch-all for identifying the oppressed, no matter its actual circumstances. It is a generalization—ironically an abstract universality—without specification. Anthony Pinn notes,

> The stigma—blackness over against whiteness—becomes a sign of excellence, or deep meaning, in that categorical racism is addressed through the transfiguration of a few vis-à-vis an altered Christ image and Christ-like postures toward the world. . . . This proposition bears significant difficulties in that *suffering* easily becomes the standard of black life—the inescapable measure of black existence.[52] [Italics added]

If we substitute the word "oppression" for "suffering," then Cone's viewpoint on Blackness is effectively captured in Pinn's summation. This vantage point on Blackness amplifies the particularity of Black oppression as constituting *the basic* Christian (theological) anchor. Undoubtedly, since Blackness—in Cone's theology—signifies the "deeper meaning" of basic ultimate reality, then the Christian God cannot exist without the underpinning of the Black experience of oppression.

Consequently, God is a theological construction, specifically a singularly Black theological construct. It follows that God is not ontologically prior to (creator of) the Black world and Black people. In fact, plenty can be said for white oppressors as the real creator. Remember, on Cone's account, the essence of Blackness is white oppression of Black people. Undeniably, this is a novel theological idea. However, can such an assumption carry on as the authentic form of Christian theology? In what manner is this an authentic formulation of Christian thought?

It appears Cone's real faith lies in Blackness—the Black community—rather than the classical notion of the Christian God. In another context, African American theologian Preston N. Williams critically notes:

> We cannot accept his [Cone's] notion that "There is only one principle which guides the thinking and action of Black Theology: an unqualified commitment to the black community as that community seeks to define its existence in the light of God's liberating work in the world. . . . Indeed we see this as the source of a fundamental contradiction in his [Cone's] work.

Williams continues:

> Either one is loyal to the God who works on behalf of the oppressed, most of whom happen to be black, or one is loyal to the blacks, most of whom may be oppressed and some of whom may have a peculiar place in the plan of God for this day. My alternative is loyalty to God or whatever symbol may stand for the ultimate and eternal source of meaning and value."[53]

However, for Cone, the symbol which stands "for the ultimate and eternal source of meaning and value" is precisely Blackness. Paradoxically, given the function of white oppression of Black people—as the essence of Blackness—then God as universal Ultimate Reality is ontologically grounded on the white oppression of Black people. Can we conclude that without white oppressors there is no God? This theological question logically follows from Cone's thesis on Blackness. The upshot is that without the white oppression of Black people—basic ultimate reality—there would be no universal ultimate reality/God. Hence, God talk is reducible to talking about Blackness as a state of white oppression.

When we shift our theological terminology from universal Ultimate Reality to the conventional notion of God, the problem becomes evident. The very meaning of the Christian God is specifically bound to the Black oppressed. In turn, the particularity of Blackness is the cardinal principle of not only Black Theology but also Christian theology itself. For this reason, we must pose the question, how can this notion sustain Christianity in universal terms? In effect, with Cone's proposition, the entirety of Christian theology basically orbits around Blackness and the corresponding condition of oppression faced by Black people.

We must query, Why is Cone caught in this theological conundrum? Why not declare that Black oppression is fundamentally social, economic, and political in character—that is, secular in makeup? Hence, why not suspend with appeals to God and ultimate reality? The answer resides in the ideological context of the late 1960s. The secular thrust of the Black power movement put on notice how Christianity was a formidable and debilitative obstacle to Black liberation. In response, Cone sought to demonstrate that Christianity was relevant to the Black power movement and hence suitably amendable to its Black nationalist proclivities and the clarion call for Black revolution.[54]

However, the stubborn fact persists that Cone is foremost a Christian theologian and ordained minister, not a revolutionary ideologue. Christian theology was the most suitable form of ideological fodder. In turn, it permitted Cone to comfortably join the fray. Rather than formulating his Black nationalist ideology on secular terms, Cone erects a theological framework. Cone firmly believed that his Black nationalist framework had to be rooted in religion. The justification for this belief centered on the contemporary and historic Christian inclinations within the African American community.

Also, by resorting to Christian theology—as the chief mechanism for Black nationalist ideology—Cone wanted to bridge the gap which conclusively differentiated the secular Black nationalist camp of Black power from the Christianity affiliated with integration. The former viewed the latter as an albatross affixed to the legacy of African American enslavement.[55] This attempt to merge Black nationalism with Christianity, successively mandated that Cone translate Christian theology in a manner relevant to the great number that had rejected Christianity as the white man's religion.

The secular Black power advocates thought Christianity to be unproductive and devoid of any actual social substance, particularly in connection with overthrowing the material conditions of racist oppression. Concretely regarding the meaning and utility of Christianity, it stands to reason that Blackness—in Cone's theology—serves as his primary theological category as well as the key social explanans. The end product of Cone's excursion is most perceptible—namely, Christian theology reductively arises as Black Theology.

Of course, there are Black Christians who fervently disagree with this kind of theology and its ancillary notion of God. In our next chapter, we examine Richard I. McKinney's critique of Black Theology. McKinney's critique stands as an essential disagreement with the central tenets expressed in Cone's theology. We now proceed to "The Critique of Black Theology: Richard I. McKinney on the Fundamental Elements of Christianity."

NOTES

1. Notable advocates of Black Theology who were non-Christians are Roy D. Morrison II and William R. Jones. See Roy D. Morrison II, "The Emergence of Black Theology in America," *The A.M.E. Zion Quarterly Review* 94(3) (1982): 2–17, and William R. Jones, "Liberation Strategies in Black Theology: Mao, Martin, or Malcolm?," in Leonard Harris, ed., *Philosophy Born of Struggle, Anthology of Afro-American Philosophy from 1917* (Dubuque, IA: Kendall Hunt Publishing, 1983). Also read William R. Jones, "Towards an Interim Assessment of Black Theology," *The Christian Century* 89 (May 3, 1972): 513–17. On Black Christian Theology, read Joseph A. Johnson Jr., "The Need for a Black Christian Theology," *The Journal of Interdenominational Theological Center* 2(1) (Fall 1974).

2. Vincent Harding, "The Religion of Black Power," in James H. Cone and Gayraud Wilmore, eds., *Black Theology: A Documentary History, 1966–1979* (Ossining, NY: Orbis Books, 1993), 40–65. James H. Cone, "Christianity and Black Power," in C. Eric Lincoln, ed., *Is Anybody Listening to Black America?* (New York: The Seabury Press, 1968). James H. Cone, *Black Theology and Black Power* (New York: The Seabury Press, 1969). Albert B. Cleage Jr., *The Black Messiah* (New York: Sheed and Ward, 1968). Henry H. Mitchell, "Black Power and the Christian Church," *Foundations: A Baptist Journal of History and Theology* 11 (April–July 1968).

3. Frank T. Wilson, "Critical Evaluation of the Theme—The Black Revolution: Is there a Black Theology?" *The Journal of Religious Thought* 26(2) (Summer 1969): 7.

4. Mark L. Chapman, *Christianity on Trial: African-American Religious Thought before and after Black Power* (Eugene, OR: Wipf and Stock Publishers, 2006). Also read "*Achieving* Blackness during the Black Power Era," which is chapter 3 of Algernon Austin, *Achieving Blackness: Race, Black Nationalism, and Afrocentrism in the Twentieth Century* (New York: NYU Press, 2006). Harding, "The Religion of Black Power," 40–65. Cone, "Christianity and Black Power."

5. Benjamin E. Mays, "The New Social Order When Integrated," *Religious Education* 58(2) (March–April 1963): 155.

6. Joseph A. Johnson Jr., "The Need for a Black Christian Theology," 19.

7. Sean Chabot, "Framing, Transnational Diffusion, and African American Intellectuals in the Land of Gandhi," in Michiel Baud and Rosanne Rutten, eds., *Popular Intellectuals and Social Movements* (New York: Cambridge University Press, 2004), 27.

8. See Vincent Harding's foreword to Howard Thurman, *Jesus and the Disinherited* (Boston: Beacon Press, 1996), 4. Thurman's text was originally published by Abingdon-Cokesbury Press, 1949. Also consult, Justin C. West, "Mysticism and Liberation: An Exploration into the Relationship between Howard Thurman's Spirituality and Black Theology," *Black Theology* 11(1) (2013): 31–57.

9. For example, none of the articles that appeared in *The Journal of Religious Thought* (Summer 1969) in which most gave voice to a critical reception of "Black Theology" appear in James H. Cone and Gayraud Wilmore, eds., *Black Theology: A Documentary History, 1966–1979* (Ossining, NY: Orbis Books, 1993).

10. Leon E. Wright, "'Black Theology' or Black Experience?" *The Journal of Religious Thought* 26(2) (Summer 1969). Richard I. McKinney, "Reflections on the Concept of 'Black Theology,'" *The Journal of Religious Thought* 26(2) (Summer 1969). Frank T. Wilson, "Critical Evaluation of the Theme—The Black Revolution: Is There a Black Theology?" Also consult Howard Thurman, "Review of J. Deotis Roberts's *Liberation and Reconciliation: A Black Theology*," *Religious Education* 66(6) (1971): 464–66. Although we

have not located a direct critique by Kelsey and Mays, consult George D. Kelsey, "The Racist Search for Self," *The Journal of Religious Ethics* 6(1) (Fall 1978), and Benjamin Mays, "Of One Blood: Scripture and Science Make No Race Description," *Presbyterian Life* (February 5, 1955).

11. Dale P. Andrews argues, "Practical theology is particularly concerned with praxis Christian ministry. It is not merely an application in systematic or constructive theology. Instead, practical theology defines the theological grounds and methods for the church's mission, presence, and practice of ministry.... However, the oppositional dialectic method of black theology does not meet functional demands of practical theology.... A methodology suited to the development of what practical theology is critically absent from black theology. Such a methodology is necessary for black theology to become the prophetic voice it seeks to be for black churches" (*Practical Theology for Black Churches: Bridging Black Theology and African American Folk Religion* [Louisville, KY: Westminster John Knox Press, 2002]). For an important theological and historical treatment of this topic (on the conflicting relationship) of the Black Theology School and the Black Church read, Raphael G. Warnock, *The Divided Mind of the Black Church: Theology, Piety, and Public Witness* (New York: NYU Press, 2014).

12. Joseph A. Johnson Jr., "The Need for a Black Christian Theology," 22.

13. Consult George Yancy, ed., *Christology and Whiteness: What Would Jesus Do?* (New York: Routledge, 2012), 24–25. Yancy's anthology presents a comprehensive theological treatment of whiteness.

14. Yancy, *Christology and Whiteness*, 26–27.

15. See John H. McClendon III, "On the Nature of Whiteness and the Ontology of Race: Toward a Dialectical Materialist Analysis," in George Yancy, ed., *What White Looks Like: African-American Philosophers on the Whiteness Question* (New York: Routledge, 2004).

16. Chapman makes the distinction between "Black" and "Negro" Theologians on the basis of differences in ideological orientation both at the level of theology and the sociopolitical implications attendant with the concept of Black power. Specifically "Black" Theology shares a Black nationalist outlook with Black power, while "Negro" Theology did not support nationalism. Instead it was more integrationist in outlook. For a scholarly treatment of theology among African American before and post–Black power, see Chapman, *Christianity on Trial*. See page 5 for Chapman's distinction between Negro and Black Theology.

17. William A. Banner offers instructive comments on Dr. Nelson, "A Christian by nurture and confession, William Stuart Nelson found common ground with those of many traditions who affirmed the freedom and dignity of all men and who believed in the significance of moral force in human affairs.... In religious thought, William Stuart Nelson was, in the language of the seventeenth century, a 'man of latitude'—a man looking beyond the dogmas and enthusiasms which divide believers to the commitments and affections which unite" ("Truth and Service," *The Journal of Religious Thought* 35(2) [Fall–Winter, 1978–1979]: 49).

18. William S. Nelson, "Religion and Racial Tension in America Today," *The Journal of Religious Thought* 2(2) (Spring–Summer 1945): 164–78. Buell Gallagher, "Conscience and Caste: Racism in the Light of the Christian Ethic," *The Journal of Religious Thought* 2(1) (Spring–Summer 1945). The editorial comment "Invitation to Imperialism" appeared in *The Journal of Religious Thought* 2(1) (Spring–Summer 1945). The quotation is from pages 3–4.

19. The editorial comment "The Christian Imperative in Race Relations" appeared in *The Journal of Religious Thought* 2(1) (Spring–Summer 1945). The quotation is from page 5.

20. William A. Banner, "The Transmission of Our Religious Heritage: Christian Ideas of Human Equality and Social Justice," *The Journal of Religious Thought* 4(2) (Spring–Summer 1947): 152–66. Charles B. Ashanin, "Afro-American Christianity: Challenge and Significance," *The Journal of Religious Thought* 16(2) (Summer–Autumn 1959): 109–19. Richard I. McKinney, "Existentialist Ethics and Protest Movement," *The*

Journal of Religious Thought 22(2) (1965–1966): 107–20. Everett F. S. Davies, "Negro Protest Movement: The Religious Way," *The Journal of Religious Thought* 24(2) (1967–1968): 13–25.

21. William Stuart Nelson, "Satyagraha: Gandhian Principles of Non-Violent Non-Cooperation," *The Journal of Religious Thought* 15(1) (Fall 1957/Winter 1958): 15–24. On Nelson's philosophy of nonviolence consult, J. Deotis Roberts, "Moral Suasion as Nonviolent Direct Action: The Legacy of William Stuart Nelson," *The Journal of Religious Thought* 35(2) (Fall–Winter, 1978–1979): 29–43. For a view of William Stuart Nelson's theology of race relations, see William Stuart Nelson, *The Christian Way in Race Relations* (New York: Harper and Brothers, 1948). For an insightful biographical look at Nelson and *The Journal of Religious Thought*, read Blanche Wright Nelson, "A Tribute to My Husband," *The Journal of Religious Thought* 35(2) (Fall–Winter, 1978–1979): 54–56.

22. In connection with *The Journal of Religious Thought*, Nelson established an annual program, The Institute of Religion, at Howard University. Frank T. Wilson notes: "For more than a quarter century, the Institute of Religion has provided a forum, and sometimes a platform, for the systematic exploration of ideas, points of view and formulations related to the broad fields of Theology, Social Ethics, the Dignity of Man and the Quest for Freedom, The Church and the World. The specific themes have derived from concern about particular aspects of human experience in the contemporary scene, as related to far-reaching and fundamental values toward which the energies of men have been directed under changing circumstances in various periods of human history. The wording of this year's theme suggests that 'Black Theology' is emerging, or has occurred, within the context of the 'Black Revolution.' Or perhaps, more appropriately, it may be said that Black Theology is one of the most noticeable manifestations of a Black revolution. At an even deeper level, one may contend that a theology filtered through the rugged terrain of Black experience is giving impetus and vitality to a Black revolution" ("Critical Evaluation of the Theme—The Black Revolution: Is There a Black Theology?" 5–6).

23. J. Deotis Roberts, "Black Theological Ethics: A Bibliographical Essay," *The Journal of Religious Ethics* 3(1) (1975): 69.

24. On Black consciousness, read J. Deotis Roberts, "Black Consciousness in Theological Perspective," in *The Black Experience in Religion*, ed. C. Eric Lincoln (Garden City, NY: Anchor Books, 1974).

25. Kelsey steadfastly argues, "When the claim, 'black is beautiful' is made as an affirmation that blackness is an authentic color among the colors of human beings and not a burnt offering to the devil, this is a valuable item of psychological reorientation and education in a world of racist imperialism based on color. But when 'black is beautiful' implies that 'white is ugly,' this is evidence that the old disease has simply been transplanted, for pseudo-species reappears under a color reversal" ("The Racist Search for Self," 251). [More on this point from Kelsey is addressed in the next chapter.]

26. Read Mark L. Chapman, *Christianity on Trial*. See page 5 for Chapman's distinction between Negro and Black Theology.

27. See Alice Echols, "Nothing Distant about It: Women's Liberation and Sixties Radicalism," in David Farber, ed., *The Sixties: From Memory to History* (Chapel Hill: UNC Press Books, 2012), 166.

28. Wright argues, "I make bold to suggest what to me amounts to a uniqueness in the Black Experience which may be capable of informing and enlarging the outlook of Christian Theology. I am, of course, realistically assuming here the fact of the uniqueness of quality in each individual life-related encounter. I am at pains also to re-emphasize the inevitable pluralism of outlook attending members of any ethnic or racial group, however closely knit. While there is, too, the quite obvious phenomenon of the geographically isolated and circumscribed pattern of Negro housing in America, all Black folks are not so confined. This being said, the fact remains of a kind of ghettoized psychology, described above and intimated by the slogan 'Black Power,' which generates an inclusive Black Experience ominously binding upon every Black

man in America. He may indeed ignore it, rationalize or forget it. However subtle the defenses employed against this involvement (and there are countless variations within each option), it is a stubborn and present fact of American life that no Black man can escape it" ("'Black Theology' or Black Experience?," 54–55).

29. James H. Cone, "Black Theology and the Black Church: Where Do We Go from Here?," in Milton C. Sernett, ed., *Afro-American Religious History: A Documentary Witness* (Durham, NC: Duke University Press, 1985), 480.

30. Eugene G. Prater, "Daniel Payne—Bishop Payne of African Methodism," *The Journal of Religious Thought* 15(1) (Fall 1957/Winter 1958): 59–70.

31. William Stuart Nelson, *The Christian Way in Race Relations* (New York: Harper and Brothers, 1948); "Satyagraha: Gandhian Principles of Non-Violent Non-Cooperation," *The Journal of Religious Thought* 15(1) (Fall 1957/Winter 1958): 15–24. On Martin Luther King's response to William Stuart Nelson's influence, consult the website to the Stanford University Encyclopedia on Martin Luther King's papers, http://kingencyclopedia.stanford.edu/encyclopedia/encyclopedia/enc_nelson_william_stuart_1895_1977/ [accessed June 30, 2017]. Also read Dennis C. Dickerson, "William Stuart Nelson and the Interfaith Origins of the Civil Rights Movement," in R. Drew Smith, William Ackah, and Anthony G. Reddie, eds., *Churches, Blackness, and Contested Multiculturalism* (New York: Palgrave Macmillan, 2014).

32. For a summary treatment of Nelson's international activism, consult Rayford W. Logan, *Howard University: The First Hundred Years, 1867–1967* (New York: NYU Press, 1969): 543–44. On Nelson's collaboration with Du Bois, see Rayford W. Logan, "Reminiscences," *The Journal of Religious Thought* 35(2) (Fall–Winter, 1978–1979): 61–62.

33. Dennis C. Dickerson, "African American Religious Intellectuals and the Theological Foundations of the Civil Rights Movement, 1930–55," *Church History* 74 (2005): 220. Among those in the civil rights movement that Thurman advised was Martin Luther King, Jr., Pauli Murray, Vernon Jordan, James Farmer, Whitney Young, Samuel Proctor, Jesse Jackson, and Bayard Rustin. Consult Reginald F. Hildebrand, "Howard Thurman: Teacher of Teachers, Leader of Leaders, and Preacher of Preachers," *The News & Observer* (February 11, 2007), http://www.unc.edu/depts/honors/docs/Food%20-%20Hildebrand.pdf [accessed August 14, 2015]. [Special note: James Farmer of the Congress of Racial Equality was the son of J. Leonard Farmer, previously mentioned in chapter 1. Consult, James Farmer, *Lay Bare the Heart: An Autobiography of the Civil Rights Movement* (Fort Worth: Texas Christian University Press, 1998). Read especially chapter 4, for the early influence of Farmer Sr. and James Farmer Jr.]

34. William Stuart Nelson, *Bases of World Understanding, An Inquiry into the Means of Resolving Racial, Religious, Class, and National Misapprehensions and Conflicts* (Calcutta: Calcutta University, 1949). Read Amiya Chakravarty, "A Tribute from a Friend," *The Journal of Religious Thought* 35(2) (Fall–Winter, 1978–1979): 58–60. A perusal of Black college newspapers would clearly document how Black theologians were typically guest speakers. For example, the theologian/philosophers Richard I. McKinney and Everett F. S. Davies, among others, were actively engaged on Black college campuses. On McKinney and Davies see, "Speakers Discuss Religion Here," *Campus Echo: North Carolina College at Durham* 14(7) (March 29, 1956).

35. Among the few on white campuses before 1960 was George D. Kelsey. After teaching at Morehouse, George D. Kelsey joined the faculty at Drew University. "In 1950, Kelsey was a guest lecturer at Drew University in Madison, NJ and taught a seminar on Christian Ethics. In 1951, he accepted the position of Associate Professor of Christian Ethics at Drew and was promoted to full Professor in 1957. In 1972, he was awarded the title of Henry Anson Buttz Professor of Christian Ethics at Drew, which he kept until his retirement in 1976." See "Biography of George D. Kelsey," in George D. Kelsey Papers, 1932–1996, Finding Aid, Drew University Library Kelsey Collection, https://uknow.drew.edu/confluence/display/Library/George+D.+Kelsey+Papers%2C+1932-1996+-Finding+Aid [accessed July 20, 2016].

36. Founded in the nineteenth century, the *A. M. E. Church Review* is the organ of the African Methodist Episcopal Church. It is a rich source for both theological and philo-

sophical thought. *The Negro Journal of Religion* was an African American interdenominational sponsored journal and located in Wilberforce, Ohio. *The A.M.E. Zion Quarterly Review* is obviously the organ of this particular historic Black Church.

37. Chapman, *Christianity on Trial*.

38. One nineteenth-entury precursor to the Black Theology School and the notion of a Black God was the A.M.E. Bishop Henry McNeal Turner. Turner emphatically stated, "Demented though we be, whenever we reach the conclusion that God or even that Jesus Christ, while in the flesh, was a white man, we shall hang our gospel trumpet upon the willow and cease to preach. We had rather be an atheist and believe in no God or a pantheist and believe that all nature is God, than to believe in the personality of a God and not believe that He is Negro. Blackness is much older than whiteness, for black was here before white, if the Hebrew word, coshach, or chasack, has any meaning. We do not believe in the eternity of matter, but we do believe that chaos floated in infinite darkness or blackness, millions, billions, quintillions and eons of years before God said, 'Let there be light,' and that during that time God had no material light Himself and was shrouded in darkness, so far as human comprehension is able to grasp the situation." Consult Henry McNeal Turner, "God I a Negro" (1898), in Edwin S.Redkey, ed., *Respect Black: The Writings and Speeches of Henry McNeal Turner* (New York: Arno Press/New York Times, 1971), 176–77.

39. Yancy, *Christology and Whiteness*.

40. Wright, "'Black Theology' or Black Experience?, 54.

41. Gayraud S. Wilmore, "The Case for a New Black Church Style," in H. M. Nelsen and R. Yokley, *The Black Church in America* (New York: Basic Books, 1971), 325.

42. Frank T. Wilson, "Critical Evaluation of the Theme—The Black Revolution: Is There a Black Theology?," 7.

43. Thurman's "Review of J. Deotis Roberts's *Liberation and Reconciliation*, 466.

44. Consult Leon E. Wright, "'Black Theology' or Black Experience?," 54.

45. Frederick Douglass, "Slaveholding Religion and the Christianity of Christ," in Milton C. Sernett, ed., *Afro-American Religious History: A Documentary Witness* (Durham, NC: Duke University Press, 1985): 104.

46. Cone, *Black Theology and Black Power*, 33.

47. For works that provide counterarguments to proofs for God's existence, consult A. C. Grayling, *The God Argument: The Case against Religion and for Humanism* (London: Bloomsbury Publishing, 2014). Michael Martin, *Atheism: A Philosophical Justification* (Philadelphia: Temple University Press, 1990). Victor J. Stenger, *God: The Failed Hypothesis: How Science Shows That God Does Not Exist* (Amherst, NY: Prometheus Books, 2008).

48. Consult John A. T. Robinson, *Honest to God* (Philadelphia: Westminster Press, 1963), 14. Also read Paul Tillich, *Biblical Religion and the Search for Ultimate Reality* (Chicago: University of Chicago Press, 1955).

49. Leon E. Wright, "'Black Theology' or Black Experience?," 54.

50. Brittany L. O'Neal, *Apologia for Black Liberation: The Concept of God in James H. Cone's Black Liberation Theology and William R. Jones' Humanocentric Theism* (Doctoral Dissertation: Michigan State University, 2015).

51. For a critique of Blackness as an ontological category, see Victor Anderson, *Beyond Ontological Blackness: An Essay on African American Religious and Cultural Criticism* (New York: Continuum, 1995).

52. Anthony Pinn, "Looking like Me, Jesus Images, Christology, and the Limitations of Theological Blackness," in George Yancy, ed., *Christology and Whiteness: What Would Jesus Do?* (New York: Routledge, 2012), 266.

53. Preston N. Williams, "James Cone and the Problem of a Black Ethic," *Harvard Theological Review* 65(4) (October 1972): 487–88.

54. Harding, "The Religion of Black Power," 40–65.

55. Harding, "The Religion of Black Power," 40–65.

THREE
The Critique of Black Theology
Richard I. McKinney on the Fundamental Elements of Christianity

The overriding presumption—regarding the defining features of Black Theology—is that it is more than merely the Blackening of white Christianity and its adjoining Christology. Black Theology in its challenge and opposition to white theology aims to radically reconstruct the substructure of white Christology and thus provide what are new fundaments for Christianity as belief system and worldview. Consecutively, it follows that Blackness becomes more than a social category descriptive of race relations and consequently assumes cardinal theological significance. Thus, the very foundation of an authentic Christology rests on the authenticity and particularity of Blackness. Yet, we uncovered that this presupposition did not stand without the critical response on the part of other African American theologians. Respecting the fundamental tenets of Christianity, Richard I. McKinney argues that Black Theology is readily open to critical assessment. He states,

> An examination of the essence of the Christian faith will be helpful toward an assessment of the validity of the "Black Theology" concept. As generally understood, central to the ethic of the Christian message is the ideal of universality, a universality which cuts across all lines of race, nation, class or even family ties.[1]

With our opening statement, Dr. Richard I. McKinney directs us in the opposite direction of Cone's previous declarations in chapter 2. McKinney is most concerned with how Christianity is fundamentally universal in its message and faith claims. From his perspective, the essence of the Christian faith—rather than the essence of Blackness—is the starting point in the evaluation of Black Theology. The classical concept of the Christian God and the universality of the Christian message come to the forefront. Sequentially, these assumptions form the presumptive context for the appraisal of Black Theology and its validity.[2]

McKinney's theology gives prime significance to the universality of the Christian message, while Cone's highlighting of Blackness—as basic ultimate reality—points toward its particularity. Here, we note that what is before us are essentially different theological positions concerning the substantive relation of Black Theology with Christianity. McKinney's charge is that we must seriously take into account the ideal that Christian universality continues as primary and fundamental. Anything less than the ideal of universality effectively diminishes Christianity to merely an aggregate of particularistic theologies. The accent on Christian theology as universality, subsequently, renders the "Black Theology" concept to critical scrutiny. In that way—and only in that manner—can we judge the validity of the "Black Theology" concept.

Yet, a counterclaim to McKinney's kind of universality is not out of the question. It could be that McKinney's notion of universality is misguided. If it is misguided, then we have not received the kind of critique of Black Theology that would warrant our attention and agreement. We could not readily offer our consent respecting how this kind of particularity fails as authentic Christian theology. A leading proponent of Black Theology, J. Deotis Roberts perhaps offers such a counterargument. Roberts declares:

> The rejoinder I hear from the theological establishment is that [Christian] theology is universal. To assert that Western theology is universal is to fly in the face of compelling evidence. It is not universal. It takes a very provincial point of view and attempts to *totalize* it. The situation now demands that theology first be contextualized. This does not rule out the possibility of partnership in a pluralistic situation. If we reach a universal situation, it must take seriously the several contexts in which theological reflection is done.[3]

We can state unequivocally that McKinney is far from belonging to the theological establishment. It could be argued, while McKinney is not a part of the establishment, he holds the equivalent viewpoint. However, we could respond that McKinney's claim of universality need not rest on "a very provincial point of view and attempts to *totalize* it." The basis for universality, in McKinney's example, could stand on different grounds.

For instance, we have the notion that Jesus's message of salvation (whatever it may be) is a universal principle. Given that a great number of Black Christians think so, therefore we ask, Are they under Western influence or rather appropriately in concert with most of the Christian world? We could very well query, What are the consequences adjoined to Roberts's critique of false universality? Does this Black form of particularity, in effect, deny that Jesus is the universal savior? Must Jesus emerge singularly as the (particular) savior of Black people?[4]

Foundationally, the idea behind Roberts's claim is the assertion that Western theology as universal is false. Even granted that we have a case here of *false universality*, it does not follow that universality—in itself—is a false idea. The search for universality may uncover false universals, yet this does not mean that universality per se is false. The conflation of the two notions overlooks the validity of universality and the need to recover it.

The charge of false universality must presume *the truth of universality* to arrive at the very *conclusion of falsity*. Hence what follows, Western theology as universality is false because of its failure to meet the criteria—the truth conditions—for universality. The pressing concern is to uncover such truth conditions for universality in making judgments about falsity. This is far from the position that universality is false. Hereafter, Roberts's critique of false universality is not an adequate criticism of McKinney's notion of universality.

Roberts, in accenting "The situation now demands that theology first be contextualized," is well taken. However, the context of particularity—for instance, Black Theology—is ultimately presumed to be an expression of the concrete universality of Christianity. The context of comparing specific (particular) things always requires a concrete universal. It follows because particularity is an instance—concrete expression—of universality.[5]

Correspondingly, the contextual universality of Christianity permits the identification of particular beliefs to serve as concrete instances of Christianity as opposed to, for example, core beliefs in other religions such as Judaism or Islam. Islam and Judaism both do not acknowledge Jesus as universal savior. The belief in Jesus as universal savior is singularly a Christian belief, which demarcates Christians from Muslims and Jews. Hence, this core belief *universally identifies* who is a Christian. Clearly, this universal identification is not the totalizing of the Western theological viewpoint. Instead, it demonstrates how universality cannot be neglected, that is if Christian theology is to make sense of its own *particularity* among other religions.

The general consensus on core beliefs—as universal principles—helps in anchoring the concrete meaning of Christianity. The key assumptions we outlined in the introduction—more or less—could be viewed as universal Christian beliefs. They were presented as the framework for establishing a broadly based consensus on what are core Christian beliefs. It seems most Christians—including Black Christians—would not find them as provincial or controversial. Can it be established that the following set of beliefs are of a distinctly Western orientation? Or instead, are they what McKinney views as "a universality which cuts across all lines of race, nation, class or even family ties?" Let us return and review the presuppositions that could possibly anchor the universality of Christianity.

1. God is a personal God and the supernatural entity that created the universe;
2. Christians must believe in the word of God and Christ, and it follows that the Bible is the inspired manifestation of the sacred word of God and Jesus Christ;
3. Christ is the Son of God, and his resurrection offers the possibility of human salvation from sin;
4. Sin is the primary condition for the spiritual and moral context of human existence on earth; and
5. Christian ethics are based on absolute morals as outlined in Biblical Scripture and in accordance with church doctrines, creeds, and traditions.

What looms over the horizon, in this discussion, is the question, Does Black Theology reject these five propositions as universal to the Christian belief system? Can the particularistic character of Black Theology point in a different direction? If it does, then it follows that Black Theology rejects the very idea that Christianity has universal utility.

Moreover, the claim of Black Theology concerning Christian authenticity becomes rather weak, if it is presumed that Christianity lacks universal value. Are we simply engaged in a plurality of particularities or does authenticity demand that Christianity has universal utility? It is precisely this rejection of Christianity's universal efficacy that fosters the attempt to critically judge Black Theology and its claim to be authentically Christian in character. Critics such as McKinney, Wilson, Wright, and Thurman are skeptical of theologies that profess to be Christian and yet discount the importance of the universal message of Christian theology.

If the particularity of race discounts the universality of Christianity, then the authentic message of Christianity goes to the wayside. It could be argued Christian beliefs are universal in nature. God, Jesus, sin, and salvation, for instance, are not limited to specific racial groups. As Dr. Benjamin Mays argues, "The creeds of Christendom have always been formulated and enforced in terms of certain beliefs about God, Jesus, sin, and salvation, never on theories about race or ethnic groups."[6]

RICHARD I. MCKINNEY AND THE CRITIQUE OF BLACK THEOLOGY: FURTHER EXPLORATIONS INTO A PHILOSOPHICAL DEFINITION

With respect to the aforementioned questions, our listing while considerable, undoubtedly is not exhaustive. Certainly, a host of other questions can immediately come to mind relating to the philosophical problem of definition. With our previous statement, from African American philosopher and theologian Dr. Richard I. McKinney, we get a sense of how the issue of Black Theology—in relation to Christianity—gains prominent attention respecting the problem of definition. College administrator, educator, scholar in religious studies, theologian, and philosopher, Dr. Richard I. McKinney astutely confronts the questions at hand.[7] McKinney asserts,

> If one heard the terms "Black Chemistry," "Black Mathematics," or "Black English Literature," he would be hard-pressed to understand exactly how such disciplines would differ from "pure" chemistry, mathematics or English literature. To what extent, therefore, is the term "Black Theology" a legitimate and viable concept? On first thought, it would appear that this term represents an attempt to mold an historic corpus of data to fit an arbitrary conceptual scheme.[8]

Undoubtedly, McKinney's declaration addresses the problem of subject matter as affixed to an academic discipline. His method is comparative and entails implicit background assumptions. For instance, what is it about *Black* Theology which makes it "Black" yet theologically consistent with Christianity? In what sense is Black Theology authentically Christian? Is the concept of "Black" in Black Theology a defining feature of its subject matter or more descriptive of the racial identification respecting its authors/practitioners?

Given the notion of Black Theology, are we to assume that Christianity is particularistic rather than based on the ideal of universality? If it is particularistic, then the idea of Jesus as universal savior no longer has the merit of justification. In other words, we cannot justify the idea of Jesus as universal savior on the basis of particularistic theology. Hence, the question, does Black theology render Jesus as something different than a universal savior?

Answers to these questions are generated by McKinney's critical observations, which are telling methodological inquiries. From our previous discussion on his first statement, it is transparent that McKinney is not in agreement with Cone's idea of God and Blackness. McKinney's inquiries bring to the forefront issues about logical coherency and theoretical consistency. What are we talking about when we refer to Black Theology? In the second proposition, McKinney astutely queries about the legitimacy and viability of the very concept. The reader should take notice of the impact of "Black" as an adjective, which is directed toward meaning.

How does the term "Black" add to the meaning of "pure" Christian theology—that is, Christian theology understood without racial labels or rather in universal terms? How important is the Black moniker? Clearly when McKinney states, "On first thought, it would appear that this term represents an attempt to mold an historic corpus of data to fit an arbitrary conceptual scheme," his query is not a wholesale rejection of the idea, "Black Theology." Instead, it is a critical appraisal at the level of a first approximation. What comes to light is a warning not to jump on the bandwagon until we thoroughly study the situation—locate the appropriate conceptual scheme—by which we might place Black Theology. The key is not falling into the trap where we have "an attempt to mold an historic corpus of data to fit an arbitrary conceptual scheme."

The avoidance of such a deception, of course, mandates that we raise the questions: How can we determine if there is an appropriate conceptual scheme for Black Theology? In other words, what are the theoretical grounds for such a conceptual scheme? Is it something we can garner from biblical texts? Or is it something that develops from the very process of doing Christian theology and how one methodologically approaches the subject? If it is an issue of methodology in the pursuit of theology, can white theologians—that master the appropriate methods—participate in Black Theology? Hence, in this sense, do they become Black theologians? This prompts the question, How does authorship shape our definition of Black Theology?[9]

Therefore, we ask, Does the adjective "Black" in Black Theology speak to the race of the author of the text? Is Black authorship a sufficient condition for defining Black Theology? Given that Farmer, Thurman, and McKinney were all Black men, does it make sense to say that they were Black theologians, that is, practitioners of Black Theology? Or is it necessary to offer a qualification, if you will, a caveat when we state that Farmer, Thurman, and McKinney are Black theologians? Such questions persist when we start from the *authentically Black* hypothesis.

Surely, it is a fact, they are Black men involved in doing and writing theology. Is there a different sense in which they are Black theologians, when reference to "Black" is based on the fact they are Black authors rather than highlighting the content of the subject matter under review? The caveat becomes necessary when the orientation and subject matter are the defining features for Blackness. Therein authorship—in terms of Black racial identity—is simply coincidental.

As we found in chapter 1, Drs. J. Leonard Farmer and Howard Thurman were theologians of African American descent—Black authors—that did not espouse Black Theology as such. The same holds true for McKinney. Since Farmer, Thurman, and McKinney were not pursuing the idea of a distinctively Black Theology, can we conclude they were actually engaged in white theology? Did they lack an authentically Black orientation to Christian theology? Were they Black theologians respecting authorship yet "white" theologians regarding theological orientation, substance, and subject matter? It seems rather odd to say that this is the case. However, this is one outcome that logically follows from a strictly binary opposition between Black and white theologies, where authorship is not a sufficient condition for defining Black Theology.

In their respective cases, the notion of Black Theology is not a description that applies to the author undertaking the academic work of theology. It makes sense to say authorship remains as an open question as to the definition of Black Theology. Subsequently, closed authorship based on race is not a constituent part of the appropriate conceptual scheme. Hypothetically, it follows that a white author could just as well participate in and contribute to the development of Black Theology. Be this as it may, we are still faced with the question of the appropriate conceptual scheme.[10]

It is vitally important that we distinguish between the appropriate conceptual scheme and the actual social context for the emergence of Black Theology. McKinney is clearly aware of the fact there is the determinate context for how the term "Black Theology" gains notoriety in the public arena. Such an entrance is not the same as uncovering the conceptual scheme, which establishes the legitimacy and viability of Black Theology.

Black Theology was the direct response to what was called the "Black Revolution." More specifically, the emergence of the Black Power movement presented a challenge for the development of a form of Christianity relevant to the circumstances related to growing Black nationalist consciousness. We have seen that a considerable number in the Black Power movement rejected Christianity as the white man's religion.[11] Furthermore, the imposition of Christianity on African American slaves was part and parcel of their oppressive conditions. Its continuance regarding post-slavery demanded a new ideological orientation away from Christianity. For most of the Black power advocates, Christianity was the oppressors' ideology.

Hence, for many in the Black nationalist camp, Christianity was a conservative and reactionary force that impeded that growth of Black nationalist consciousness and the attainment of Black Power. The impact that Black power had on nationalist thinking among Black youth specifically moved many away from the Black church and Christianity. A different sense of racial/national identity became more pronounced, and the Christian emphasis on love and the philosophy of nonviolence, thereby rendered as impotent. In many ways, Black Theology was a Christian response to such criticism and alienation. Specifically, it was a particular form of Black religious nationalism.[12] In 1969, McKinney responded to this "Black Revolutionary" context when he wrote,

> Now, today, as part of the "Black Revolution," we are presented with proposals for the construction of a "Black Theology." Obviously, like other terms characteristic of this movement, the term "Black Theology" is a term of protest. It can be seen as a protest against the hypocrisy of certain White Christians who have failed to recognize either in their preachments or in their actions the relation of the Christian gospel to the needs of the Black community.[13]

If Black Theology boils down to "a protest against the hypocrisy of certain White Christians who have failed to recognize either in their preachments or in their actions the relation of the Christian gospel to the needs of the Black community," then its primary audience becomes not Black people but rather "a certain group" of white Christians. In this sense, McKinney is not far from Black Theologian Joseph A. Johnson's position on Black Theology. For Johnson, we observed, argued that Black theology was a *reaction* to white theology and theologians. In both instances, the protest or reaction is on behalf of Black Christian interests as they relate to the white Christian—hypocritical—pronouncements and practices.

McKinney makes this point crystal clear—namely, "the relation of the Christian gospel to the needs of the Black community" become the Black interests that are—with respect to Black Theology—protest phenomenon.[14] Despite their theological differences, what is key is that McKinney and Johnson both presume some kind of an authentic Christianity which is free of such hypocrisy. Or as we found in Johnson's brisk phrasing, free from the "gross perversion of the Christian faith."

In contrast to McKinney and Johnson, Farmer and Thurman were convinced that what officially—should we say authentically?—became Christianity was, in theological terms, vastly different from the teachings of Jesus. Given our discussion—in chapter 1—about the disjunction of the religion of Jesus and the emergence of Christianity, we must ask, How is the Christian gospel related to the needs of the Black community? Maybe the Christian gospel is not related at all. Obviously, the notion of some kind of relation all depends on our definition of Christianity.

Given our definition, advanced by Thurman, it makes sense to ask, Are we actually witnessing a white failure of recognition with respect to "the Christian gospel to the needs of the Black community?" Or instead are we observing Christianity per se—that is, what Howard Thurman points out as the Christian religion adopted by the Roman oppressors of Jews? Perhaps if Thurman is right, then the perceived failure is no more than a misconception concerning Christianity. Christianity is not the religion of Jesus and we should not define it in that manner. If the latter is the case, then, we have a misdirected protest on the part of Black Theology.

Misdirected since Black Theology begins with the wrong supposition—namely, that white Christianity persists as an inauthentic form. It could very well be that—in historical terms—white Christianity is nearer to the mark regarding the origins/authenticity of Christianity. This means that rather than the case of white hypocrisy among certain Christians, we are facing the real legacy of authentic Christianity. Granting the idea of an original Christianity as oppressive—in distinction from the religion of Jesus—the very fight over the authenticity of Christianity is ill advised.

Although, a philosophically challenging thought to reflect upon, this conclusion is not where McKinney intends on taking us. His search for the appropriate conceptual scheme presumes a different sort of Christianity and Christian theology than Thurman's. McKinney thinks that the historical Jesus and Christianity are identical. In McKinney's estimation, Christian theology in substance is universal because God is universally ultimate reality and Jesus represents all of humanity. Furthermore, the Christian core belief system—particularly its ethical dimension—is universal in its scope; not to mention the universal implications respecting the articles of faith embodied in Christianity. Black nationalist religious orientation—Cone's Black Theology—is incompatible with McKinney's principle of Christian universality.

Hereafter, there is a different sort of theology than what Cone proposes for us. Does this quest for universality lead us to white theology? Or can universality ground particular efforts to concretize how Black people and the Black experience are properly located in the needed conceptual scheme? This understanding of Christian universality is McKinney's starting point. Perhaps McKinney's first statement will help us along the road of discovering the proper conceptual scheme. Let us return to it and see how it permits us to shed further light on discovering the appropriately suited conceptual scheme.

BLACK THEOLOGY, UNIVERSAL CHRISTIAN FAITH, AND THE BLACK CHURCH

As theologian and philosopher, McKinney is not inclined to reach any hasty conclusions about the matters at hand. He is concerned that we make a careful judgment in view of the call for Black Theology. The context of his remarks is the year of 1969, when Black Theology was gaining public attention. Crucially, the validity of Black Theology is grounded on making the correct discovery of its conceptual scheme. This search for the appropriate conceptual scheme is the driving force in his critical analysis of Black Theology. Let's return to McKinney's first statement. He informs us,

> An examination of the essence of the Christian faith will be helpful toward an assessment of the validity of the "Black Theology" concept. As generally understood, central to the ethic of the Christian message is the ideal of universality, a universality which cuts across all lines of race, nation, class or even family ties.[15]

This statement unfolds how McKinney views the essence of the Christian faith and Christian ethic vis-à-vis the validity of Black theology. Concurrently, the essence of Christian faith becomes the litmus test in evaluating any theology that claims to be Christian in character. Moreover, the ethic behind the Christian message is universality. "The ideal of universality, a universality which cuts across all lines of race, nation, class or even family ties," effectively renders a critical judgment on the particularity of Black Theology.

McKinney argues that the ideal of universality overrides all particular interests. He is not far from Paul's rendering of Christianity. Paul states, "There is neither Jew nor Greek, there is neither bond nor free, there is neither male nor female: for ye are all one in Christ Jesus" (Galatians 3:28, King James Version). Paul's transcendent concept of universality, nonetheless, harbors a neglect of criticism about the real material conditions that engender oppression. If bond and free are one in Christ, we ask, is this unity in Christ rather a call for the spiritual escape from the critique of such material conditions? We must further query, Does this mean not changing these oppressive conditions in the here and now? African American philosopher Robert C. Williams amplifies these points of deliberation about Paul when he provocatively questions,

> As persons called into a community of freedom, are slaves free to exist beyond the external conditions of bondage? Is not Paul's discussion of freedom more related to sin and spirituality than to social circumstances? Many theologians use Paul's counsel to Philemon, as regards the status of Onesimus the slave, to indicate a definite proslavery position on Paul's part.[16]

When McKinney argues, "The ideal of universality, a universality which cuts across all lines of race, nation, class or even family ties," with the idea of "which cuts across," he seems to imply *transcendence* of race, nation, class, or family ties. Such universalism, in its transcendent character, is an abstract rather than concrete universal. Thus, it does not offer a concrete solution to slavery and its vestiges. Can we with validity claim that this is authentically Christianity? If it is authentic Christianity, then it falls woefully short as a liberation theology. Of course, we could ponder, why presume Christianity is a liberation theology? McKinney's (and Paul's) transcendent universality seems to be more a matter where the focus is on *personal salvation* rather than collective liberation. Given this difference in focus, we can infer that McKinney's stance implicitly challenges the very idea of liberation theology, whether it is Black or not.[17]

McKinney's claim concerning the universality of the Christian message must wrestle with the implications of such transcendence as we find with Paul's dictum. McKinney's stance appears to be, on our interpretation, in accord with Paul's position on the universality of Jesus Christ. Other interpretations may be possible, which we will not address in the body of the text.[18] What we do know is that in McKinney's estimation, the issues of race and nation are not consistent with authentic Christian theology. He argues that this universal ideal is even manifested in the concrete experiences of Black Christians. McKinney emphatically states,

> Historically, as everyone knows, Black people were taught Christianity by Whites. It is admittedly anomalous that a people enslaved should be

taught a gospel of brotherly love by those who sanctioned a system which denied the humanity of those whom they taught. Yet the Blacks accepted and appropriated this gospel, for its basic message was pertinent to their situation.

McKinney continues,

> [T]he Black church became the bulwark of spiritual and moral strength for the Black community. But throughout this development, it was never thought that the Christianity of the Black people was a *specialized faith*, but rather that people of all races and colors were expected to incorporate *the same basic principles* in their religion and in their lives.[19] [Italics added]

The same basic principles of Christianity—found in the white church—were manifested in the Black church. McKinney contends there is no real theological divide concerning the Black church and its white counterpart. If Black Theology claims to have derived from the Black Christian experience and particularly its associated churches, then McKinney—a scholar on this very topic of the Black church—sets out to make the record clear.[20] It is McKinney's viewpoint, the Black church "never thought that the Christianity of the Black people was a specialized faith," hence, requiring something like "Black Theology" and a "Black Christ."[21]

McKinney argues that Black Theology then is not the product of the historic Black church and everyday Black Christian experience. The Black church did not espouse a theology that diverted from *the same basic principles* that Christians of all races and colors were committed to respecting their convictions and how they led their lives. Plainly, the racial divide regarding the Christian church, although overtly racist, however, did not encompass ancillary theological distinctions; wherein a different set of Christian principles were operative.

The Black church did not historically emerge as grounded on any distinctive theological orientation. He explains why Black people would embrace the religion of slave masters. McKinney illuminates,

> It is also a matter of wonder that these slaves could accept the religion of their masters as freely as they did. The explanation may be found in the fact that the Christian faith was a religion which offered *salvation and spiritual security to all persons regardless of their status in life*. The Blacks accepted wholeheartedly this particular aspect of the Christian religion and, in doing so, recognized that those who taught them this religion did not always practice it themselves.[22] [Italics added]

McKinney affirms that Black acceptance of Christianity was due in large part to its universal elements. Namely, "Christian faith was a religion which offered salvation and spiritual security to all persons regardless of their status in life." Furthermore, the advent of Black churches was not the product of theological divergence pertaining to white Christians. Rather than the matter of white theology, McKinney contends that racism pushed Black people out of the white church, thus forming their own congregations. His remarks are instructive: "In this respect, it can be said that in large measure the Negro church is a child of protest; for had the Whites been willing to accept Negroes on a basis of equality in their congregations, it is hardly likely that the Negroes would have been constrained to establish their own centers of worship as they did."[23]

If Black churches did not harbor ideas about Black Theology, it also stands that biblical texts are far from providing the needed documentation for African American churches deliberating about some form of Black Christology. In similarity with Thurman, McKinney acknowledges that Jesus was a Jew and further adds that in all likelihood was not white. McKinney is not caught in the snare that Christian universality renders Jesus as a white man. He states, "With respect to the claim that Jesus was a Black man, a good argument can be made that he was hardly as Caucasian in his appearance as he is often represented. Travellers to the Holy Land have often been struck by the dark complexions of many of the people there, and the claim is made that Negro blood has been mingled with Jewish blood."[24]

McKinney thus emphasizes, "Whatever may be the case here, the fact is that Jesus evidently considered himself a Jew, *no matter the hue of his skin*, and he apparently considered himself as one in the long line of Hebrew prophets. But *the thrust of his message is basically universal*, and the attempt to make it limited to only one race represents a distortion of history"[25] [Italics added].

So, therefore, we return to the topic of Christology and the historical Jesus outlined in chapter 1. The questions we addressed centered on who was Jesus and what is his relationship to Christianity? Is this relationship linked in a particular manner to the Black experience? How would a Black Christology enter the theological picture? Does making theology Black—in its orientation—successively engender Black Christology?

The presumption here with Black Theology is that Black Christology ultimately facilitates the African American quest for the historical Jesus. Could this perhaps be the basis for which we find the appropriate conceptual scheme of Black Theology? Now we ask, How would McKinney respond to such questions about Black Christology and the historical Jesus? From the above argument, McKinney argues Jesus was neither primarily focused on Judaism nor was he a religious—Jewish—nationalist of any stripe. On this issue—Judaism and Jesus—McKinney joins ranks with Farmer's stance about the inconsequential nature (respecting the theological position) of Jesus's connection to Judaism.

Indeed, McKinney's article, "Reflections on the Concept of 'Black Theology'" stops nothing short of conveying this fact. Let us return to his comment on the historical Jesus. "Whatever may be the case here, the fact is that Jesus evidently considered himself a Jew, no matter the hue of his skin, and he apparently considered himself as one in the long line of

Hebrew prophets. But the thrust of his message is basically universal, and the attempt to make it limited to only one race represents a distortion of history."

Unlike Thurman, McKinney differentiates Jesus's Jewish identity from race. Remember that for Thurman Jewish identity was synonymous with racial designation. While McKinney claims that although Jesus is a Jew and perhaps dark in complexion, race is not of any theological significance. The historical Jesus offers a universal message shorn of any racial particularity. Herein, we observe that McKinney advances a claim about the historical Jesus. His historical judgment is based on the idea that if Jesus limited his efforts to only one race or people it follows we would have a distortion of history.

Yet, we discover pertinent biblical text that makes the very point about Jesus dealing with one group of people. The Matthean Jesus clearly says, "Go nowhere among the Gentiles and enter no town of the Samaritan, but go rather to the lost sheep of the House of Israel. And proclaim as you go, saying, 'The kingdom of heaven is at hand'" (Matthew 10:5-6 ESV).

The thrust of this message, from the Matthean Jesus, is far from basically universal and indeed is antithetical to universality. However, the principle of universality is the cornerstone of McKinney's rejection of Black Theology and its ancillary Christology. Those partisans of the Black Theology School could very well find this passage from the Matthean Jesus materializes as confirmation of the particularistic viewpoint. McKinney's cornerstone is considerably weakened when we take the above Matthean passage into account. Biblical justification for McKinney's Christian universalism confronts a formidable roadblock in terms of the Matthean Jesus. Yet, McKinney has no need for trying to construct a Black Christology on the basis of particularistic theology. A Black Messiah leading a chosen people—Black people—is not on his theological agenda. (More on the topic of Black Messiah in our next chapter.) Now let us address the problem of Christology in view of biblical texts.

CHRISTOLOGY, UNIVERSAL THEOLOGY, AND BIBLICAL TEXTS

At source, the basis for McKinney's presumption about a Christology of universality occurs from a different reading of biblical texts than found with the Matthean Jesus. Can we gather that the Bible is a stumbling block for McKinney's universalist position? Is McKinney entangled in the Eurocentric interpretation of biblical texts? Can we surmise that the very idea of universality as a conception is the by-product of Eurocentric reading? In response to the charge of Eurocentrism, we have already established that McKinney is not claiming that Jesus is white—in fact for McKinney race has no theological significance—although he finds that

Jesus's message is universal and available to white and Black people alike.²⁶

Perhaps we have other concerns regarding the hermeneutics (interpretation) of biblical texts. The problem could be in our very understanding of Jesus's relation to the New Testament. What can we take from the Bible respecting the universality or particularity of Christology? African American theologian and biblical scholar Peter Gomes offers some intriguing perceptions regarding this issue. Gomes argues,

> I suggest that the Bible, in its entire complex splendor, is but a means to a greater end, which is good news, the glad tidings, the gospel. Jesus came preaching—we are told this in all the Gospels and but nowhere in the Gospels is there a claim that he came preaching the New Testament, or even Christianity. It still shocks some Christians to realize that *Jesus was not a Christian,* he did not know "our" Bible, and that what he preached was substantially at odds with his biblical culture and with ours as well.²⁷ [Italics added]

On a path similar to Thurman, Gomes brings to our attention that biblical texts are problematic to establishing the particularity or the universality of Christianity vis-à-vis the historical Jesus. It is transparent—from the standpoint of the historical Jesus—that McKinney cannot stand on sound biblical foundation for establishing Christian universality. Thus, we must ask, On what grounds does McKinney's claim on the Christian message of universality finds its moorings? As we found with Thurman, if it is the historical Christianity contra historical Jesus, then the concern of how Christianity became the official religion of the Roman Empire is no small matter. Universality—catholic in the etymological sense of the word—is intimately linked to Roman imperialism. It is no coincidence that the Roman church eventually claimed (in the fourth century) the status of "Catholic" or universal church.²⁸

Nonetheless, we can see that for McKinney, given the universality of the Christian ethic, the idea of any appropriate conceptual scheme for Black Theology, of the particularistic sort, is also a mistaken notion. In fact, with Black Theology not only is its Christology inaccurate but also the very idea of God becomes distorted. This is a major pitfall because any theology that distorts the concept of God is essentially a flawed and false theology. McKinney unequivocally declares,

> And how do the Black theologians think of God? Is he also black? And are Black people his chosen ones? The concept of "Black Theology" suggests that God, in whatever form he is conceived, is primarily pro-Black. And this, of course, negates the fundamental conception of a deity who is impartial to all his creatures. Only such a deity is universal. Only such a deity can be considered as the creator and judge of all the world.²⁹

Transparently, the centerpiece of Christian theology is the concept of God. McKinney goes directly into what he thinks is problematic about the racialized focus on God in Black Theology. Three points are pertinent: First, Black Theology claims that God is pro-Black. Second, this pro-Black stance expresses God's partisanship, while McKinney's notion of authentic Christian theology posits an impartial God. (And this idea of an impartial God relating to authentic Christianity is consistent with our earlier observation on Frederick Douglass.) Third, the Christian God is universal—manifested as creator and judge of the whole world—therefore this God, unlike Black Theology's conception, is an impartial judge of the world. Consequently, rather than a God that harbors a Black orientation on the issues in the world, the Christian God includes Black people among others in the world on equal terms. McKinney thinks this is the content behind the Christian message of universal ideal.

McKinney's critique of Black Theology is directed at how the adjective 'Black' in Black Theology denotes a theological orientation, which is racial in substance and distorts the historical Jesus as well as the Christian ethic of universality. We should keep in mind that McKinney's critique does not overlook the particularities respecting racism. Nor does he neglect the vestiges of Black oppression—from a religious point of view—resulting from how white Christians have been culprits in this process. McKinney's Christian universal ideal does not disregard this particularity. The concrete particularity of racism that white churches fostered had a major impact on Black psychological makeup. He states,

> The systematic suppression and exploitation of many generations of Black Americans have had their toll in the sense of inferiority and even self-hatred among many of them. Certainly there is need for the correction of the evils of the racist aspects of our society, especially as those evils stem from religious ideologies and institutions. The question remains, however, whether the concepts of a "Black Christ" and a "Black Theology" are legitimate means of achieving this end.[30]

In McKinney's considered opinion, the concepts of "Black Christ" and "Black Theology" are questionable means for addressing white racism. Although, he is conscious of the fact that the sense of inferiority and self-hatred in the African American community mandates a drastic psychological change and direct confrontation with racist religious ideologies and institutions. Writing in 1969, when these ideas of "Black Christ" and "Black Theology" were initially gaining currency, he notes,

> [T]he concept of "Black Theology" smacks of the mood of irrationality which characterizes much of the revolution in progress in this country, among Blacks as well as Whites. We should not have to invent "way out" ideologies in order to effect the kind of transformation of society which is desirable. That transformation can be made within the context

of a close adherence to the essence of the Christian message as we find it in the record of Jesus' life and teachings.[31]

Given that for McKinney it appears that "the record of Jesus' life and teachings" is a reference to Biblical Scripture then—as we have previously noted—his notions about "the essence of the Christian message" for social transformation, thus, resting on biblical foundations is open to considerable argumentation. In this respect, Black Theology can also point to supporting biblical texts to advance its counterposition as well.[32] Therefore, from a Christian perspective, we would have a theological stalemate rather than a progressive step forward. The Bible as well as biblical theology itself could be our juggernaut. Certainly, it is imperative that we acknowledge that neither paradigm—universality nor particularity—holds supremacy. It appears this conflict may not find resolution within Christian biblical theology.

In his observations, Peter Gomes brings into bold relief how Christians often misunderstand the import of biblical Scriptures. Instead of one central message of universality, there are several messages of a conflicting nature. The writers of biblical texts often had their own theological agenda, which was often expressed through the person of Jesus.[33] Nevertheless, at core, for McKinney, the problem with Black Theology is that in its particularity it negates the universality of Jesus's teachings and the Christian message.

In McKinney's estimation, this ethic of universality does not allow for God siding with one group of people against another. God is an impartial deity and this stamps his universality. Can we deduce from this that God is not on the side of the oppressed because that would make him opposed to the oppressors as a particular social group? Will God decide that all white people are oppressors, or must this become a matter of individual behavior?

Similarly, the Black oppressed in this fight against oppression cannot expect that God would join the Black oppressed against their white oppressors. In turn, could God stand against white oppression and still remain free of the antiwhite proclivities of Black Theology? If McKinney holds to the latter, we can see why he is at odds with how Black Theology defines itself. For McKinney whiteness is not reducible to Black oppression, and here he departs from Cone's Black Theology.

Does God's impartial judgment render a verdict in terms of this worldly existence or must we wait on the heavenly reward? If it is a worldly judgment, what are the issues under review? We can assume it is sin, yet we are still faced with concretely deciding on what is sin. Does racism count as sin? Granting that racism is a sin, how can institutional racism lead to a verdict? Who stands as guilty?[34]

While Black Theology can very well point to white institutions, McKinney's Christian universality seems to address the matter of sin in more personal terms—individual salvation. This theology lacks a social dimension because McKinney's Christian universality is *transcendent* in character. McKinney's transcendent or abstract universality appears to be situated on an aggregation of individuals that are removed from any *concrete* social designations. God's judgment of the whole world begins and ends with the individual. If this inference holds true, then McKinney's view of God's ultimate judgment (eschatology) significantly remains devoid of the social breadth offered by Black Theology.[35]

In all fairness to McKinney, he is not opposed to constructing a theology which insists on social transformation. However, it must not be revolutionary in character. Hence, it must be guided by the universal principles of Christianity, which from McKinney's perspective is not revolutionary. He thinks revolutionary ideologies are irrational and "way out," consequently we can construe that McKinney's Christian theology—in political terms—is closer to a type of moderate (reformist) liberalism that does not rule out a healthy dose of racial pride, albeit circumscribed by a humanitarian sense of personal dignity.

McKinney concludes his essay outlining what he considers as the appropriate conceptual scheme for Black Theology. This appropriate conceptual scheme is conditional and thus restricted by the Christian principle of universality, which remains irreversible. This appropriate fit comes by acknowledging that the quest adjoined to overcoming racism's psychological impact on the Black community does not point in the direction of a narrow particularism. It follows that from McKinney's theological viewpoint, Black Christian Nationalism cannot outweigh Christian universality.[36]

While there is the possibility that Black Theology and Black Christology might facilitate overcoming the psychological damage of racism on the Black community, the possible danger of this move (concerning the ideal of Christian universality) cannot be ignored. The Christian ideal of universality, for McKinney, fosters a sense of personal dignity not just for Black people but also it importantly includes all people. McKinney states:

> We may conclude, then, that to the degree that the basic thrust of the concept of "Black Theology" is in the direction of an increased awareness of all people, Blacks and Whites alike, of the essential dignity and worth of all members of the human race, without, at the same time, doing violence to the concept of a universal God and of a Jesus who is concerned for all humanity, to that extent, it is a viable concept. Otherwise, we may ask, what justification can there be for it?[37]

McKinney's statement accents that Black Theology must be consistent with "the essential dignity and worth of all members of the human race." Hence, it stands to reason that Black Theology must not stand in any fashion in opposition to Christian universality. This is due to the fact that Christianity upholds "the concept of a universal God and of a Jesus who is concerned for all humanity." Because Jesus as Christ stands with all people, Jesus cannot be a Black Messiah, either literally or symbolically.[38]

Likewise, since God is universal, then in terms of the Christian deity, God is not ontologically meaningful due to any sort of meaning attached to Blackness or for that matter whiteness, however defined. McKinney's Christian God transcends race and racial monikers. McKinney, nevertheless, grants a possible theological space for Black Theology. However, this space requires a significant reformulation, in actuality a *redefinition* regarding what we found with Cone and other advocates of Black Theology under review.

With McKinney's *definitional qualification* granted to Black Theology, he renders its resultant particularism as subject to the overriding principle of Christian universality. This is a significant theological caveat. For McKinney, herein lies the appropriate conceptual scheme for Black Theology—a conceptual scheme that allows for the universality of the Christian message, while acknowledging that racism among white Christians and their institutions persists as a theological problem for Black people. McKinney emphasizes that this kind of oppressive theology is particularly harmful for those trapped in the psychological confinement of racism.

Racism becomes and remains an assault on human (personal) dignity. This is why, at heart, the Christian universal message is at odds with racism—that is, racism undermines the personal dignity of all humanity. Accordingly, Blackness—in its particularity and respective ethnocentric proclivities—cannot be the pivotal point of authentic Christian theology. McKinney fervently believes that centering Christian theology on Blackness in a singular manner effectively dissipates the critical edge separating the universality of Christianity from the particularity of racism. This conceptual scheme places not only Cone's Black Theology into question, for at root, it also has consequences for the recovery of authentic Christianity and its universal message of human dignity.

CONCLUSION

In a similar manner, the African American philosopher and theologian Dr. George D. Kelsey offers insight into the very thrust of the movement for Black awareness and pride. Prior to the advent of the Black Theology movement, Kelsey wrote extensively on the topic of racism and Christianity. Although not a member of the Black Theology school of thought, Kelsey undoubtedly inspired early members of the Black Theology movement. Particularly his critique of racism as sin (in the form of idolatry) had a lasting effect on generations to come.[39]

Yet, it has been noted, Kelsey's critique is not appropriately expressed on the principles of the Black Theology School. One result of this understanding is that we must be aware that Kelsey's critique of racism does not amount in reducing the opposition to racism to antiwhiteness. In this sense, Kelsey would not agree with Cone and Yancy, namely "Love is the refusal to accept whiteness." As Leon E. Wright brings to our attention,

> George Kelsey pronounces prophetic judgment upon the "racism" characteristic of Black-White involvement in America. Methodologically, Kelsey has impressively utilized moral and ethical insights culled from his own Judaeo-Christian perspective to indict cant and equivocation within the Christian church itself. It would be *incorrect to label the norms so applied as "Black" or otherwise.* They are rather such as are *universally recognized*—justice, love, truth, "faith"—as *fundaments of any specifically Christian moral order.* His ethical perspectives with regard to the "Christian Understanding of Man" would thus quite neatly correspond with any normative statement of Christian theology under this heading.[40] [Italics added]

Although, his stance does not begin on the theological particularity of Blackness, Kelsey is keenly aware of the psychological damage on Black people relating to racist imperialism. Kelsey's universally recognized Christian principles—justice, love, truth, faith—are not antithetical to the promotion of Black racial pride, albeit without the encumbrance of the antiwhiteness stance associated with Black Theology. Kelsey clearly argues that the affirmation of Black identity has great psychological merit in a white racist society. Here Kelsey is in concert with McKinney. Kelsey proffers,

> When the claim, "black is beautiful" is made as an affirmation that blackness is an authentic color among the colors of human beings and not a burnt offering to the devil, this is a valuable item of psychological reorientation and education in a world of racist imperialism based on color. But when "black is beautiful" implies that "white is ugly," this is evidence that the old disease has simply been transplanted, for pseudo-species reappears under a color reversal.[41]

Can it be that the defining feature of Black Theology—with its accent on Blackness in its particularity and antiwhiteness as its cardinal principle—ultimately reduces to a theological form of color reversal? Since Kelsey and McKinney, among others, were apprehensive of these elements of Black Theology, is it justified that we question their locus as Black theologians in terms of some notion of authentic Blackness? Only from a Black nationalist religious sensibility can we think that such an assumption can be justified. Who are Black theologians need not be encumbered by belonging to the late 1960s "Black Theology" School of Thought.

Moreover, we cannot overlook that the Black Theology School's claim on Black authenticity was simultaneously a claim for authentic Christianity. Does authentic Christianity mandate the recovery of authentic

"Blackness"? Yet, let us not forget the important words of Leon E. Wright,

> [I]t should not be supposed that one advances the cause of a "Black Theology" merely by painting faces black or partisanly juggling spiritual preferences before God, respecting persons or groups. Whatever the case for Black Theology may turn out to be, let us not cavalierly create a set of mythological assumptions whose credibility deserves only to be "de-mythologized" at the same instant. If racism is bad, it cannot achieve respectability by masquerading within any preferred ethnic or racial stock.[42]

In what way can it be demonstrated Black Theology is authentic Christianity? How can we determine if authentic Christianity is particularistic or universal, even liberatory or oppressive? In the offering, is a Black Messiah an authentic Christian or mythic portrayal? Has Black Theology created "a set of mythological assumptions whose credibility deserves only to be 'de-mythologized' at the same instant?" At base, these are questions that demand historical inquiry into the origins and development of Christianity, precisely for the resolution of the matter regarding authenticity. Therefore, in an effort to answer these questions, we will explore in the next chapter, "Black Messiah as the Authentic Christ: Alternative Biblical Myth or Real History?"

NOTES

1. Richard I. McKinney, "Reflections on the Concept of 'Black Theology,'" *The Journal of Religious Thought* 26(2) (Summer 1969): 12.

2. While not directly critiquing Black Theology, Benjamin Mays strongly advocated the universal message of Christianity. "This universalism in the Gospel is climaxed and attested to by the fact that Christ died for all mankind. . . . In both the ancient and medieval church, the basis of membership was faith, in Jesus Christ, our Lord. The basis of membership was faith, not race; Christ, not color; creedal acceptance and not nationality." Freddie C. Colston, *Dr. Benjamin E. Mays Speaks: Representative Speeches of a Great American Orator* (Lanham, MD: University Press of America, 2002), 217–18.

3. J. Deotis Roberts, *Black Theology in Dialogue* (Philadelphia: Westminster Press, 1987), 13.

4. Black theologian James T. Murphy poses the question, "If God has made salvation possible for everyone through Jesus Christ, why are some oppressed in society based upon the color of their skin?" For a detailed discussion of salvation and Black Theology read James T. Murphy, Jr., *Defining Salvation in the Context of Black Theology* (Bloomington, IN: Xlibris Corporation, 2012), 82. Especially consult chapter 5, "Salvation within Black Theology."

5. Consult "Concrete Universal," in Nicholas Bunnin and Jiyuan Yu, eds., *The Blackwell Dictionary of Western Philosophy*. Blackwell Publishing, 2004. Blackwell Reference Online. September 14, 2016 http://www.blackwellreference.com/public/book.html?id=g9781405106795_9781405106795.

6. Colston, *Dr. Benjamin E. Mays Speaks*, 218.

7. John H. McClendon III, "Dr. Richard Ishmael McKinney: Historical Summation on the Life of a Pioneering African American Philosopher," *American Philosophical Association Newsletter on Philosophy and the Black Experience* (Spring 2006). Joan Morgan,

"Teaching the Young Keeps Him Young: 90 Year Old Dr. Richard McKinney of Morgan State Still Going Strong," *Black Issues in Higher Education* (August 22, 1996).

8. McKinney, "Reflections on the Concept of 'Black Theology,'" 10.

9. For a work by a white theologian in Black Theology, consult Patrick Bascio, *The Failure of White Theology: A Black Theological Perspective* (New York: P. Lang, 1994).

10. For works written by white theologians that advance the idea of a Black theological perspective, consult James W. Perkinson, *White Theology: Outing Supremacy in Modernity* (New York: Palgrave Macmillan, 2004); Bascio, *The Failure of White Theology*; and Theo Witvliet, *The Way of the Black Messiah* (Oak Park: Meyer & Stone, 1987).

11. Chapman notes, "During these turbulent years young African Americans, especially those in the ghettos of the urban North, quickly turned away from the ideologies of integration and nonviolence to embrace the philosophies of Black Nationalism and self-defence [sic]. Also important for understanding the emergence of Black Power, however, is the frustration African American youth directed toward the Black church, an institution they considered unresponsive to their radical, nationalist consciousness" ("Defending the Faith: Nascent Black Theology as an Apology for Christianity," *The Journal of the Interdenominational Theological Center* 20[1–2] [Fall–Spring, 1992–1993]). See also Vincent Harding, "Black Power and the American Christ," *Christian Century* (January 4, 1967). James H. Cone, "Black Theology and the Black Church: Where Do We Go from Here?," in Milton C. Sernett, ed., *Afro-American Religious History: A Documentary Witness* (Durham, NC: Duke University Press, 1985), 477–88.

12. Vincent Harding, "The Religion of Black Power," in James H. Cone and Gayraud Wilmore, eds., *Black Theology: A Documentary History, 1966–1979* (Ossining, NY: Orbis Books, 1993), 40–65. Gayraud Wilmore, "Black Power, Black People, Theological Renewal," in James H. Cone and Gayraud Wilmore, eds., *Black Theology: A Documentary History, 1966–1979* (Ossining, NY: Orbis Books, 1993), 125–40. Harding, "Black Power and the American Christ." W. H. Becker, "Black Power in Christological Perspective," *Religion in Life* 38(3) (Autumn 1969).

13. McKinney, "Reflections on the Concept of 'Black Theology,'" 11.

14. For a more complete treatment of McKinney's concept of protests and dissent, consult Richard I. McKinney, "Existentialist Ethics and Protest Movement," *The Journal of Religious Thought* 22(2) (1965–1966): 107–20; "Ethics of Dissent," *The Journal of Religious Thought* 29(2) (Autumn–Winter 1972): 68–79.

15. McKinney, "Reflections on the Concept of 'Black Theology,'" 12.

16. Robert C. Williams, book review, "Amos Jones Jr., *Paul's Message of Freedom: What Does It Mean to the Black Church?*" *Horizons* 12(2) (Fall 1985): 376. For a scholarly yet different treatment than Williams provides—of Paul and slavery—see Brad Ronnell Braxton, *No Longer Slaves: Galatians and African American Experience* (Collegeville, MN: The Liturgical Press, 2002); and Amos Jones, Jr., *Paul's Message of Freedom: What Does It Mean to the Black Church?* (Valley Forge, PA: Judson Press, 1984).

17. Murphy, *Defining Salvation in the Context of Black Theology*.

18. On the impact of Paul and Christian conduct, Leon E. Wright notes, "There is, then, this painfully wide chasm between Pauline thought and any observably effective bearing upon Christian conduct. The curious fact remains, therefore, that, outside of outright rejection, Christian scholars, ministers and laymen seem singularly reluctant openly to test what is meant by the confessional implications of Paul's schema for today's world" ("Paul Revisited: From Cult to Cosmos," *The Journal of Religious Thought* 32(1) (Spring–Summer 1975): 112.

19. McKinney, "Reflections on the Concept of 'Black Theology,'" 11.

20. Richard I. McKinney, "The Black Church: Its Development and Present Impact," *Harvard Theological Review* 64(4) (October 1971): 452–81.

21. For a contrasting viewpoint, see James H. Cone, "Black Theology and the Black Church: Where Do We Go from Here?," in James H. Cone and Gayraud Wilmore, eds., *Black Theology: A Documentary History, 1966–1979* (Ossining, NY: Orbis Books, 1993), 266–75.

22. McKinney, "The Black Church: Its Development and Present Impact," 454.

23. McKinney, "The Black Church," 457.
24. McKinney, "Reflections on the Concept of 'Black Theology,'" 13.
25. McKinney, "Reflections," 13.
26. Cain Hope Felder, "Beyond Eurocentric Biblical Interpretation: Reshaping Racial and Cultural Lenses in Christian Education," *The Journal of the Interdenominational Theological Center* 40(1) (Fall 2014): 5–20
27. Peter J. Gomes, *The Scandalous Gospel of Jesus: What's So Good about the Good News* (New York: HarperCollins Publishers, 2007), 14.
28. "The word Catholic (katholikos from katholou—throughout the whole, i.e., universal) occurs in the Greek classics, e.g., in Aristotle and Polybius, and was freely used by the earlier Christian writers in what we may call its primitive and non-ecclesiastical sense. . . . The combination 'the Catholic Church' (he katholike ekklesia) is found for the first time in the letter of St. Ignatius to the Smyrnaeans, written about the year 110. The words run: 'Wheresoever the bishop shall appear, there let the people be, even as where Jesus may be, there is the universal [katholike] Church. . . . Although belief in the 'holy Church' was included in the earliest form of the Roman Creed, the word Catholic does not seem to have been added to the Creed anywhere in the West until the fourth century." Consult *New Advent Catholic Encyclopedia*, http://www.newadvent.org/cathen/03449a.htm [accessed July 22, 2016].
29. McKinney, "Reflections on the Concept of 'Black Theology,'" 13.
30. McKinney, "Reflections," 12.
31. McKinney, "Reflections," 13.
32. Reginald F. Davis, "African-American Interpretation of Scripture," *The Journal of Religious Thought* 57(2)/58(1–2) (2001–2005): 93–105. James H. Cone, "Biblical Revelation and Social Existence," in James H. Cone and Gayraud Wilmore, eds., *Black Theology: A Documentary History* (Ossining, NY: Orbis, 1993), 159–176. Charles B. Copher, *Black Biblical Studies: Biblical and Theological Issues on the Black Presence in the Bible* (Chicago: Black Light Fellowship, 1993). Vincent L. Wimbush, *The Bible and African Americans: A Brief History* (Minneapolis: Fortress Press, 2003). Michael Joseph Brown, *Blackening of the Bible: The Aims of African American Biblical Scholarship* (Harrisburg, PA: Trinity Press International, 2004).
33. Bart D. Ehrman, *Forged: Writing in the Name of God—Why the Bible's Authors Are Not Who We Think They Are* (New York: HarperCollins, 2011). Robert M. Price, *The Incredible Shrinking Son of Man: How Reliable Is the Gospel Tradition?* (Amherst, NY: Prometheus Books, 2003). Gerd Lüdemann, *The Great Deception: And What Jesus Really Said and Did* (Amherst, NY: Prometheus Books, 1999). Paula Fredriksen, *From Jesus to Christ: The Origins of the New Testament Images of Jesus* (New Haven, CT: Yale University Press, 1988).
34. Theologian and philosopher George Kelsey argues that racism—a species of idolatry—is a sin. See George Kelsey, *Racism: The Special Problem for Christianity* (Nashville: Christian Life Commission, SBC, 1964). George Kelsey, *Racism and the Christian Understanding of Man* (New York: Charles Scribner's Sons, 1965).
35. Murphy, *Defining Salvation in the Context of Black Theology*. On eschatology, see Dale P. Andrews, *Practical Theology for Black Churches: Bridging Black Theology and African American Folk Religion* (Louisville, KY: Westminster John Knox Press, 2002), 26, 47–49.
36. The key advocate of Black Christian Nationalism was Albert B. Cleage. Consult Albert B. Cleage Jr., *Black Christian Nationalism: New Directions for the Black Church* (New York: Morrow, 1972).
37. McKinney, "Reflections on the Concept of 'Black Theology,'" 13–14.
38. For a literal reading, see Albert B. Cleage Jr., *The Black Messiah* (New York: Sheed and Ward, 1968), and for a symbolic interpretation, consult Gayraud S. Wilmore, "Black Messiah: Revising the Color Symbolism of Western Christology," *The Journal of the Interdenominational Theological Center* 2(1) (Fall 1974).
39. George Kelsey, *Racism and the Christian Understanding of Man*.

40. Leon E. Wright, "'Black Theology' or Black Experience?," *The Journal of Religious Thought* 26(2) (Summer 1969): 52–53.

41. George D. Kelsey, "The Racist Search for Self," *The Journal of Religious Ethics* 6(1) (Fall 1978): 251.

42. Consult Leon E. Wright, "'Black Theology' or Black Experience?," *The Journal of Religious Thought* 26(2) (Summer 1969): 54.

FOUR

Black Messiah as the Authentic Christ

Alternative Biblical Myth or Real History?

For the opponents of the Black Theology School, the racialization of Christianity was a significant departure from authentic Christianity as universal in character. Leon Wright was quite clear in his admonition. "[I]t should not be supposed that one advances the cause of a 'Black Theology' merely by painting faces black or partisanly juggling spiritual preferences before God, respecting persons or groups. Whatever the case for Black Theology may turn out to be, let us not cavalierly create a set of mythological assumptions whose credibility deserves only to be 'demythologized' at the same instant."[1]

Yet, often the clarion call for universality remained silent about the iconography that persists as dominant in Western Christian institutions. Such universality frequently offered a Eurocentric imagery of Jesus as Christ. Given the historical, geographical, and cultural circumstances surrounding this iconography effectively meant that calls for universality were often demonstratively a façade for the kind of racialized imperialism that we previously uncovered with George D. Kelsey's penetrating critique.[2]

In the early formation of the Black Theology School, there developed important challenges over the iconic presentation of the white Christ as symbolic of authentic Christianity. This iconic display was considered particularly disturbing, when it appeared in Black churches and homes. The cultural ramifications of white religious icons—especially in the Black context—were deemed racist intrusions and white distortion of the authentic Messiah and Christianity. It was assumed that this iconography—with its corresponding images of white Jesus—perpetuated white hegemony in religious form. Moreover, some Black clergy's acceptance of white religious symbolism facilitated such detrimental aims.[3]

Likewise, this challenge was not limited to the iconic aspects of Christology alone; it also encompassed confronting its historical and theological grounds. Issues pertaining to the question of the Jesus of faith and the historical Jesus were no doubt integral to the discussion on Black Christology. Questions about the divinity and humanity of Jesus also became vital topics of deliberations. Consequently, the issue of the historical Jesus becomes entwined in theology.[4]

Nevertheless, the framing of Black Christology usually sparked—as its centerpiece—the notion of the Black Messiah. Most in the Black Theology School were inclined on demonstrating that a Black Messiah was of the upmost theological significance as well as crucial to biblical interpretation. In 1968, Rev. Albert B. Cleage led the fight to reclaim "Black Jesus" with his text—comprising a collection of sermons—*The Black Messiah*.[5]

We now explore the ramifications of how the white Christ conception was superseded by the Black Messiah notion. The Black Messiah idea arose as the cardinal principle and core belief for the Black Christology movement. Integral to this core belief—Black Messiah—was also the objective of recovering the historical Jesus. The primary questions, which will guide our considerations, in this chapter, were posed earlier in the introduction. Hence, the following list:

1. How can we make the determination whether Jesus is Black rather than white?
2. When such adjectives as Black and white come into play—thus signifying racial categories—are we speaking symbolically or literally?
3. Do we have an anachronistic reading, when race is inserted into the question of Jesus's identity?
4. Can it be historically confirmed that Jesus was a Black Messiah?
5. Is such a Black Messiah the product of faith commitments and mythological construction?
6. Why does the racial identity of Jesus Christ theologically matter?

Our answer to the first question—how we can make the determination whether Jesus is Black rather than white?—significantly depends on how we approach the definition of these two terms. Granting that Blackness and whiteness specify a definite set of material (social) conditions and relations, it follows such specifications command we should deal primarily with social rather than theological categories. Explicitly—regarding the race of Jesus—the social category determinations command we engage in historical inquiry respecting the precise context for uncovering ideas about contemporaneous racial identity. Falling short of this mark ultimately results in an anachronistic reading.

An anachronistic reading comprises the inappropriate imposition of our contemporary categories of definition and description on past conditions, circumstances, and persons. One approach toward testing—if we have successfully avoided the pitfall of an anachronistic reading—comes about by inquiry into past notions adjoined to self-identification and self-definition. The context for this inquiry includes the specified time period, place, and people. This problem of concrete specification of racial categories versus ethnic or religious identity is a crucial factor in comprehending ancient social relations. Without a correct historical assessment of how social relations were constituted, then anachronistic reading becomes a real impediment.

For illustration, how would Jesus and his contemporaries respond to the notion that he was the Black Messiah? In all probability, given what contemporaneous notions about race and ethnicity were, it would more likely appear as a rather strange question. Ancient Jewish identity did not entail today's exercise of phenotypical—racial—description as essential to self-definition. Yet, on the supposition that Jews were a Black nation, in a white Roman empire, Albert B. Cleage argues for the Black Messiah concept. He declares, "I believe that Jesus, The Black Messiah was a revolutionary leader sent by God to rebuild the black nation, Israel and liberate black people from powerlessness and exploitation of the white Gentile world."[6]

We contend this supposition is an anachronistic rendering that confuses race with ancient ethnic, religious, and class relations. What recent scholarship makes transparent is that all social categories (including gender) were stamped by considerations of ancient Jewish ethnic, religious, and class relations in juxtaposition with Roman circumstances and sensibilities. Subsequently, the critical reader must not confuse these social elements with present-day racial categories.[7]

A concrete analysis of the conditions surrounding social relations of that time—in all of its complexity—is requisite. It stands to reason that we should not conceive of ethnicity and race (during antiquity) as reducible to the racial categories operative in contemporary United States. As Lloyd A. Thompson insightfully informs us, "In Roman society Jews (*Iudaei*) were not a race (visible or invisible) in the sociological sense."[8]

Given they were not even considered a race, logically speaking Jews could not have been a Black race. In turn, the idea that Jesus was either Black or white is fundamentally a category mistake resulting from an anachronistic reading. Consequently—as we customarily find in our existing U.S. racial context—dark complexion in itself may not suffice as a descriptor of Blackness. Various social groupings—we would now designate as nonwhite or people of color—in antiquity were more engaged with self-definitions that were in accord with the prevailing ethnic, religious, and class affiliations of the period. While not entirely absent, phenotypical description respecting skin color was not primary to social identification in antiquity.[9]

Lacking the needed specification and details regarding the social context of group self-identification, phenotypic description remains an abstraction without determinate content. We should not overlook the fact that our racial designations of today are historically and socially specific. Even now a very dark person from India is not necessarily a Black person according to U.S. or Indian racial standards of the present day. It follows that contemporary categories of race cannot apply to ancient history; that is short of careful scrutiny of definitive social relations in antiquity.[10]

How someone is selected according to present-day racial designations involves three important considerations—namely, phenotypic description (physical makeup), genotypic classification (genetic ancestry), and the actual social (historical-legal) context for cultural identification.[11] A Black person in the United States may come under another racial designation if born in a different country. A person deemed Black in the United States could very well not be considered so if native to Brazil. However, when such definitions extend beyond the description provided by our racial categories and social contexts, then we approach our second question on the list.[12]

Our second question—"When such adjectives as Black and white come into play, are we speaking symbolically or literally?"—now becomes the principal concern. Not all advocates of the Black Christ agree on the meaning attached to Blackness. Depending on whether a literal or symbolic method is functioning, supporters for Jesus as Black Messiah can have widely differing conceptions and images. This results from the fact that all efforts at literal reading are reliant on historical evidence.[13]

In contrast, symbolic treatment need not rest on this foundation. For example, Gayraud Wilmore thinks that fellow Black Theologian Albert Cleage's literal idea of Black Messiah misses the boat. Wilmore proffers,

> It is the *symbolic meaning of blackness in relation to redemptive suffering*, and not the claim that Albert B. Cleage makes for the actual skin color of Jesus, that gives warrant to our designation of Jesus as the Black Messiah. *To call Christ the Black Messiah is not to infer that he looked like an African*, although that may well have been the case considering the likelihood of the mixture of the Jewish genetic pool with that of people from the upper Nile, Nubia and Ethiopia. *Nor are we implying, by calling him the Black Messiah, that other people may not find it meaningful to speak of Christ as the White Messiah, or the Yellow Messiah, or the Red Messiah!*[14] [Italics added]

Wilmore's symbolic treatment of Black Messiah has important historical and theological consequences. First, the notion of Black Messiah finds its ontological anchor in theological construction rather than history. We reach this conclusion because when Wilmore argues, "It is the symbolic meaning of blackness in relation to redemptive suffering," from which we derive the Black Messiah, then redemptive suffering becomes the overriding principle for his color symbolism. Moreover, we know that *redemptive suffering* is clearly a theological category. For redemptive suffering only makes sense in view of how one renders God's relationship to human suffering, what theologians refer to as theodicy.[15]

Second, in Wilmore's view, Blackness—in terms of Black Messiah—is not an actual racial description of the historical Jesus. Rather it is a *theological signifier* about God. Namely, we have the precise relation of God to Black existence, while adjointly conferring value to redemptive suffering. When Blackness emerges as theological signifier, the door opens to Wilmore's color symbolism and thus his Black Messiah conceptualization. Although Wilmore does indicate that there may be some warrant to the historical context about "the likelihood of the mixture of the Jewish genetic pool with that of people from the upper Nile, Nubia and Ethiopia," it remains that "to call Christ the Black Messiah is not to infer that he looked like an African."[16]

Hence, Blackness of the Messiah is detached from existing historical and social designations. Wilmore is not attempting to uncover the Black Messiah in any sort of racial manner, either in terms of the ancient past or today. Instead, we observe that the Black Messiah is one of several possible theological paradigms, which includes the White Messiah paradigm as a legitimate possibility. On Wilmore's accounting, redemptive suffering does not exclusively pertain to the Black experience. Hence, *white redemptive suffering* correspondingly yields its respective White Messiah.[17]

Furthermore, the plurality of theological constructs—White Messiah, Yellow Messiah, or the Red Messiah—ontologically speaking (in reality) indicates that the racialized Messiah concept is an open rather than closed option. In this respect, not only is Wilmore's notion of Black Messiah symbolic in character but also a significant departure from many in the Black Christology camp. The general principle of redemptive suffering as applicable to all racial groups leads directly to a racially pluralist conception of Messiah that surfaces as foremost concerning what becomes symbolic in makeup.[18]

Historical facts about the person of Jesus—respecting race/ethnicity— need not restrict faith claims to a Black Messiah. Wilmore states,

> To speak of the Messiah figure in terms of the ontological significance of the color black is to provide both black people and white people, if the latter are open to the possibility, with a way of understanding the relevance of the Person and Work of Christ for existence under the condition of oppression, and to call both the Black and the White Church to the vocation of involvement in the liberation of the oppressed in history.[19]

While Wilmore leaves room for both Black and White Messiahs, a Black Messiah does not exclude white participation in the corresponding liberation struggle against oppression since Black Messiah is an inclusive notion with ontological (real world) utility for Black and white people and their particular churches. Wilmore's notion of Blackness is a broadly conceived theological category that offers up a principle for racial reconciliation. He states,

> If blackness is made to stand for conflict, oppression, suffering and death, we may say that God became black! In the symbolism of the liberation Christology, God became black in order to show that blackness is the ultimate reality for all men and that the final reconciliation of blackness and whiteness, of the oppressed and the oppressor, of death and life, is not in man's making of history, but in God himself.[20]

Wilmore's Black Messiah as symbolic concept provides for addressing Black oppression through Black and white cooperation toward Black liberation. With Blackness as symbolic and not literal in character, then Blackness can serve as "the ultimate reality for all men and that the final reconciliation of blackness and whiteness" which transpires as a divine intervention. Humans are God-dependent respecting the resolution of social problems such as exploitation and oppression.

Wilmore's appeal to establishing racial conciliation, along with his idea about reconciliation between oppressor and oppressed, effectively constrains the notion of Black liberation. Rather in any fundamental transformation of real—material—structures and relations that effectively overthrows the oppressors, liberation is reduced to reconciliation. In fact, liberation actually includes the oppressors. Instead of liberation from oppressors, Wilmore conveys, "And in the anguish and suffering of that same struggle the oppressors come to know the judgment of God upon their sinful attempt to become gods over their fellowmen. In that judgment is the possibility of their salvation."[21]

Moreover, Wilmore notes that the material struggle for liberation has a higher calling than secular objectives. He states, "What then is the meaning of the earthly struggle of the oppressed for liberation? Is it all a mirage, a divine hoax, a cruel joke? No, because in the anguish and suffering of the struggle itself the oppressed come to the revelation of the meaning of existence on earth and of their gracious union with the Oppressed One."[22]

Wilmore's notion of liberation effectively surordinates the material reality of oppression and exploitation to the religious aim of salvation and redemption. Instead of a rigorous stance on obtaining freedom in the secular confines of material circumstances, Wilmore gives the nod to divine liberation. He explains:

> The most profound meaning of the liberation of the oppressed is the consciousness of the meaningfulness of the struggle for life and hope

and the vindication of their determination to be human beings conformed to the command of God to be free for him.... Now the stage is set for the manifestation of the liberation of the Oppressed One in the resurrection and exaltation. That is the ultimate liberation, for without diminishing the significance of historical freedom, political, economic and cultural liberation can only refer penultimately to an incomplete and fragmentary experience which inevitably yields to the temptation to exercise mastery over others.[23]

Furthermore, Wilmore's Christology has a more multiculturalist slant than an unyielding Black nationalism rooted in the antiwhiteness orientation. Consequently, Wilmore's idea of pluralist Christology does not discount white Christology, rather it can be symbolically reconcilable with Black Christology. As well, we can infer that the White Messiah confronts the problems adjoined specifically to white oppression. It is not clear—from Wilmore's statement—whether the idea of White Messiah has the same implications for Black people that Black Messiah evokes for whites. Specifically, whether Black people join in the fight for white liberation from oppression. It does seem that the composite—Black and White—Messiahs present the opportunity for whites to engage on two fronts against oppression—that is, Black and white liberation struggles, respectively.

Unlike what we found—in an earlier chapter—with Cone's reflections on Blackness and oppression, Wilmore does not constrict oppression simply to the Black experience.[24] Instead, he universally grants that redemptive suffering anchors the general definition for the Messiah concept. Thus, it logically follows that Wilmore's "White Messiah" concept presumes redemptive suffering is also applicable to white people. This necessitates that Wilmore's notion of oppression becomes universal rather than particularistic in scope.[25]

In no uncertain terms he declares, "But more than that, it is to find in the mystery of Christ's death and resurrection a theological explanation of *all suffering, oppression* and an ultimate liberation"[26] [Italics added]. Although, mystery clouds the explanation of Jesus's death and resurrection, nonetheless, it is not only the foundation for the general principle of redemptive suffering, it is also considered a historical fact. Clearly, Wilmore's theological position on Christ's death and resurrection presumes that these events are actually historical in character. While Wilmore's notions about the Blackness of the Messiah is a symbolic matter, the resurrection of Jesus is a literal event. Yet, if the resurrection of Jesus is literal in character, then it must be subject to historical scrutiny as with any other claim regarding historical facts.[27]

It is evident that Wilmore does not consider the conflicting New Testament reports on the crucifixion or the historicity of the resurrection. He is not concerned with who was fundamentally responsible for Jesus's execution, nor what the motivations for this action were and why Jews—

rather than Roman officials—were chiefly held accountable in the New Testament and especially the Book of John.

Such questions are left unanswered due to Wilmore's greater emphasis on the theological dimension of the crucifixion—redemptive suffering—than a critique of biblical testimonies. Therein, Wilmore's supposition about the execution and resurrection of Jesus lacks the required content for standing as a confirmed historical statement.[28] Biblical scholar Gerd Lüdemann explains,

> An examination of the historicity of Jesus' resurrection is called for because according to early Christian testimony it is an event in time and space. . . . Therefore "this event has come to us in the form of historicizing reports." The evangelist Luke follows the earliest witnesses, including Paul, who asserts that the original one was not a spirit but Jesus Christ himself.[29]

Here, Wilmore is in alignment with the view that Christianity has universal efficacy. Jesus Christ's death and resurrection addresses all suffering and oppression. It is not limited either symbolically or literally to Blackness as we respectively find with Cone and Cleage. Yet, Wilmore's universality gains expression in the variously racialized—particular—forms affixed to the Messiah idea. Wilmore's universality allows for particularity in theology via his open-ended color characterization (symbolism) adjoined to the Messiah concept.

With regard to our third and fourth questions, Wilmore—at first appearance—looks as if he takes an ahistorical approach to the person of Jesus and his racial identity. Hence, in answer to "Do we have an anachronistic reading when race is inserted into the question of Jesus's identity," Wilmore could respond by stating that Jesus is relevant to Black people—that is as Black Messiah—only to the extent that "the mystery of Christ's death and resurrection [is] a theological explanation" of Black suffering and oppression. While this theological explanation removes Jesus's racial identity from history, Wilmore does not intend in removing Jesus entirely from history.[30]

For we must believe that this mystery of Christ's death and resurrection is a historical fact. Thus, to that extent, we uncover that Wilmore resorts to the mythological explanation of Jesus's resurrection as a matter of history. Hereafter, we have a *mythological and theological claim on history* instead of an attempt at the historical presentation of the facts about the crucifixion and resurrection of Jesus.[31]

JESUS'S CRUCIFIXION AND RESURRECTION: FAITH CLAIM OR HISTORICAL FACT

The matter of the who, the what, and the why of the crucifixion and resurrection lack historical details in Wilmore's account. Perhaps Wilmore's omission results from his understanding regarding the Gospel texts. One chief factor could be that the Gospel text presentations offer conflicting accounts on the details surrounding the crucifixion and resurrection. Hence, it should come as no surprise that prominent Christian theologians such as Emil Brunner and Rudolf Bultmann deny the historicity of the resurrection yet affirm its importance on the theological grounds of *Christian faith*.[32]

Both Brunner and Bultmann argue that Jesus's resurrection is an "eschatological fact" or "eschatological event." Yet, an "eschatological fact" or "eschatological event" speaks to God's judgment on the whole of history and not to the verifiable facts regarding specified historical events[33]—in other words, it does not pertain to the subject matter we normally encounter with human history and in carrying out historical research. For Brunner and Bultmann, theology rather than history holds sway in this matter.

In divergence from Brunner and Bultmann, Wilmore ostensibly supports the idea that the resurrection was a historical event. Nevertheless, the historical treatment of Jesus's resurrection should not only be consistent with early Christian testimony; it is mandatory we establish some form of historical verification concerning this theological claim. Short of such historical verification, the theological claim about Jesus's resurrection is no more than empty conjecture. Gerd Lüdemann argues,

> Indeed, the defenders of church tradition of the second century have emphasized that claim by introducing the doctrine of the fleshly nature of Jesus' resurrected body. . . . [T]he historical question of "the basis and justification for this testimony . . . remains decisive." Without this basis any theology of resurrection, even the theology of the New Testament, is groundless speculation.[34]

However, Wilmore simply views the death of Jesus in terms of Isaiah's notion of the suffering Servant of God. Consequently, the extent to which the resurrection is considered a historical event, it becomes wrapped in theological rhetoric. For Wilmore, it is this cardinal Christian theological belief, which becomes the compelling factor that links the Black Messiah to contemporary Black oppression. In upholding this belief, Wilmore's Black Christology does not depart from the conventional (white?) Christian idea about Jesus as suffering Servant of God. He simply gives a Black coloring to a very traditional Christian belief.[35]

Nonetheless, Wilmore's theological explanation requires symbolic Blackness and not an actual racial label for Jesus. This theological explanation amounts to the assertion that "God reveals himself in solidarity with the affliction of the oppressed by the revelation of his Son, Jesus Christ, as the Oppressed One of God."[36] Surely, we can infer from this that God stands in opposition to oppression.

It is noteworthy the idea that God is one with the oppressed is not specific to Black Theology alone. Proponents of the Social Gospel, long before Wilmore, have supported this particular theological position. Among past African American clergy there is the pioneering advocate of the Social Gospel school, Rev. Reverdy C. Ransom of the A.M.E. Church. Additionally, we have African American preacher and socialist George Washington Woodbey. Today he remains quite notable among this group of early progressive clergy.[37]

In many respects, regarding the social implications for change in the material conditions of Black life, Ransom and Woodbey's theological positions were more advanced and challenging in relation to Christian orthodoxy than Wilmore's Black Christology. Obviously, when Jesus achieves the exalted status as the Son of God and "the Oppressed One of God," Wilmore is certainly following the traditional New Testament rendering on Jesus. In this sense, he resorts to Blackening one of Christianity's primary tenets.[38] We will shortly see that Albert Cleage's literal Black Messiah concept departs from the suffering Servant thesis affixed to the crucifixion and resurrection of Jesus.[39]

In contrast to the historical Jesus, the divinity of Jesus becomes pivotal to Wilmore's symbolic Blackness. "The Oppressed One of God" becomes the cardinal bond—rather than the flesh and blood Jesus—that cements the Black Messiah to present-day Black experience. The historical Jesus is relegated to the background and the divinity of Jesus to the foreground. Historical evidence of Jesus as a Black man is not required for Wilmore's Black Messiah.[40]

What we unearth is that one must have a faith commitment about the divinity of Jesus for embracing Wilmore's idea of Black Messiah. Put simply, Wilmore's Black Messiah notion only makes sense for the Christian who believes that Jesus is more than a mortal human being and thus characterized as the Son of God. Faith commitment instead of historical facts are requisite for this particular conception of the Black Messiah.

In regard to Wilmore's approach, subsequently, our impression would be—no, in committing to an anachronistic reading. His symbolic Blackness as theological explanation provides a detour around the fallacy of an anachronistic reading. Furthermore, Wilmore's criticism of Cleage's literal take on Jesus as Black also demonstrates this point. If Jesus is not considered as literally Black, then there is no need to compare our contemporary ideas about race with ancient ones. In this respect, we uncover that Wilmore's theological symbolism trumps Cleage's historical literalism.

In other words, Wilmore's symbolic treatment of Jesus does not allow for contemporary racial categories to impose themselves on ancient history. Hence, the fourth question, "Can it be historically confirmed that Jesus was a Black Messiah?," has no real relevance. Wilmore is removing us from historical facts about Jesus and race, and he situates the Messiah concept on theological (faith) commitments. Such faith commitments are founded on how one understands the theological function of redemptive suffering in Black Christology.

Sequentially, the Black Messiah conceptually depends on the treatment of redemptive suffering and its connection to Black people. We look not to the historical Jesus but rather to the theological construction of the Black Messiah. In the main, Wilmore's project is a Christological one, which is removed from the literal or historical accounting of Jesus's race.

With the aforementioned in mind, it is the fifth question—"Is such a Black Messiah the product of faith commitments and mythological construction?"—that emerges as fundamental. Rather than a mythological construction per se, we have the historicizing of myth, which results in a theological conceptualization based on faith commitments surrounding "the mystery of Christ's death and resurrection." Faith in the mystery of Christ's death and resurrection suffices as grounds for apprehending how Blackness is adjoined to redemptive suffering.[41]

Although, we should add, the idea of the historicizing of myth involves that Jesus's resurrection is presented as an actual historical event. Nevertheless, the resurrection actually falls into the domain of myth. We have noted that biblical scholars such as Gerd Lüdemann make a strong case for why—on examination—the belief in the resurrection as a historical fact requires the critical scrutiny of historical research and documentation of the event. At best, this belief in the resurrection remains as the speculative—rather than historical—grounds for faith claims about Jesus in the capacity of the Messiah. The mythic dimension emerges as substantially important for faith commitments.[42]

However, this particular problem about Wilmore's views on the resurrection issue is not our primary concern at this juncture. What becomes of immediate import centers on why the theoretical weight of the resurrection event anchors Wilmore's symbolic erection of the Black Messiah. With his symbolic premise, we can see how Wilmore would respond to our last question—"Why does the racial identity of Jesus Christ theologically matter?" It matters precisely because the very idea of Black Messiah, in his estimation, is not a historical description of Jesus in antiquity.

Actually, it's a Christological creation that addresses contemporary racism and thereby not indicative of ancient race relations. Black Messiah theologically matters because it is essentially a theological presumption, which fosters a religious meaning adjoined to present-day Blackness and the reality of Black suffering affixed to racism. Wilmore declares, "To speak of Christ as the Black Messiah is rather to invest blackness in Western civilization, and particularly in the United States and South Africa, with *religious meaning* expressing the preeminent reality of black suffering and the historical experience of black people in a racist society"[43] [Italics added].

In the first chapter, we previously queried: Who was Jesus and what is his relationship to Christianity? How is this relationship linked to the Black experience? How would a Black Christology enter into the theological picture? Wilmore's response to these questions is instructive. "Black people have been struck, not only with the similarity of what seemed to be their inexorable fate as a race and the Messianic vocation of suffering, but also with the profound, if not exact correspondence between their experience of blackness in Western civilization and the description of the Messiah."[44]

The notion of description—respecting the Messiah—that Wilmore posits is not a physical (phenotypical) description of Jesus as a living human being with notable features that are African/Black. Wilmore's description is a Christological one that in turn commands the use of symbolism. This theological description—based as it is on redemptive suffering—is the link that binds the existing Black experience to his Black Messiah concept. The Black Messiah is a suffering Servant of God and to that extent he becomes—symbolically—Black. Wilmore's grounding assumption is that Black people also have historically experienced the plight of suffering Servants of God. Hence, contemporary Black people can theologically relate to Jesus as Black Messiah, particularly at the level of symbolism.

Blackness emblematically becomes a theological description and explanation. Meanwhile Blackness is only one option among several relative to the notion of a "racialized" Messiah. It follows that this "Black" Messiah as a theological description is not a solitary connection to the historical Jesus. White, Yellow, and Red Messiahs, Wilmore contends, are in the picture as well—that is as long as redemptive suffering is a present condition. This plurality (of Messiahs) is possible because theology rather than history is the determinate factor. We must understand that Wilmore's symbolic idea of Black, White, Yellow, and Red—racialized—Messiah is a *theological projection* resting on constituent forms of redemptive suffering.[45]

We can infer from this that Wilmore suggests that Jesus—in the capacity of Messiah—is not one singular person. We reach this conclusion precisely because the various forms of racialized Messiah are not attached to a *historical person* as such. This symbolic method allows for various theological interpretations concerning who is the Messiah. More properly, rather than Jesus is *The* Messiah, we should say Jesus is *A* Messiah—that is, situated according to the Christology of given racial groups. The theological impact of Wilmore's symbolic method has significant and dire consequences for uncovering the historical Jesus in terms of the identification—Black Messiah.

For instance, Wilmore's color symbolism creates a huge paradox for anyone seeking an explanation that historically attempts to explain how Jesus is the one and only Black Messiah. This follows since Wilmore's color symbolism has to consider the manifold of several Messiahs. If Jesus is a Messiah, then it becomes a matter of theological production as to how many we have. Wilmore clearly establishes that the Black Messiah — as historical person — is not found in the pages of the Bible or in the annals of history. Black Messiah in substance rests on theological symbolism.

Moreover, his Black Messiah is not only symbolic in nature, it is also a theological projection onto the history of Western civilization. Since Wilmore intends to invest Blackness with *"religious meaning"* then the concomitant historical meaning must derive from his theological projection. The very connotation of Blackness in the history of Western civilization must ultimately assume religious form. The substance behind Black symbolism, in the history of Western civilization, becomes a concern of *theological imagination* not historical investigation.

Uprooted from history by means of theological symbolism, Jesus becomes fair game for a host of theologies. Granted, it can be demonstrated that the specified theology offers a symbolic description of how the Messiah-concept represents the condition of redemptive suffering. Consequently, since all possible forms of oppression without a doubt exceed specified forms of racial oppression, then to the degree that we have oppressed social groups, it follows we should have a particular kind of Messiah. Theological imagination is the only limitation to the production of possible Messiahs.

If gender and race are the basis of oppression, sequentially there could be a constituent gendered/racialized Messiah. Accordingly, a Black womanist Christology should not be out of reach. No androcentric conception of a Black Messiah can be found here. In Wilmore's Christology of multiple Messiahs, Jesus is effectively removed from the fact he is a male. Theological imagination can allow for such abstractions as the Messiah in the form of Black woman. This follows since the Black Messiah idea does not have a restrictive relation of one-to-one correspondence with the singular historical person of Jesus as male or white.[46]

On the foundation of Wilmore's account, while there is one historical Jesus, there are in turn many theologically created Messiahs. Therein, the Messiah concept becomes a theological — very human — projection. This theological projection of the Messiah concept is transparently open-ended. Based on Wilmore's thesis, the possibility of an infinite number of "specified" Messiahs — that correspond with different oppressed groups and their experience of redemptive suffering — is not out of the question. From Wilmore's perception, Jesus conventionally becomes *A* Black Messiah rather than *The* Black Messiah. We uncover that the matter of *theological consideration* (imagination) emerges as the conceptual grounds for such pluralistic determinations based on racialized or in fact other idealizations respecting the concept of Messiah.

This pluralistic conception of Messiah separates Wilmore from many in the Black Theology School. Although the notion about the White Messiah—as a corruption of authentic Christianity—is held by a number in the Black Theology School, such thoughts are not on Wilmore's Christological agenda. Wilmore cannot in principle stand in opposition to the idea of a White Messiah—that is to say, he cannot consider the White Messiah notion as in some manner the corruption of authentic Christianity. This is because his creation of theological symbolism (instead of historical literalism) is at base how Black Messiah gains warrant.

The singular notion of the Black historical Jesus would limit the options to one and only one Messiah. As we have observed, Wilmore's starting point discards the singular historical person—Jesus—as the Black Messiah. This is why we say that Wilmore approaches the matter of a Black Messiah from an ahistorical standpoint. From his point of view, the actual race (or gender) of the historical Jesus is immaterial. In fact, the historical Jesus disappears all together in Wilmore's Christology.

One must, however, theologically commit to the crucifixion and resurrection of Jesus as well as the Son of God notion in consenting to Wilmore's symbolic Black Messiah. This is why we contend that redemptive suffering becomes the overriding principle in Wilmore's Christology of the Black Messiah. The only "historical" factor is that the mythic story of the crucifixion and resurrection of Jesus is historicized, that is, interpreted as if it is a historical event. Once we allow for Wilmore's historicizing of mythology—surrounding the crucifixion and resurrection—the way is open for theology as surrogate for history. Wilmore's Black Messiah is not only symbolic, more significantly it is a *theological claim* respecting *the history* of the resurrection of Jesus.

Additionally, the crucifixion and resurrection are fundamental dimensions of Wilmore's Christology. Yet, its historicity is actually established outside the realm of historical inquiry. Wilmore gives expression to faith commitment in the crucifixion and resurrection of Jesus. This is why we submit that the historical Jesus disappears all together in Wilmore's Christology. In sum, we are dealing with theology and not history when it comes to his symbolic Black Messiah. Strictly speaking, Wilmore's position on a symbolic Black Messiah idea prominently stands outside of historical confirmation.

Meanwhile, ostensibly Albert B. Cleage's approach to the Black Messiah concept is literal and historical, rather than symbolic and ahistorical. In Cleage's estimation, history grounds the literal truth that there is one and only one Messiah within the Christian tradition. This presumed historical fact—Jesus is the Black Messiah—entails it has substantive theological significance. Black Christian faith is a theological matter rooted in ancient Black history. Thus, we have Cleage's Black Christian Nationalist creedal statement, "I believe that Jesus, The Black Messiah was a revolutionary leader sent by God to rebuild the black nation, Israel and liberate black people from powerlessness and exploitation of the white Gentile world."[47]

ALBERT CLEAGE AND HIS LITERAL NOTION OF THE HISTORICAL BLACK MESSIAH

Cleage's historical methodology remains all-encompassing with respect to theology, biblical interpretation, mythic texts, historic truth, and the idea of the Black Messiah. There is no resort to rendering Jesus as symbolically Black. Cleage's ostensible historical realism is crucial to the racial description of Jesus. In Cleage's estimation, the historical Jesus and the Black Messiah are one and the same. There is also the theological and biblical import of racial terms and hence their significance is vitally attached to the Black Messiah. Cleage's Black Messiah concept requires a theology that conforms to a different reading of biblical texts than the Christian traditional—white—approach. With this in mind, his reading presumably discloses the historic elements in the Bible. Cleage remarks,

> So we have to deal with the theology that restructures interpretations of the Bible. We have to restructure, using the historical basis for the interpretation of the Bible. Moving toward a theology which goes back to the original historical elements—the historic elements— such few elements as there are in the Old Testament and the New Testament. . . . Fantasy is everywhere—the Old Testament, New Testament.[48]

He continues,

> We're dealing with mythological kinds of developments but yet the whole mythology—the Old Testament, the New Testament—carries some kind of historic truth and they say truth is what we're really interested in and the historic truth is that we're dealing with a revolutionary black leader who's fighting for the liberation of black people in the New Testament and the Old Testament we're dealing with the struggle of an enslaved black people who liberated themselves.[49]

When Cleage argues "we have to deal with the theology that restructures interpretations of the Bible," we discover that this process of restructuring evolves as pivotal to his whole theological project. He assumes the orthodox—white Christian—interpretation of the Bible does not provide a basis for overcoming the mythological roadblocks that hinder biblical interpretation from uncovering the historic elements in the Bible. The theology that restructures interpretations of the Bible recognizes that all that is in the Bible is not self-evidently true and the appearance of fantasy brings this point home. On the face of it, Cleage is calling for a method of biblical interpretation that issues forth the need to *demythologize* biblical texts.[50]

In Cleage's view, if we are to uncover the historical elements buried in biblical texts, we must displace the mythological structures—fantasy—that impede the historical interpretation of the Bible. It seems that he presumes that once the mythological obstructions—fantasy—are dislodged from the Bible, one can unearth "the original historical elements" which constitute the substantive truth of biblical texts.[51]

Thus, the course of biblical interpretation is fraught with the primary tension concerning how mythological fantasies obscure historical elements in the Bible. However, this tension also reflects a different set of circumstances. This is evident when Cleage states, "We're dealing with mythological kinds of developments but yet the whole mythology—the Old Testament, the New Testament—carries some kind of historic truth."

Here we have a different kind of emphasis than what we formerly uncovered. Formerly, it was the matter of dislodging historic elements from mythological fantasy. Now it appears that "historic truth" is actually bound up in mythology. Mythology is not simply obstructive forms of fantasy, because it also retains the element of historic truth. With this latter interpretation, plainly historic truth actually resides within the very structure of mythology. Indeed, mythology appears not only as residence for the historic truth but also it divulges such truth to us.[52]

Cleage's phrase, "yet the whole mythology . . . *carries some kind of historic truth,*" visibly makes this manifest. When the whole mythology . . . *carries some kind of historic truth* it becomes transparent that mythology is not simply fantasy. Some measure of truth resides in mythology, and historic truth at that. Now we observe that a certain degree of ambiguity and contradiction surround Cleage's treatment of myth and historic truth. On the one hand, historic elements must be dislodged from the fantasy attendant with myth and on the other, 'the whole [biblical] mythology—the Old Testament, the New Testament—carries some kind of historic truth." Therefore, we must ask, is mythology simply fantasy that obstructs the truth or is it the medium that not only hosts but also reveals the historic truth?

We contend that this ambiguous treatment of myth and historic truth is by no means a small matter. This is due to the fact that the former approach speaks to the need for ridding ourselves of the fantasy attached to myth, while the latter supposition actually undermines such an effort. The idea that there is some kind of truth bound within the whole of biblical myth is directly in conflict with dislodging historic elements from the fantasy adjoined with the function of myth.

This contradiction is all the more important when we examine the conclusion of Cleage's argument—namely, "they say truth is what we're really interested in and the historic truth is that we're dealing with a revolutionary black leader who's fighting for the liberation of black people in the New Testament and the Old Testament we're dealing with the struggle of an enslaved black people who liberated themselves."

How do we determine, that is, how do we know that Jesus is a revolutionary black leader and in what way is it documented in the Old and New Testament? Cleage's contradictory notion about myth does not render an immediate solution to the problem. Indeed, Cleage's contradictory approach is the basis for the dilemma before us.

In other words, is this "historic truth" about Jesus—"as a revolutionary black leader who's fighting for the liberation of black people in the New Testament and the Old Testament"—mythic truth or a historical fact? Can it be that Jesus is a real historical person, a Black revolutionary, which however we detect that biblical texts—with their mythic fantasy—obstructs from our sight? In contrast, does Jesus remain a mythic figure whereby we can still ascertain that this fantastic portrayal of his life story reveals historic truth that subsequently has contemporary relevance for Black liberation? Similar questions have been presented about biblical—mythic—figures such as Moses. We should note that Moses and the exodus myth has had a particular impact on African American notions of liberation.[53]

The difference in connotations (as reflected in these contrasting questions) is no trivial matter. This is because the problem of biblical mythology and its relationship to historic truth becomes front and center as the chief predicament for a coherent delineation on the conceptual locus of myth. Is the Black Messiah a historic truth bound up in myth? What does it mean to be a historic truth wrapped up in myth or fantasy? Can myth as fantasy become a medium for truth? Or do we have a contradiction in terms?

This contradiction is all the more noteworthy because Cleage emphatically argues that the idea of a white Jesus is a matter of myth. This mythic factor becomes the basis for the complete dismissal of a white Jesus as real historical person. Rather than truth bound in this myth, what we have here is pure fantasy. White Jesus as mythic character is eliminated from the pages of history as a false proposition. The whole of biblical mythology—as a carrier of historic truth—is now fractured with the myth of white Jesus and Christianity.

Cleage states, "Anthropology proves that anyone objective and who can divorce himself from the white establishment can establish for himself that there is no way in the world Jesus could have been white, no way in the world Israel could have been white, no way in the world that the whole background basis of Israel and Christianity could have been white." He then adds, "But the fantasy element is very important. The reason black people have been so chained to the church is the fact that the mythical fantasies of white Christianity were so basically meaningful to an enslaved, insane black people—because the mythology of white Christianity is basically insane. So it was an insanity speaking to insanity."[54]

For Cleage, the mythical fantasies of white Christianity are not only distortions of historical reality but also patently insanity. Such a strong claim about mythical fantasies of white Christianity squarely puts Cleage, in this instance, in the role of dislodging the truth of Black Jesus from the falsehood—fantasy—and insanity of white (mythical) Jesus and Christianity. The demythologization of white Christianity, in Cleage's estimation, brings both truth and sanity to the discussion via the recovery of the Black Messiah.

As to our first question, "How do we make the determination whether Jesus is Black rather than white?" Cleage suggests that science—anthropology—rather than mythology provides the answer. In view of the scientific evidence, it would be insane to think of Jesus and Christianity as white. Unlike Wilmore, Cleage leaves no room for a white Messiah—that is, short of falling into the clutches of the white establishment and the grip of insanity.

Yet, there still remains the nagging problem concerning how the idea of the Black Messiah is bound up in biblical mythology. Therefore, while science points to the truth of the Black Messiah, nonetheless we also discover so does the whole of biblical mythology. Despite his arguments to the contrary, Cleage readily embraces myth since the whole of biblical mythology "carries some kind of historic truth, namely the truth of the Black Messiah." Let us return to Cleage's statement on this question.

> We're dealing with mythological kinds of developments but *yet the whole mythology—the Old Testament, the New Testament—carries some kind of historic truth* and they say truth is what we're really interested in and the historic truth is that we're dealing with a revolutionary black leader who's fighting for the liberation of black people in the New Testament and the Old Testament we're dealing with the struggle of an enslaved black people who liberated themselves.[55] [Italics added]

The Old and New Testament mythology as well as anthropology provide us with an accounting of the Black Messiah. Consequently, we have two conflicting propositions—about myth and science—as to where the historic truth of the Black Messiah resides. In this case, the whole of biblical mythology is no longer merely fantasy. Yet, we have *myth as fantasy* if Jesus is declared white. We contend that quite obviously the underlying problem resides in Cleage's ambiguous treatment of myth. This inconsistency is most transparent in his statement on African mythology and its relationship to biblical texts. Cleage states,

> When we go back we find that *all the basic mythology* in the Old Testament is the mythology of Africa which was taken from Africa. From traditional Africa—that's the Africa before the white man. The concept of the chosen people, the concept of creation—all those ideas—*that has any validity* in the Old Testament and the New Testament stems from Africa.[56] [Italics added]

Subsequently, Africa provides "all the basic mythology . . . that has validity" (within biblical texts), hence we gather that Cleage is suggesting we need to recover the original—authentic—African mythology. We must conclude that since it emerges from Africa, this mythology has some particular value—historic truth—for Black people today.

If this is the case, what happens to Cleage's idea that mythology is fantasy? How does African mythology—fantasy—escape the peril of distorting historic truth? Why does African mythology offer validity to the stories of the creation and of the chosen people? Simply because a myth has African origins, Cleage presumes that it must be true. However, do not judgments concerning the validity and truth of any mythological system, without exception, still require demonstration and justification? If science disproves the idea that Jesus is white, why not conclude that science overturns African creation mythology? On Cleage's accounting of myth as fantasy, the significance of the truth affixed to African mythology becomes a confused proposition.

Granting Cleage's Black nationalist outlook, it could be argued that the very notion of mythology has expressly a *contradictory character*. If it is *African mythology* we have some element of historic truth and validity. However, if it is *white mythology* we observe instances of fantasy and the distortion of history. While such a bifurcation seems arbitrary and capricious, we must still face the question, does the dual *character* approach best map out how Cleage deals with mythology?

Although it continues as explicitly tied to his method, Cleage cannot rationally justify such an ethnocentric approach to the problem of mythology. Either African mythology is fantasy or it is the basis for some kind of historic truth, and the same principle should rationally hold true for white mythology. Nevertheless, for myth to retain historical truth, it has to sustain criteria that are open to empirical verification. Wherein, the facts of the case are gathered from references and sources open to public scrutiny and not just conventional belief in mythology.

This ambiguity concerning the general treatment of myth has an immediate impact on how Cleage renders the historical Jesus as a Black man. With regard to our second question, "When such adjectives as Black and white come into play—thus signifying racial categories—are we speaking symbolically or literally?" Evidently, Cleage is speaking literally. Such literal depiction of Jesus as Black, he claims, must be established on historical grounds. Such grounds depend on the restructuring of the theological interpretations of the Bible. Paradoxically, the theological interpretation of the Bible is not removed from African mythology.

Herein, Cleage's Black Theology both rejects white mythology—along with its white Messiah—as well as confirms African mythology as the basis of the historical truth for the Black Messiah. Moreover, the whole of biblical mythology—which Cleage contends is basically African mythology—is said to be a carrier of historic truth. Cleage's arguments tendered against biblical mythology are actually undermined by his simultaneous embrace of it, albeit this embrace is filtered through the affirmation that

African mythology serves as the basis for biblical mythology. Obviously, Cleage's mishandling of the idea of mythology lands him in a serious predicament respecting the literal treatment of the Black Messiah.

We know that Cleage rejects symbolic Blackness—based on redemptive suffering—therefore that is not an option. Clearly, there is a vast chasm between Cleage and Wilmore on this point. Due to the presumption that racial categories of Jesus's era are consistent with our contemporary times, sequentially Cleage believes that phenotypic description is in order. Cleage's response to the question—Do we have an anachronistic reading when race is inserted into the question of Jesus's identity?—would certainly be an emphatic no.

Yet, given he assumes that contemporary racial categories are identical with the ancient ones of Jesus's times, Cleage must demonstrate why he is not engaged in an anachronistic reading. For example, do biblical texts give support to the claim that Jesus identified himself as a Black Messiah? Or that Israel viewed itself as a Black rather than Jewish nation? Was Roman citizenship conferred on the basis of race? Is it not the case that some Jews were actually granted Roman citizenship? Biblical texts indicate that Paul was a Roman citizen, and Paul was a Jew who claimed he was a Pharisee. Can it be validly argued that Paul was Black and a Roman citizen? [57]

What extrabiblical sources indicate such self-identification on the basis of Blackness? Lacking such references, how can it be confirmed that Jesus and those around him held to the view that he was Black? As we earlier indicated, perhaps the idea that Jesus was a Black Messiah would have been a strange idea for a Palestinian Jew of this historical period. From our previous chapters, we noted that Howard Thurman viewed Jews as a race, while Richard McKinney thought of Jewish identity as something apart from race. Neither confirm that Jesus was literally Black nor identified himself as such.

Furthermore, phenotypical description in itself cannot provide the necessary answer to the complexity of race and ethnic identity, not to mention corresponding religious affiliation and relations during antiquity. For example, certain Jews during the time of Jesus held Samaritans in contempt. According to biblical scholar Bruce Chilton, even Jesus was not exempt from such a contemptuous view about Samaritans. Notably we find that differences with Samaritans is pronounced throughout the Bible. Yet, confusion over the very origins of the Samaritans is often encountered in the misreading of biblical texts.[58]

Such differences between Jews and Samaritans relate to religion and ethnicity rather than our modern notion of race and race relations. Hence on what grounds did Jews view Samaritans? Surely present-day racial categories would not apply in this instance. Can the same be said about Romans and their relationship to Jews? The implication of this question pertains to the fact that Cleage assumes Jews were Black and Romans were white.[59]

Class, ethnic, and religious differences in antiquity are not reducible to our present-day notions about race and racism. Historical specification of the actual past state of affairs—concerning social relations and attendant conflicts—is requisite for exercising a literal reading with regard to the racial identification of the subjects under review. Theological commitments should not obstruct this vital sociological and historical dictate. If this mandate is neglected, then an anachronistic reading is in the offering.[60]

CLEAGE'S BLACK MESSIAH: MYTH AND THEOLOGY

This mandate concerning historical specification is of particular importance in our deliberations on Cleage's Black Messiah. We reach this conclusion since his literal reading on the race of Jesus—Jesus is a Black Messiah—is established by resorting to a theological claim on history, along with mythological considerations. The former is thought to be the basis for restructuring theology for biblical interpretation. Yet, when we examine Cleage's notion of theology, there is an assumption that theology is intimately tied to mythology as fantasy. Cleage argues,

> *The fantasies of Christianity are very important to black people* and they prove one thing—that *theology is important to black people*. We will never get free as black people until we change our theology. *We got to forget the fantastic mythological element and we got to forget the idea that Jesus on Calvary freed black people.* We were not saved by anything Jesus did on Calvary. If Jesus freed white people on Calvary that's for them to figure out. But certainly black people were not freed on Calvary, *because we're still not yet free.*[61] [Italics added]

With this statement, it appears that Cleage views this form of (white) theology as the fantasies of Christianity. Therein, this theology is misdirected and "We got to forget the fantastic mythological element." Thus, "we got to forget the idea that Jesus on Calvary freed black people. We were not saved by anything Jesus did on Calvary." Plainly, Cleage does not agree with Wilmore on the importance of the crucifixion. We should not forget that this matter of crucifixion and resurrection was the lynchpin for Wilmore's color symbolism and the Black Messiah.

Cleage rejects the idea that the crucifixion of Jesus was a liberating event for Black people. Here Cleage is most emphatic, "certainly black people were not freed on Calvary, because we're still not yet free." Now we encounter a contradiction in Cleage's argument. Previously we were told that by means of mythology "the historic truth is that we're dealing with a revolutionary black leader who's fighting for the liberation of black people in the New Testament and the Old Testament we're dealing

with the struggle of an enslaved *black people who liberated themselves*"⁶²
[Italics added].

Let's examine Cleage's two statements about Black people and liberation. Cleage simultaneously claims, on the one hand, that Black people liberated themselves, and, on the other hand, that Black people were never liberated and still now are not free. If we assume the former notion—of successful liberation—and Calvary is not the liberation event, then what becomes our marker of liberation? Simply put, how did Jesus liberate Black people in the past? If such an event remains as the historic truth—which we gather from mythology—then how can that event be documented?

What is before us is a theological claim about Black liberation as a historical event. The matter of verifiable documentation is not only crucial for establishing the truth of his claim but also the validity surrounding the very idea of Jesus as Black Messiah. This is due to the presupposition about Jesus as Black Messiah historically leading a successful Black liberation movement. Moreover, this movement—under Jesus' leadership—has relevance for the contemporary Black struggle. The dilemma is a glaring one. Without an actual liberation event—led by Jesus—then the very status of the Black Messiah is called into question. Cleage's Black Christology is crucially grounded on the historical Jesus as Black liberator.

In a real sense, for Cleage, "Black" people of antiquity and Black people in the contemporary United States are one and the same. Yet, we have previously pointed out that Jewish ethnic identification of this period was not self-consciously Black or even of nonwhite identity. Additionally, Jesus's status of Messiah was more properly a question concerning ethnic and religious affiliation in the context of Judaism and the subsequent formation of Christianity. Specifically, there ultimately occurred a wide gulf between the Jewish concept of Messiah and what later develops as the Christian belief in Jesus as the Christ or Messiah.

The theological implications of this divergence have a telling impact on the perspective that Christianity maintains concerning the legacy of the historical Jesus. As Peter Gomes insightfully demonstrated, in an earlier chapter, Jesus was not a Christian. If Jesus was not a Christian, then Christianity—even when it is presumed Black—cannot rectify the misdirected belief that Christianity points us in the direction of the historical Jesus. Hence, Cleage's Black Messiah is far from offering a solution to the problem of the historical Jesus. Put simply, by identifying with Black *Christian* Nationalism rather than Judaism, Cleage ignores the significance of Jesus as Jew and not Christian. Therefore, Cleage confuses the historical—Jewish—Jesus on two accounts, namely with Jesus designated as both Black and Christian.⁶³

This historical point about ethnic and religious identity amplifies Cleage's misunderstanding regarding Jesus and the liberation of Black people. Most prominently, contra Cleage's belief, Jesus could not and did not lead Black people to liberation because the very idea of the ancient Jews as Black is no more than an anachronistic reading. This arises from Cleage's literal take on Jesus as the Black Messiah. His view on Jesus as Black Messiah thus fosters the idea about the continuation of the same Black predicament lasting over two thousand years.

We submit that since the crucifixion of Jesus was not a liberating event, it follows that, for some *Jews*, Jesus was a failed Messiah. Importantly, we must not overlook that Jesus and his early followers were Jews and not Christians. These Jewish followers had differing perspectives on the meaning attached to the crucifixion. Hence, David C. Sim raises the question,

> In terms of early Christians, the belief that Jesus of Nazareth was the crucified and resurrected Messiah necessitated a reevaluation of all the issues associated with Jewish ethnic affiliation and social identity. An integral component of Christian identity was belief in Jesus' messiahship, but what did this mean in terms of the contemporary Jewish mode of self-definition. Did faith in Christ replace the traditional Jewish identity markers or merely was it an extra one that supplemented the others.[64]

Cleage's anachronistic reading neglects the complexity of this matter of contemporaneous Jewish self-definition. Nevertheless, his latter admission that Jesus's death on Calvary did not free Black people is a novel theological position for a present-day Christian. For most Christians, the idea of Jesus as universal savior is a core belief that follows from the crucifixion. Yet, evidently Cleage rejects this idea about the crucifixion being affixed to Jesus as universal savior. In turn, we could ask, What value is a Black Messiah that fails in leading his people to liberation?

In ancient Jewish history, it is documented that there were a number of failed Messiahs. One response to the continuation of Jewish oppression — in the wake of failed predictions of a liberating event — was the mythic idea that the Messiah would emerge as miracle worker. However, Cleage shuns the idea that Jesus was a miracle worker for the notion that he was a Black nationalist revolutionary. What is missing from Cleage's account is the documentation of the successful revolutionary overthrow of the Roman oppressor.[65]

If Jesus failed two thousand years ago, then what relevance does he have today for any Christian, Black or otherwise? Herein lies the importance of the Christian resurrection myth. Despite death on the cross, Jesus returns to life on earth and remains undefeated. The hope for liberation/salvation remains alive because Jesus continues to live. However, Cleage rejects this option with respect to the crucifixion and resurrection of Jesus. In this vital sense, his Christology diverts from Wilmore and several others in the Black Theology School. Cleage declares,

> The resurrection story is obviously a religious mythology. The whole concept of Jesus arising from the dead on the third day obviously is mythology. You can build all kinds of theologies about it—presupposing that it actually happened and it is a historic fact. . . . We are dealing with mythology in the whole Easter story, but the mythology is important because of later additions. The whole concept of Easter rising has no relationship to Jesus but with Apostle Paul but it points to the ultimate escape beyond death.⁶⁶

Cleage continues,

> Jesus nailed to the cross on Calvary provided the possibility for people in all generations . . . to be saved—whatever "saved" means in that context—to be saved. A person living in all kinds of poverty and degradation and powerlessness is to be saved by something Jesus did two thousand years ago. Now that is *basic myth*.⁶⁷ [Italics added]

Given his statement on Easter and the resurrection, we now observe that Cleage returns to debunking religious myths. Rather than upholding the view that myth contains some kind of historic truth, Cleage boldly challenges the Easter myth of Jesus's resurrection. In fact, his comments are a telling indictment on how the Christian notion of salvation—based on the resurrection myth—ideologically preserves the status quo of Black "poverty and degradation and powerlessness." We get no pie in the sky or Jesus ascending to heaven from Cleage.

> They say that Jesus ascended into heaven, but the mythology is important that people would actually go down through time believing that it's possible for a man to ascend—a resurrected body to ascend into heaven. Bodies don't ascend into heaven. We're dealing with fantasy and slaves always prefer fantasy. The more powerless they are the more they prefer fantasy, because reality is unpleasant and it makes difficult demands on them. Fantasy is the easy kind of solution.⁶⁸

Moreover, the ideological illusion of personal salvation is readily exposed. Cleage makes a sharp distinction between a soteriology of personal salvation—which he views as based on individualism—and the collective liberation of a people. Therein, Cleage is theologically at odds with McKinney's soteriology. We cannot overlook that McKinney's universal savior designation respecting Jesus implicitly encompasses personal salvation. Yet, in Cleage's estimation,

> The whole concept of the individual communing with God is not there. God speaks to an individual only that he may convey a message to a people. God saw Israel as a chosen people. God is communicating through people is basic and black people have to recapture that because God is not going to speak to any individual black person. All those nights you've spent praying that God would ease your burden and let you fly away home when you die has been wasted, because

unless you will function as a black person, part of a black nation, and part of a black movement, God could not waste time listening to you.[69]

Cleage further added, "The old time Black church when you used to pray people into the church—the old church would come together and pray somebody into salvation. Well then, the process was O.K., but the idea wasn't what salvation was. It was very naïve and simple because the idea of salvation has to do with personal sin that God would have no concern about."[70]

When Cleage's argues—"God speaks to an individual only that he may convey a message to a people. God saw Israel as a chosen people. God is communicating through people is basic and black people have to recapture that because God is not going to speak to any individual black person"—obviously collective liberation is the chief aspect of his Black Theology.

The Black movement is the determining factor in the theological structure behind Cleage's conception of communication with God. Petition prayers—of a personal kind—to God are not on his agenda. God's primary concern is collective Black interests. Of course, we must ask, How does Cleage know his view on God is the correct one? What theological rationale provides the needed justification? More importantly, does Cleage's theology facilitate or obscure uncovering historical Jesus as Black Messiah? We contend that the basis for Cleage's conception of God emerges from his reading of the Old Testament. He explicitly states,

> So in the Old Testament we find a blue print for the kinds of things black people have to do. That's not to say in your Old Testament you find a higher concept of God than the relationship with man that we find in traditional African religion, because to me there is an authentic unity that's developed in traditional African religions that's much more developed, much more a complete a concept than found in the thesis . . . of Jesus. Jesus had a rather aborted ministry. His ideas were not totally put together.[71]

In Cleage's view, Black Christian Theology is quintessentially a liberation theology and the Black church should foster a liberation movement. He argues, "Now we have to realize that when you talk about dealing with a liberation movement with some kind of sanity . . . that you have to develop a process—a process whereby black people can be changed. This is where the Church, the Black Church has failed totally."[72]

Plainly, Cleage's Black Christian Nationalist theology is a departure not only from conventional white Christian theology but also from most theologians in the Black Christian Theology School. Cleage's Christology situates the historical Jesus as foundational, with Jesus removed from the exalted status as divinely placed and hence standing above life and death. The immortality of Jesus Cleage concludes is an unacceptable myth. In stark contrast, Wilmore's symbolic Blackness is squarely located in Jesus' death and resurrection as the suffering Servant.

Yet, due to his ambiguous treatment of mythology—in more general terms—Cleage is not entirely free from the pitfalls of religious mythology. What is critical here is that a literal interpretation requires historical facts—that is, empirical verification from publicly available source materials. While he rejects myth as fantasy, Cleage also primarily depends on mythology—rather than history—to anchor his belief that Jesus is the Black Messiah and liberator of Black people. We submit that Cleage's ambiguity about mythology is the main reason why his efforts at a literal reading fall short of the mark.

At best, we have a theological claim on history regarding the Black Messiah. At worst, no amount of theological restructuring (juggling?) can act as a substitute for historical analysis or documentation. Thus, we return to the question, "Does Cleage's theology facilitate or obscure uncovering historical Jesus as Black Messiah?" The following comment from Thomas L. Thompson is most helpful for our reflection. In his text, *The Messiah Myth: The Near Eastern Roots of Jesus and David*, Thompson remarks,

> Before asking whether episodes and scenes that structure the story of Jesus' life are based on events, we need to look at the function of stories in antiquity. The stories of Jesus's birth and baptism, of his preaching and miracle working, of his suffering and crucifixion—as well as the story of his resurrection—fulfill a clearly defined, coherent function. Together they embody a well-defined tradition of discussion that formed the Judaism to which the Gospels belong. That they might create expectations among the readers of the tradition does not define their intended function.[73]

Rather than grapple with the totality concerning the mythic functions of such stories, Cleage's method comprises selectively picking and choosing what myths are acceptable from those that are not. This judgment is confirmed when we previously examined Cleage's contradictory treatment of African and white mythology. Moreover, Cleage's ambiguity concerning myth—whether it was fantasy or the carrier of a form of historical truth—clearly indicated that a mythic interpretation of the Bible was far from out of the order.

If we are to take Thompson's charge seriously, then Cleage's failure becomes even more fundamental in its repercussions—namely, his failure to recognize that biblical texts are not history books. What remains as the intended function of the ancient authors—of biblical texts—was not history but rather the construction of mythic stories with theological intent. Cleage's attempts at historicizing the Bible—to establish the historic presence of the Black Messiah—is at root a theological endeavor. Instead of presenting us with the historical Jesus, Cleage offers up an alternative—historicized—version of the mythic story about Jesus. Albeit Cleage's Jesus is a Black and not a white Messiah.

If our evaluation of Cleage is correct, then our question, "Is such a Black Messiah the product of faith commitments and mythological construction?" immediately directs us to faith commitments based on mythological construction. It is precisely mythological construction that holds sway in Cleage's literal depiction of the Black Messiah.

The dominant form of historical realism that marks Cleage's literal depiction of the Black Messiah actually occludes its essence which is specifically his particular take on the historicizing of myth. It is historicized mythology instead of historical inquiry that anchors Cleage's Black Messiah. Put simply, Cleage's literal rendering is no closer to history than Wilmore who is unabashedly ahistorical in his approach to the symbolic Black Messiah.

In both instances, with Wilmore and Cleage, we have in the offering a particular form of Black Christology anchored on the presumption of faith commitments—theology—rather than history. Besides, we have effectively demonstrated that their theologies rest on mythic grounds. For Wilmore, it is the myth of the crucifixion and resurrection of Jesus—as the suffering Servant of God—which serves as the chief anchor. In the case of Cleage, it is the supposition that the whole of biblical texts and its adjoining mythology carry the historical truth of the Black Messiah.

The theological differences between Wilmore and Cleage's perspectives on Christology are only apparently a matter comprising sharp differences based on a symbolic and literal reading of the historical Jesus. In each instance, the overriding factor of mythology is the sustaining principle that anchors both conceptions of Christology. In a nutshell, the dividing line is firmly situated within contrasting mythological presumptions. This methodological issue—concerning the use of mythology—is our root problem. In this sense, Wilmore and Cleage share more in essence than what is apparent. Both are engaged with wrestling with mythology as the primary means for founding their respective notions of Black Messiah. In our comparative study of Wilmore and Cleage, what essentially remains at stake are contending mythological presumptions, with regard to Black Christology.

CONCLUSION

In conclusion, we must return to the pronouncement on cautiously pursuing Black Christology. Leon Wright perceptively warns,

> [I]t should not be supposed that one advances the cause of a "Black Theology" merely by painting faces black or partisanly juggling spiritual preferences before God, respecting persons or groups. Whatever the case for Black Theology may turn out to be, let us not cavalierly

create a set of mythological assumptions whose credibility deserves only to be "de-mythologized" at the same instant.[74]

Although Wright's critique of Black Theology intends on advancing an alternative theological position, our aim in this chapter is straightforwardly a philosophical critique of theological claims. Hence, the philosophical relevance of Wright's warning is that it speaks to the danger of Black Theology resorting to mythology and mythic explanations.

From our philosophical analysis, what is most evident is that the notion of Black Messiah—as the authentic Christ—is no more than an alternative biblical myth. Hence, there is no empirical basis verifying that the idea of the Black Messiah is any closer to the historical truth than is the notion of white Messiah. The reader could very well ask, How do we reach this conclusion?

First, we should note that both paradigms concerning a racialized Messiah are entangled in mythic reading of ancient history. From Cleage we have an anachronistic reading and with Wilmore the mythic treatment of the crucifixion and resurrection. Second, the difference between the two viewpoints is fundamentally one of conflicting theological opinion rather than historical evidence. This conflict boils down to divergent faith claims, and therefore the historical Jesus remains shrouded in biblical mythology. Additionally, Black mythology—even when biblical in character—cannot advance our knowledge of history. Thus, with the Black Messiah notion, the historical Jesus remains prisoner to theological commitments established on mythological assumptions.[75]

Hence, when we return to our primary question under deliberation, namely the topic of our chapter, "Black Messiah as the Authentic Christ: Alternative Biblical Myth or Real History?" we can conclude with certainty that Wilmore and Cleage's notions about Black Messiah are no more than alternative biblical myths. Now we will proceed to our next chapter, "Whiteness and Christology: Why does the Racial Identity of Jesus Theologically Matter?"

NOTES

1. Consult Leon E. Wright, "'Black Theology' or Black Experience?," *The Journal of Religious Thought* 26(2) (Summer 1969): 54.

2. For the idea of race in antiquity, read St. Clair Drake, *Black Folk Here and There, Volume 2* (Los Angeles, CA: Center for Afro-American Studies University of California, Los Angeles, 1990); Frank M. Snowden, *Blacks in Antiquity; Ethiopians in the Greco-Roman Experience* (Cambridge, MA: Belknap Press of Harvard University Press, 1970).

3. Gayraud Wilmore argues, "Only a few black leaders like Bishop Henry M. Turner of the AME Church and Bishop George Alexander McGuire of the African Orthodox Church had the intellectual courage and prophetic zeal to speak of a Black God, or to attempt a basic revision of the color symbolism of Christianity. Most had been so smitten by the white symbolism of the culture that dominated their conscious and subconscious life that they could not personally authorize a structure of religious

belief that gave blackness a positive and constructive meaning without falsifying daily experience" ("Black Messiah: Revising the Color Symbolism of Western Christology," *The Journal of the Interdenominational Theological Center* 2(1) [Fall 1974]: 12).

4. Diana Hayes, "Christology in African American Theology," in *The Oxford Handbook of African American Theology*, ed. Katie G. Cannon and Anthony B. Pinn (New York: Oxford University Press, 2014).

5. Albert B. Cleage Jr., *The Black Messiah* (New York: Sheed and Ward, 1968). Aswad Walker, "Princes Shall Come Out of Egypt: A Theological Comparison of Marcus Garvey and Reverend Albert B. Cleage Jr.," *Journal of Black Studies* 39(2) (November 2008): 194–251. For a historical accounting of the notion of Black Christ, read Kelly Brown Douglas, *The Black Christ* (Ossining, NY: Orbis Books, 1994). With regard to biblical interpretation see Herbert Robinson Marbury, *Pillars of Cloud and Fire: The Politics of Exodus in African American Biblical Interpretation* (New York: NYU Press, 2015). Also read Edward J. Blum and Paul Harvey, *The Color of Christ: The Son of God & the Saga of Race in America* (Chapel Hill: University of North Carolina Press, 2012).

6. Albert B. Cleage, "Black Religion and Black Revolution," Item ID: daams 01023032 Box 1, Folder 23 Black Religion Symposium, 1972 Department of African and African American Studies Records. On April 8, 1972, Duke University Black Studies under the direction of Prof. Walter W. Burford sponsored a symposium, "Black Religion and Black Revolution." Rev. Albert B. Cleage was the keynote speaker. A transcription of the Cleage speech is the source of reference for all citations from Rev. Cleage in this chapter. The online record of this symposium is by courtesy of Duke University Libraries—Rubenstein Library—Guide to the Department of African and African American Studies records, 1966–1981. http://library.duke.edu/rubenstein/findingaids/uaafro/ Duke University Archives, David M. Rubenstein Rare Book & Manuscript Library, Duke University. Please note that the pagination of this transcript has been omitted.

7. Consult Lloyd A. Thompson, "Rome and Race," The University Lectures, 1981, University of Ibadan (Ibadan: University of Ibadan, 1987), 71.

8. Hayim Lapin, "The Law of Moses and the Jews: Rabbis, Ethnic Marking, and Romanization," in Natalie B. Dohrmann and Annette Yoshiko Reed, eds., *Jews, Christians, and the Roman Empire* (Philadelphia: University of Pennsylvania Press, 2013). Drake, *Black Folk Here and There, Volume 2*. Snowden, *Blacks in Antiquity*.

9. Edwin M. Yamauchi, *Africa and Africans in Antiquity* (East Lansing: Michigan State University Press, 2001).

10. Snowden, *Blacks in Antiquity*.

11. For a materialist philosophical treatment of race, see John H. McClendon III, "On the Nature of Whiteness and the Ontology of Race : Toward a Dialectical Materialist Analysis," in George Yancy, ed., *What White Looks Like: African-American Philosophers on the Whiteness Question* (New York: Routledge, 2004). For the legal aspect on race in the United States, consult Malik Simba, *Black Marxism and American Constitutionalism* (Dubuque, IA: Kendall Hunt Publishing Co., 2016).

12. John H. McClendon III, "Act Your Age and Not Your Color: Blackness as Material Conditions, Presumptive Context, and Social Category," in George Yancy, ed., *White on White, Black on Black* (Lanham, MD: Rowman & Littlefield, 2005).

13. Hayes, "Christology in African American Theology."

14. Wilmore, "Black Messiah: Revising the Color Symbolism of Western Christology," 13.

15. William R. Jones, "Theodicy and Methodology in Black Theology: A Critique of Washington, Cone, and Cleage," *Harvard Theological Review* 64 (1971): 541–57. Also consult, Stephen C. Ferguson II, "Teaching Hurricane Katrina: Understanding Divine Racism and Theodicy," *APA Newsletter on Philosophy and the Black Experience* 7(1) (Fall 2007): 1–5.

16. Wilmore, "Black Messiah," 13.

17. Wilmore, "Black Messiah," 14, 16.

18. The general thrust of most proponents of Black Christology derives from the diametrical opposition to white Christology and whiteness more generally. The significance of Wilmore's distinctive position we later address in chapter 5.

19. Wilmore, "Black Messiah," 14.

20. Wilmore, "Black Messiah," 16.

21. Wilmore, "Black Messiah," 16.

22. Wilmore, "Black Messiah," 16.

23. Wilmore, "Black Messiah," 17.

24. The reader must remember that Cone states, "The fact that I am black is my ultimate reality. My identity with blackness [a term for one who is oppressed], and what it means for millions living in a white world controls the investigation" (*Black Theology and Black Power* [New York: Seabury Press, 1969], 33).

25. The particularity of Blackness is the overwhelming trope of the Black Christology school. Hence, what we gather from James Cone, Joseph A. Johnson, William L. Eichelberger, and Albert Cleage, among others, is an accent on particularity that directs Black Theology on a collision course with white theology.

26. Gayraud S. Wilmore, "Black Messiah," 16.

27. Read the insightful treatment of Robert Greg Cavin, "Is There Sufficient History Evidence to Establish the Resurrection of Jesus?," in Robert M. Price and Jeffery Jay Lowder, eds., *The Empty Tomb: Jesus beyond the Grave* (Amherst, NY: Prometheus Books, 2005).

28. Michael Martin, "The Resurrection as Initially Improbable," in Robert M. Price and Jeffery Jay Lowder, eds., *The Empty Tomb: Jesus beyond the Grave* (Amherst, NY: Prometheus Books, 2005).

29. Gerd Lüdemann, *The Resurrection of Christ: A Historical Inquiry* (Amherst, NY: Prometheus Books, 2004), 11–12.

30. Gerald Sigal, *The Resurrection Fantasy: Reinventing Jesus* (Bloomington, IN: Xlibris, 2012).

31. Geza Vermes, *The Resurrection: History and Myth* (New York: Doubleday, 2008).

32. Brunner states, "The New Testament witnesses do not speak with one voice.... We may regard the variety of Easter narratives as a sign of the fact which they report is in the strict sense of the word an 'eschatological fact,' that is, the beginning of the coming of eternal Consummation, of the new world, which cannot be apprehended by the categories of this special-temporal world" (*The Christian Doctrine of the Church, Faith, and the Consummation: Dogmatics: Vol. III* [Eugene, OR: Wipf and Stock Publishers, 2014], 409). Also read Sigal, *The Resurrection Fantasy*.

33. Rudolf Bultmann declares, "It [the resurrection of Christ] is an object of faith because it is an eschatological event. And it is for this reason it cannot be an authenticating miracle" (*New Testament Mythology and Other Basic Writings* [Minneapolis: Fortress Press, 1989], 38).

34. Lüdemann, *The Resurrection of Christ*, 12.

35. Brunner, *The Christian Doctrine of the Church, Faith, and the Consummation*.

36. Wilmore, "Black Messiah," 13.

37. Calvin S. Morris, *Reverdy C. Ransom: Black Advocate of the Social Gospel* (Lanham, MD: University Press of America, 1990). Philip S. Foner, "From Slavery to Socialism: George Washington Woodbey, Black Socialist Preacher," in Jacob Henry Dorn, ed., *Socialism and Christianity in Early 20th Century America* (Westport, CT: Greenwood Press, 1998).

38. Of course, Wilmore's Blackening of Christianity is a symbolic gesture that does not in any fashion reconstruct basic Christian tenets.

39. Cleage states, "The resurrection story is obviously a religious mythology. The whole concept of Jesus arising from the dead on the third day obviously is mythology. You can build all kinds of theologies about it—presupposing that it actually happened and it is a historic fact.... We are dealing with mythology in the whole Easter story." Consult "Black Religion and Black Revolution."

40. Wilmore argues, "Generations of the oppressed have pondered the meaning of the Suffering Servant of God in relation to their own condition, but none more consistently than the sons and daughters of Africa—the black people of the world" ("Black Messiah," 13).

41. On this question about faith, Wilmore is not far from Bultmann's position. See note 33.

42. Vermes, *The Resurrection*.

43. Wilmore, "Black Messiah," 13–14.

44. Wilmore, "Black Messiah," 13.

45. On the idea of theological projection see Ludwig Feuerbach, *The Essence of Christianity* (New York: Barnes & Noble Books, 2004).

46. Jacquelyn Grant, *White Women's Christ and Black Women's Jesus: Feminist Christology and Womanist Response* (Scholars Press, 1989). Kelly Brown Douglas, "Teaching Womanist Theology: A Case Study," *Journal of Feminist Studies in Religion* 8 (Fall 1992). Kelly Brown Douglas, *The Black Christ* (Ossining, NY: Orbis, 1994). For practical application of womanism in theology respecting counseling, read Markeva G. Hill, *Womanism against Socially Constructed Matriarchal Images* (New York: Palgrave Macmillan, 2012).

47. Cleage, "Black Religion and Black Revolution."

48. Cleage, "Black Religion."

49. Cleage, "Black Religion."

50. Susan Ackerman importantly notes, "While . . . the term 'myth' is used in New Testament literature with negative connotations, much in the New Testament is in fact mythic in character" ("Myth," in Bruce M. Metzger and Michael D. Coogan, *The Oxford Companion to the Bible* [New York: Oxford University Press, 1993], 541).

51. Also read Rudolf Karl Bultmann, *Jesus Christ and Mythology* (New York: Scribner, 1958); *Kerygma and Myth* (New York: Harper & Row, 1961).

52. In this sense, Cleage is not far from Rudolf Bultmann's conception of demythologization. On Rudolf Bultmann and demythologization, Van A. Harvey states, "demythologization refers to a type of interpretation of the New Testament first systematically proposed in 1941 by Rudolf Bultmann. He argued that the message of the New Testament with couched in the language of primitive and prescientific mentality that, from the standpoint of the history of religion must be called mythological. . . . Theology should accept the entire message is having a mythological form and seek to interpret the whole consistently. This interpretation is possible, Bultmann continued, because mythology also has certain elements of truth, even though that truth is stated in an outmoded form. Myth expresses certain fundamental intuitions about human existence and its relations to the powers that man experiences as the ground and limit of his life. In order to understand these intuitions, however, it is necessary to separate them from their outmoded form, that is, it is necessary to demythologize" (*A Handbook of Theological Terms* [New York: Touchstone, 1992], 67). Also consult Bultmann, *Kerygma and Myth*.

53. D. M. Murdoch, *Did Moses Exist?: The Myth of the Israelite Lawgiver* (Seattle, WA: Stellar House Publishing, 2014). Marbury, *Pillars of Cloud and Fire*. Rhondda Robinson Thomas, *Claiming Exodus: A Cultural History of Afro-Atlantic Identity, 1774–1903* (Waco, TX: Baylor University Press, 2012).

54. Cleage, "Black Religion and Black Revolution."

55. Cleage, "Black Religion."

56. Cleage, "Black Religion."

57. On Jews and Roman citizenship, see Paul Trebilco, *The Early Christians in Ephesus from Paul to Ignatius* (Grand Rapids, MI: Wm. B. Eerdmans Publishing, 2007), 42; and James S. Jeffers, *The Greco-Roman World of the New Testament Era* (Downers Grove, IL: Inter Varsity Press, 2009), 14. Lloyd A. Thompson, "Rome and Race," 71. Frank M Snowden, *Before Color Prejudice: The Ancient View of Blacks* (Cambridge, MA: Harvard University Press, 1983).

58. Bruce Chilton, *Rabbi Jesus: An Intimate Biography* (New York: Doubleday, 2000), 67–70. Another scholar in Samaritan studies, Magnar Karveit brings to our attention, "Many Bible readers will think chapter 17 of the second book of Kings refers to the origins of the Samaritans. . . . On closer inspection, however, it turns out that 2 Kgs. 17:29 does not refer to the Samaritans but to the 'people of Samaria,' whose relation to the Samarians is not immediately clear." Karveit further adds that the Samaritans have their "own story of their origins. . . . These documents were created in the late Middle Ages . . . and they provide us with an origin story which assumes that the Samaritans represent the true Israel from the time of Jacob, whereas the Jews split off from this true Israel by following the aberrant priest Eli" (*The Origin of the Samaritans* [Leiden: Brill, 2009], 1–2).

59. Also read Lloyd A. Thompson, *Romans and Blacks* (New York: Routledge, 2015). Cleage, "Black Religion and Black Revolution."

60. On Jesus and his encounter with the Samaritan woman, consult Chilton, *Rabbi Jesus: An Intimate Biography*, 67–70. Also consult Richard Coggins, "Samaritan," in Bruce M. Metzger and Michael D. Coogan, eds., *The Oxford Companion to the Bible* (New York: Oxford University Press, 1993), 671–73. The scholarly literature on Black people in antiquity is quite broad. See Charles B. Copher, "Three Thousand Years of Biblical Interpretation with Reference to Black Peoples," in *African American Religious Studies: An Interdisciplinary Anthology*, ed. Gayraud S. Wilmore (Durham, NC: Duke University Press, 1989); David M. Goldenberg, *The Curse of Ham: Race and Slavery in Early Judaism, Christianity, and Islam* (Princeton, NJ: Princeton University Press, 2003); Denise Eileen McCoskey, *Race: Antiquity and Its Legacy* (New York: I. B.Tauris, 2012); Thompson, *Romans and Blacks*; Yamauchi, *Africa and Africans in Antiquity*.

61. Cleage, "Black Religion and Black Revolution."

62. Cleage, "Black Religion."

63. Peter J. Gomes, *The Scandalous Gospel of Jesus: What's So Good about the Good News* (New York: HarperCollins Publishers, 2007), 11. L. Michael White, *From Jesus to Christianity* (San Francisco: Harpe, 2004). David C. Sim, "Jews, Gentiles, and Ethnic Identity in Matthew," in Geoffrey Dunn and Wendy Mayer, eds., *Christians Shaping Identity from the Roman Empire to Byzantium* (Leiden: Brill, 2015). Lapin, "The Law of Moses and the Jews."

64. Sim. "Jews, Gentiles, and Ethnic Identity in Matthew," 27.

65. Jerry Rabow argues, "To keep hope alive during desperate times, Jews began to emphasize the version of the Messiah myth predicting the arrival of the messianic era would be preceded by the infliction on the world of 'terrible birth pangs' (a term used by Isaiah). . . . Because of the seemingly unbridgeable contrast between the miserable reality of Jews lives and their sweet dreams of universal peace, it was natural for Jews to believe that it would take a miracle worker to bring on the change. In this manner, the Jewish Messiah figure from an ordinary leader to a man of miracles. . . . Of course, one difficulty with the requirement that the Messiah must be divine, miraculous being is what to do when the Messiah is not ultimately successful" (*50 Jewish Messiahs: The Untold Life Stories of 50 Jewish Messiahs since Jesus and How They Changed the Jewish, Christian, and Muslim Worlds* [Lynbrook: Gefen Books, 2002], 2–3).

66. Cleage, "Black Religion and Black Revolution."

67. Cleage, "Black Religion."

68. Cleage, "Black Religion."

69. Cleage, "Black Religion."

70. Cleage, "Black Religion."

71. Cleage, "Black Religion."

72. Cleage, "Black Religion."

73. Thomas L. Thompson, *The Messiah Myth: The Near Eastern Roots of Jesus and David* (New York: Basic Books, 2009), 31.

74. Leon E. Wright, "'Black Theology' or Black Experience?," 54.

75. Blum and Harvey, *The Color of Christ*.

FIVE

Whiteness and Christology

Why Does the Racial Identity of Jesus Theologically Matter?

In this chapter, our inquiry into the relation between whiteness and Christology embarks from the standpoint of philosophical analysis. Rather than offering an alternative theological proposal, our philosophical investigation is an appraisal on the theological claim—the incompatibility of whiteness with Christology. The main philosophical concern involves identifying why and how whiteness is viewed as incompatible with Christology as well as critically reviewing the corresponding justifications and counterarguments for this belief.

Additionally, the theoretical impact of this identification points directly to if and how we should categorize Jesus in racial terms. If such racial categorization theologically matters, then it has special import respecting the compatibility or incompatibility of whiteness with Christology. For example, when Jesus is presumed as white, it follows that there should not be any question about the compatibility of whiteness with Christology. However, presumably if Jesus is alternatively the Black Messiah, we could suppose that the notion of the Black Messiah and thus Black Christology correspondingly offers a corrective to white Christology? Therefore, how would the compatibility of whiteness sustain any relevance to Christology? The answer to this question would entail that whiteness is problematic from the standpoint of Christology.

On this Christological question, concerning the problem of whiteness, George Yancy provides a compelling argument, however from a different vantage point than Black Christology. African American philosopher George Yancy argues, "Through a hermeneutical lens that sees Jesus as the embodiment of love and justice for those who suffer, *the problem of whiteness*, as a site of hegemony, must be approached through a Christological framework of that important Nazarene carpenter who was the very embodiment of caritas."[1]

We should point out that this citation comes from an edited work (published in 2012) by Dr. Yancy. He informs us that his text, *Christology and Whiteness: What Would Jesus Do?* is specifically designed to address the problem of whiteness from the perspective of Christology.

> Personally, my objective was neither to argue for the historical reality of Jesus nor for his metaphysical status as divine. For me, this is a point of narrative embarkation, a place woven out of *hope, love, and desire*. This text specifically asked theologians, religionists, and social ethicists whether Jesus' life and work can or cannot address the question of contemporary forms of white privilege.[2]

Let's review the main objective of the text, namely "*Christology and Whiteness: What Would Jesus Do?* is specifically designed to address the problem of whiteness from the perspective of Christology." Certainly, Yancy views whiteness as incompatible with Christology. Indeed, this presumption of incompatibility stems from how Christology operates as his very conceptual framework for the examination on the problem of whiteness. We submit that there are several philosophical questions, which are pertinent regarding Yancy's authorial intentions. Let us now outline our queries on the topic.

First, the question "What would Jesus do?" presumes having already answered, "Who was Jesus?" We contend the latter question—Who was Jesus?—is the starting point with any Christological investigation. Once we identify Jesus within the respective theological framework and coinciding historical context, then we can determine what he would do.[3] Second, what is problematic about whiteness? Are we to assume that it is more than simply the racial description attached to given social groups? Third, if it is more than a racial descriptor, does it follow that whiteness is the same (or at least in the same categorical realm) as white privilege or white racism? Fourth, must we presume there is only a singular approach pertaining to Christology when addressing whiteness or is it the case there are multiple points of Christological entry?[4] Fifth, if there are multiple Christological perspectives, then we inquire, how do we determine, which is the appropriately suited Christological viewpoint for interrogating whiteness? Sixth, is the proposed aptly suited Christological viewpoint essentially what is meant by authentic Christology? Seventh, what is the justification for our decision about what constitutes the correct thesis on an authentic Christology? Eighth, does Black Christology, in turn, point us in the direction of authenticity?[5] Ninth, how does this thesis about authenticity square with the historical facts about multiple Christologies?[6]

Rather than addressing these questions at this point, they frame our discussion throughout the chapter, thus collectively forming the heuristic framework for our analysis. What turns out to be immediately apparent is that Yancy presumes whiteness is problematic from the Christological position. Accordingly, the incompatibility of whiteness with Christology becomes axiomatic. This axiom functions in concurrence with the notion that whiteness operates within the same categorical realm as white privilege/racism. Yancy is not alone in this judgment. For instance, Black Theologian Joseph A. Johnson Jr. exclaims:

> The tragedy of the interpretations of Jesus by white American theologians during the last three hundred years is that Jesus has been too often identified with the oppressive structures and forces of the prevailing society. His teachings have been used to justify wars, exploitation of the poor and oppressed peoples of the world. In his name, the vicious form of racism has been condoned and advocated. In a more tragic sense this Jesus of the white church establishment has been white, straight-haired, blue-eyed, Anglo-Saxon; that is presented in the image of the oppressor. This "whiteness" has prevailed to the extent that the black, brown, or red peoples of the world, who had accepted Jesus as Lord and Savior, were denied full Christian fellowship.[7]

In Johnson's estimation, white Christianity is fundamentally oppressive and even denies people of color full participation in the halls of Christian fellowship. Sequentially, the racial makeup of the oppressor, Johnson contends, is transparently none other than white. Therefore, the iconography that depicts a white Jesus has the symbolic function of giving expression to oppression and, hence, it cannot serve as authentic Christology. It follows that Johnson concludes that whiteness is incompatible with Christology.

In fact, he contends the problem of whiteness has persisted for over three hundred years. Thus, clearly having origins with the advent of slavery and therein whiteness—white Christology—is in the same categorical realm with white privilege/racism. Apparently, Johnson and Yancy are in concert about the incompatibility of whiteness with Christology. The incompatibility of whiteness with Christology immediately denotes that authentic Christianity should be free of whiteness. It stands to reason that not only is whiteness essentially oppressive, but also it significantly entails that authentic Christology must be removed from such attributions.

Consequently, the question of the authenticity of Christianity is pivotal to the presumptive context about compatibility and incompatibility of any racial designation. For most Black Christologists, this presumptive context becomes the primary line of distinction between white and Black

Christology. Yet, we detect that lurking within the background remains a hidden presumption.

This hidden presumption—if you will—is that Black Christology is in concert with authentic Christianity. However, as a matter of logical concern, the formal justification about why Black Christology is authentic, in turn, becomes a mandatory stipulation. From our review of Johnson's declaration, we find he lacks the necessary proof for establishing that Black Christology is singularly what must be deemed as authentic Christianity. Nevertheless, in Johnson's view, white Christology is an inauthentic form, and it persists as the compelling point of departure for our analysis.

In summation, Johnson's definition of whiteness—as oppressive in its essential features—thus renders white Christology as inauthentic. Based on Johnson's definition of whiteness, then it continues that whiteness would be incompatible with Christology. This clearly explains why, for Johnson, the incompatibility of whiteness with Christology stands as axiomatic. In this respect, we think, Johnson is in accord with Yancy's notion that whiteness—as a tenacious problem—constitutes the object of Christological investigation.

Therefore, whiteness fails as any kind of descriptive feature of Christology. Formulated as an affirmative theological category, then, white Christology (by the definitions attached to the two terms) would amount to an oxymoron. Two key ideas come into play with this formulation; namely, whiteness is definitively oppressive, while Christology—in its essential meaning—is far removed from being oppressive in character.

Subsequently, on this dialectical assumption, whiteness and Christology are extreme polarities, indeed antagonistic opposites. This all follows from the presupposition that oppression is the defining feature of whiteness. Therein, lies the theological significance of why authentic Christology must be removed from whiteness and particularly in terms of any definitive characteristic of Christology. By its very definition and meaning, whiteness is oppressive. Sequentially, authentic Christology challenges all forms of oppression.

Given this proof for demonstrating the grounds for authentic Christology, then, Christology becomes the suitable framework for the critical analysis of whiteness. It follows that the notion of suitable framework—for judgments about whiteness—is established by indicating that the authenticity of Christology maintains the requisite status associated with fundamental characteristics that are free of oppression.

We submit, however, that this consideration on inauthenticity—regarding white Christology—does not exhaust the scope of possible Christological options. Therefore, let us turn now and instead consider the possibility of the *compatibility* between whiteness and Christianity. Let's grant that there are those Christian devotees who uphold the compatibility of whiteness with Christology. In this way, we can approach this relationship without premature closure on the subject.

One way of fashioning the essential compatibility of whiteness with Christology is via the affirmative formulation of "white Christology." White Christology—as an affirmative premise—obviously presupposes the compatibility of the two terms. Given specified racial notions about the nature of Christianity vitally serving as the foundation for Christology, white Christologists could argue that white Christianity cannot be removed—without adequate justification—from the realm of Christological alternatives.

Of course, this pluralistic method pertaining to Christology can just as well serve as the justification for Black Christology. Thus, the affirmative stance for white Christology is not an exception to the rule, rather it is in concert with the way all racialized Christologies—including Black Christology—could be justified as consistent with Christianity. The methodological shift from a line of demarcation based on a monolithically conceived authenticity to the pluralistic method continues as the basis for the legitimacy of racialized Christologies. Pluralism in Christology is confirmed by historical data; this stands in contrast to the foundational (theological) presupposition on authenticity. From its advent, the history of Christianity, we will discover, has always given way to multiple expressions with attendant Christologies. Therefore, white Christology is far from an aberration.[8]

In philosophical terms, what is operative in this instance (of plurality) is a principle of difference that persists without transforming into a relation of mutual exclusion. By relation of mutual exclusion, we mean that Black and white Christology stand in opposition, such that it becomes an *either/or* dichotomy. Either Black Christology is authentic or white Christology assumes this mantle. Both cannot simultaneously serve as representative of authentic Christology.

However, only on the presupposition that Christological legitimacy requires some form of authenticity—in an approximately monolithic sense—are we bound to the idea that Black and white Christology are mutually exclusive. Earlier, in chapter 4, we discovered in fact that Black Christologist Gayraud Wilmore adopted such a pluralist approach to Christology and sequentially affirmed the legitimacy of white Christology. Subsequently, we unveiled that the mutual exclusion of Black and white Christology is not a necessary condition for establishing the legitimacy of white Christology.

In short, the legitimacy of white Christology could rest on the premise that historically there have been multiple expressions of Christianity, which also includes white Christianity. Logically, this is the first step toward exploring how white Christology could stand on an affirmative basis. On this logical basis, we can reasonably argue that white Christianity accordingly would have its own supplementary white Christology.

What cannot be overlooked is that on Johnson's account white Christology fails because it is considered as an oppressive imposition on a supposed authentic Christianity, which is thought to be free of such attributions.

The multiplicity of Christologies eliminates the presumption that legitimacy must rely on a monolithic authenticity. In this pluralistic sense, Christianity can be legitimated on historical grounds. In other words, over the course of history—rather than one viewpoint consisting as *the* authentic Christianity—we uncover there have been multiple forms of Christianity of which white Christianity stands among that order.[9] In turn, white Christology can function as the legitimate expression of this white Christianity. With that said, unquestionably the very meaning of white Christianity, with its respective history, requires closer inspection.

How we define white Christianity is crucial in any inquiry on whiteness and its compatibility/incompatibility with Christology. For example, it could be presumed—by proponents of white Christology—that when it comes to Christianity, the notions of "Western" and "whiteness" are synonymous adjectives. We think this is a long-prevailing assumption among scholars. For a considerable time now, in Western scholarship, there has been the predominant idea that Western European history is the basis and context for what constitutes the core meaning behind the designation—white culture. For some, this historical progression of white (racial) development reaches all the way back to ancient Greece.[10]

In going back to ancient Greece, there is the assumption that ancient Greek society emerges as the cradle of so-called white civilization.[11] While the notion that civilization is racial in makeup is an anachronistic conception, notably, a considerable number of Black scholars hold to this same presupposition about the Greek origins of white civilization as synonomous with Western civilization.[12]

However, Black scholars tend to disagree with the supplementary ideological position that the advancement of *world civilization* is one and the same with European/white cultural progression. We must point out that this presumption as to how world civilization is primarily white European cultural development simply amounts to Eurocentrism. By Eurocentrism, it is meant that world civilization centers on the European experience.[13]

Moreover, from this Eurocentric stance, there is the belief that the emergence of Western Christianity was at the center of this historical progression on civilization. The nineteenth-century German philosopher Hegel was one of the leading exponents of this viewpoint.[14] Hence, from this perspective, white Christianity involves the entire legacy of the Western European church experience. It follows, in establishing Western Christianity, that the so-called Fathers of the Church are simultaneously responsible for the advent of white Christianity and its subsidiary Christology. On this basis, Augustine, Cyprian, and Tertullian, despite their African ancestry, become purveyors of white/Western Christianity.[15]

We ask, therefore, Are the Catholic Church and Protestant denominations of Western Europe representative of white Christianity? Is it plausible therefore to submit that Western Christianity engenders white Christology? If this is the case, the legitimacy of white Christology is sustained by the very history of Western Christianity. Consecutively, the critique of white Christology entails incisively searching into the actual basis of Western Christianity, whatever it may be.[16]

In counterposition, it could be argued the idea of an actual "Western" basis of Christianity is mythic in character. Walter Homolka claims, "The litany of wars, persecution, and hatred in European history in many ways prove, despite ubiquitous claims to the contrary, there has never been a truly *Christian* 'Christian Occident' or 'Christian West.'"[17]

With Homolka's claim in mind, it could very well be the notion—"Western Christianity"—is a trope that captures a kind of self-identity on the part of white Christians respecting their European heritage as embodied within Christianity, a way of justifying why European/Western dominance is vital to the world on religious grounds. Subsequently, the following questions are posed: With the arrival of European colonization in the Western hemisphere, does Western European Christianity thus continue as an existent white Christianity with roots in ancient Greece? Or does white Christianity originate at the point cojoined with European colonization and the successive emergence of African slavery?[18]

This demarcation is not a minor concern for determining the conceptual basis of white Christianity. Several critics of white Christology proclaim that this form of Christology originates with European colonization and African slavery rather than the entire history of Western Christianity as such. This is most evident with Johnson's prior remarks. In turn, it is argued that European colonization and African slavery are deviations from Western Christianity, which is thought to be authentic Christianity.[19]

Evidently, the historical interpretation of Western Christianity—as white Christianity—is ensnared with conceptual challenges of both historical and theological substance. One thing we can know with certainty, Christianity—in terms of the Western European experience—in conjunction with the rise of capitalism, set the stage for the African slave trade and "the peculiar institution" of African enslavement. The African slave trade and slavery were often touted as the Christianizing mission to save African heathens. Paul Harvey observes, "For much of the eighteenth and nineteenth centuries race and religion defined 'civilization.' Christianizing others involved civilizing them. Sometimes this meant brutally stripping African Americans of the garments of their own civilization."[20]

The historical background for this chauvinistic outlook toward non-Christians was established in the earlier period of the so-called Christian/

pagan dichotomy. Consequently, the idea of paganism and heathenism denoted any non-Christian religious belief system. This derogatory outlook toward pagans and heathens was usually adjoined with the conviction that such groups lacked civilization. Wherein civilization—in the broadest sense—was presumed to be synonymous with Western civilization and its accompanying Christianity.[21]

The historical development of Christianity therefore is the key indicator for the assumption that Christianity assumed different forms over the course of its history. Only on the presupposition that Christianity is a static phenomenon, standing outside of historical formation, is it possible to think that Christianity did not assume various arrangements, including white/Western Christianity. This fact about historical formation considerably strengthens the claim for white Christology. The main historical point consists in the plurality of various forms of Christianity.

Here our analysis is not dependent on theological commitments, which are connected to notions about authentic Christology. Instead, the historical review of Christianity in its process of development becomes paramount. In part, the perspective that Christianity is a static phenomenon—outside the parameters of history—is the result of conceptualizing Christianity in theological terms, where the authentic form remains immutable and any other formations are simply deviations of the original— authentic—arrangement.

A HISTORY OF MULTIPLE CHRISTIANITIES: THE ROADBLOCK TO THE THEOLOGICAL IDEA OF AUTHENTIC CHRISTOLOGY

The historical review of antiquity indicates that even the early dedicated followers of Jesus consisted of multiple and completely different—conflicting—groupings, what biblical scholar Bart Ehrman refers to as the "Lost Christianities." Building on the earlier research of Walter Bauer, Ehrman's text clearly shows that the origins of Christianity are far from monolithic. Hence, the idea of the singular original—authentically based—Christianity is no more than a theological misnomer based on nonhistorical presumptions. Even before the advent of Western Christianity, we had multiple forms of Christianities.[22]

Therefore, the achievement of "authentic" Christology has less to do with historical antecedents. At root, we have a theological construction with the notion of authentic Christology. In specific terms, the decisive factor for authenticity resides in the theological polemics surrounding Christian orthodoxy and heresy. Herein, authenticity is synonymous with a presumed "monolithic" orthodoxy, and where the interpretation of Church dogma comprises orthodoxy as "right opinion" and heresy designates "wrong belief."

With the label of orthodoxy, it is supposed, we have the attainment of Christological authenticity. Notably, Church declarations on orthodoxy and heresy have shifted over the course of Western Christianity. Since yesterday's orthodoxy often becomes today's heresy, authentic Christology (as orthodoxy) is subsequently a dynamic rather than inert conception. Within this polemical framework—orthodoxy versus heresy—the historical locus of authentic Christology is neither singular nor static.[23]

It follows that any critique of white Christology as inauthentic must consider all the above factors. One cannot dismiss white Christology without establishing sufficient theological and, moreover, historical grounds for dismissal. Sequentially, the advocates for white Christology are not merely unreasonable with their affirmative stance. Such theological differences are at base contending Christologies and no one Christology can claim authenticity outside of the specified—historical—context under review. Consequently, there is considerable warrant for the claim that white Christology legitimately stands among the host of Christological alternatives.

Of course, we have the several kinds of Christianity before and during the medieval period. We should not disregard, for example, the decisive split between the Roman Catholic Church and the various Orthodox Churches of Eastern Europe; the formation of the Coptic Church and Ethiopian Orthodox Church in Northern Africa, and later the Protestant Reformation. All of which attest to the fact that there were/are varied expressions of Christianity. We discover that theological differences leading to major divisions in Christianity often centered on the matter of rival Christologies. Yet, the determination as to what is the authentic form of Christianity/Christology is an open theological question, which is grounded in determinate circumstances.[24]

What we can decipher is that with the various forms of Christianity, there are corresponding notions about Christology. This same principle should hold true for any judgment about the reality and authenticity of white Christology. Despite controversy vis-à-vis authenticity, white Christology—like it or not—has a real historical presence among Black Christians. In fact, we discover, white Christians were intimately engaged in the African slave trade and slavery. After all—from a historical perspective—it was white people who introduced Christianity to—more precisely imposed it upon—Black slaves.

The African American adoption of Christianity during slavery, among other things, came at the expense of prevailing indigenous African religions. Hereafter, the ideological imposition of Christianity became a crucial element of capitalist dominance over African Americans during slavery and postslavery. Whatever the measure of the conceptual distinction—offered by Black Theologians—respecting whiteness and Christology, it ultimately leads to the wall of stubborn historical facts about how

Christianity facilitated capitalism as an exploitative and oppressive system.[25]

In his groundbreaking study *Capitalism and Slavery*, Eric Williams astutely remarks, "Queen Victoria sent a message to two African chiefs: 'England has become great and happy by knowledge of the true God and Jesus Christ.' To the Manchester capitalist, 'Jesus Christ was free trade, and Free Trade was Jesus Christ.'" Indeed, the English slave-trader John Hawkins "Christened" his slave ship with the name, "Jesus."[26]

From concrete historical inspection, we uncover that whiteness/white racism and Christianity were inseparable ideological components respecting the capitalist exploitation of Africans. As correlative categories, which ideologically facilitated enslavement, neither category is extricable from the other, in any practical sense. We reach this conclusion particularly since this constitutes the ideological substance behind capitalist (material) domination. Therefore, the argument for the incompatibility of whiteness with Christianity is a philosophically idealist perspective that sorely neglects the material reality surrounding slavery and its ideological justification.

The idealist separation of whiteness from Christianity overlooks that the ideological function of Christianity regarding African slavery was decisively and intrinsically linked to whiteness/white racism. Christianity as religious ideology was multifaceted, and it included racist and nationalist forms of expression. Thus, the accent on whiteness/white racism as an ideological prop for (capitalist) slavery is a correct view for deciphering how Christianity as religion functioned within this ideological matrix. We must not forget the previous remarks from Paul Harvey. "For much of the eighteenth and nineteenth centuries race and religion defined 'civilization.' Christianizing others involved civilizing them. Sometimes this meant brutally stripping African Americans of the garments of their own civilization."[27]

Hence, theologian Moni McIntyre's statement, "Whiteness infected the attitudes of slave-holders—indeed whiteness made slavery possible," can also (in this same regard) include Christianity.[28] For instance, it could be argued, "Christianity infected the attitudes of slave-holders—indeed Christianity in ideological terms—made possible the sustaining presence of slavery within the associated capitalist milieu."

Moreover, just as we find that Christianity served as the decisive (ruling) ideological mechanism during the time of the Roman Empire—with its attendant modes of oppression and exploitation—the same can be said about Christianity during slavery in the United States. Whether presumed to be distinctively white/Western respecting its essential characterization or attached with some alternately specified designation, nonetheless Christianity has a long history as the ideological facilitator of oppression and exploitation.[29]

Hence, it is important to note that the Christian sanction of slavery did not begin with African enslavement. Junius P. Rodriquez declares,

> The advent of Christianity did not have a significant impact upon the practice of slavery in the Roman world. Like the Jewish tradition from which it developed Christianity neither questioned the morality or legitimacy of the institution of slavery. The teachings of Jesus included no official condemnation of slavery, and both the Old and New Testaments of the Bible contain passages that reflect an acceptance of the social and political conditions of the times—including an acceptance of slavery as it existed.[30]

We contend that this historical state of affairs is why white Christology cannot be counted as inauthentic Christianity—that is, maintain the stance of blanket rejection of white Christology entirely based on its oppressive character. Here, we think that Joseph A. Johnson's and Walter Homolka's previous charges about white/Western Christianity miss the mark. On the results of historical investigation, Christianity as religious ideology—along with its auxiliary Christology—in the ancient past has not been removed from oppression and exploitation. Therefore, the search for an authentic Christology, which is ideologically detached from oppression and exploitation, rests on an ahistorical and philosophically idealist accounting of Christianity.

Certainly, Christianity was an ideological instrument that buttressed African American enslavement, which successively worked hand in glove with white racism, national oppression, and capitalist exploitation. Furthermore, given Christianity was an ideological imposition on African slaves, in the context of brutal (capitalist) exploitation, then it was not—in any manner—an invitation to become members of the broader Christian—white—church community. The mission of Christianity—regarding African American slaves—was not to save souls but rather to ruthlessly exploit and degrade Black people in the pursuit of capitalist profits. The bottom line was that Christianity served as a hegemonic ideology in the service of capitalist—chattel—slavery.

Black womanist theologian Katie Cannon brings to our attention how religion and capitalism are so conjoined. Drawing on the works of the profound Black sociologist of capitalism, namely Oliver C. Cox, Cannon adeptly notes that Cox argued,

> Religion must become virtually inseparable from capitalist philosophical assumptions, science, and economic thinking. In other words, religion must be subordinated to economic interests, so that nothing challenges the dictum that "wealth in a capitalist society should be made to produce more wealth." Religious scruples against wealth and worldly activities must cease to interfere with the unconstrained enhancement of material welfare.[31]

The ideological function of Christianity vividly brings to light that resorting to Christian ideals and rituals as an explanatory framework for concluding that whiteness/white racism are deviations from authentic Christianity demands our critical scrutiny. This logically follows since Christianity—as religious ideology—cannot be removed from its function in preserving exploitive relations of production. Indeed, theologian M. Shawn Copeland perceptively brings to our attention:

> Not even the sacrament of baptism could redeem black flesh from the damnation and predation of slavery; rather baptism served to tame, to temper, to discipline the slave for ease of subjugation and *profitability of service or sale*. Hence, the slave would come to perceive grace only as emancipation or freedom or escape, but more likely as the release of death.[32] [Italics added]

Copeland's observation amply supports the prior statement about Christianity as an oppressive ideology that sustains exploitation. Furthermore, it should be noted that long before African enslavement, the idea that baptism stood in concert with the status quo—inclusive of slavery—indeed it was a critical aspect of the Hebrew/Christian religious ritual and thinking. In his *Baptism in the New Testament*, George Raymond Beasley-Murray conveys, "Heathen slaves on their entry into a Jewish house were compelled to receive a baptism . . . 'in the name of slavery i.e. to become slaves.'" [33]

Clearly, when we encounter the extended history—within the ancient Judeo-Christian tradition—the prior conception of baptism was not anything close to signaling freedom from slavery. Long before the idea of white Christology and African slavery, the ancient ritual of Christian baptism steadfastly endorsed slavery. It could very well be the case; Copeland's observations about baptism and Black slavery point us to the very Judaic origins of Christianity. Rather than any supposed deviations associated with white Christianity, the primary and original intent of Christian baptism was not freedom from enslavement. From the start, the Christian viewpoint on baptism affirmed the status quo—slavery.

Up until now, we detected, some Black Christologists argue that white Christology is a unique aberration that distorts the authenticity of Christianity. They maintain white Christology stems from the white Christian legacy of racism with its origins in slavery through contemporary times. Furthermore, they additionally claim that such racist practices are not in accord with authentic Christianity. As an alternative to white Christology, Black Christology, it is believed, becomes decisive for the return to authentic Christianity and away from "fraudulent" Christianity.[34]

Of course, based on our previous analysis, the idea of "true" or genuine Christianity is bereft of any historical justification. Granting the ahistorical basis for this assumption, then we are left with theological rather than historical grounds supporting the claim of authenticity. Hereafter, theologically speaking, whether white Christianity is "true" Christianity (or not), we find that the proposed answers are intimately related to the substance of the given Christological outlook inspecting the matter. With Black Theology, it follows that "authenticity" is the objective measure for the equivalent suitable Christology. However, given the historical fact that rival Christologies are in contention without any external measure—which can provide some standard for authenticity—means that this plurality directs us to relativism, a relativism that stands without some objective criteria.

In effect, we have competing theological claims about the nature of authentic Christology sans historical verification and justification. Subsequently, the premise that Christology is a viable means—for the critique of whiteness—must seriously take into consideration all the above. We submit that the failure to take heed of the previous admonitions renders the suitability of any form of Christology, including Black Christology—functioning in terms of a critical framework—as empty of any real substance.

Therefore, the idea that white Christology is a deviation from authentic Christianity is a theological claim that has no historical validity. Thus, authenticity cannot serve as justification for dismissing white Christology. In fact, this theological outlook on authenticity obscures the accurate comprehension of the history of Christianity. The key problem is that Christianity itself has a history, which is linked to oppression and exploitation. Consequently, this vital historical fact gets lost within the process of theological shuffling about authenticity. Accordingly, all efforts at Blackening Christology—with the aim of recovering authentic Christianity—must come under our critical inspection.[35]

CHRISTOLOGY IN BLACK AND WHITE: THE PROBLEM OF AUTHENTICITY

For now, it should be noted that how one considers the compatibility/incompatibility relationship between whiteness and Christology is primarily centered on the respective Christological viewpoint that is in place. Beforehand, for instance, we explored how Black Christology critically opposed white Christology as a deformation of Christianity. We submit that this Black Christological outlook suitably facilitates demonstrating, from at least one theological perspective, the incompatible affiliation between whiteness and Christology.

Nevertheless, this critique is based on the presumption that Black Christology is in concert with the genuine form of Christianity. We contend this presumption about maintaining the posture of authentic Christianity demands justification. This is ever more significant, given that white Christology proffers the same, on its own behalf. Therein, let us inspect what are the pitfalls associated with this theological quest for authenticity.

Obviously, this Black Christological standpoint is a return to the a-historical method, concerning the analysis of Christianity and Christology. With Black Christology, the important fact that Christianity has a prolong historic connection to oppression and exploitation—prior to the advent of so-called white Christology—is effectively ignored. Second, Black Christology effectually dismisses the historical fact that Christology—over the course of history—has had countless modes of expression.

The dichotomy between conceiving of some ideal form of authentic Christology contra the material reality of multiple forms of Christianity (in history) cannot be rectified by resorting to the claim that Black Christology is a return to authenticity. We cannot escape the stubborn reality of history—Christianity in its multiple forms includes white Christology—by resorting to idealist fantasy that Black Christology can recapture so-called authentic Christianity.

The theological view about a singular authentic Christianity ultimately becomes a surrogate for real historical analysis. This is one reason why, we argue, Black Christology embraces philosophical idealism. Theological commitment to the ideal of authentic Christianity holds sway over the concrete analysis of real—material—conditions. Moreover, this idealist (nonhistorical) approach fundamentally grounds the claim that Black Christology is in accord with Christian authenticity. Thus, the Black Christology claim to authenticity is in effect a theological argument that dismisses both the plural character of Christology as well as the extended historical presence of Christian ideological and material oppression.

Considering the embrace of philosophical idealism, "authentic" Christianity sequentially appears as a religious worldview free of oppression and exploitation. It follows that ethical appeals to Christian ideals of justice, equality, love and the like are viewed as sufficient conditions for rendering Christianity as pristine and liberatory. Yet, we must note that this idealist standpoint (on Christianity) is no more than an ideological illusion that sorely overlooks the harsh (material) reality of the Christian legacy, an ideological illusion which is also complicit in disguising the very role of Christianity within the ideological realm of social relations.

In its ideological function, Christianity operates as preserver of the status quo, operating decisively in the real world of living human beings. We have already discovered that Christianity has been historically situated quite prominently in circumstances where the broad masses—caught in various modes of production—face exploitation. Therein, Christianity ideologically sanctions such conditions in the name of God. This ideological appeal to the Christian God, in support of exploitation, is replete throughout history. Furthermore, the historic use of violence to carry out war, plunder, and abuse on a broad scale has on many occasions found its justification in Christian dogma.[36]

In comparison, Black Christologists consider authentic Christianity — as such — in terms of being pristine and thus free of any oppressive and exploitative aspects. Herein resides the theological idea that white Christology is a deviation from authentic Christianity. Hence, the oppressive character of white Christology becomes fundamentally distinct from a putatively unspoiled Christianity. Subsequently, philosophical idealism holds sway, and the material circumstances affixed to the history of Christianity assumes backseat.

In contradistinction to its critical view on white Christology, Black Christology openly embraces and identifies with the reputed form of authentic Christianity. Therefore, with its accompanying critique, we find that Black Christology remains engaged in a fierce contest with white Christology for theological legitimacy. In line with this thinking about white Christology, Black theologian William L. Eichelberger argues,

> When one moves studiously into the realm of Black Christology, there is an important follow-up action which must be taken. One must initiate immediately an analysis of that which stands in dialectical opposition to the discipline he is articulating; therefore, any person beginning a study of Black Christology must surely deal with White Christology. One has to do an analysis of it. The analysis will divulge the fact there is a form of misanthropy in certain aspects of white Christology. There is a kind of corruptiveness in white Christology. One begins to see readily that white Christology is a vehicle of enslavement, a vehicle of brutalization, an instrument of invidious oppression of a substantial part of the human family.[37]

Of course, the assumption "There is a kind of corruptiveness in white Christology" should be rationally demonstrated, thus based on the notion of — compared with — a differing kind of (antiwhite) Christology, which is established as authentic in character and free of oppressive ideology. Without historical proof of authenticity, then what we can gather is that Eichelberger merely asserts what must be proven. It could very well be that instead of white Christology as the culprit, the real perpetrator of these tribulations was Christianity pure and simple. In sequence, we contend, Black Christology as a form of Christianity is not a suitable alternative, given its own Christian roots. What is at stake is the presumption that authentic Christianity remains pristine and removed from oppressive attribution.[38]

The legitimacy of the authenticity claim must stand the test of critical review, relating to Christianity's essential makeup as nonoppressive. Precisely with Eichelberger's claim, we unearth that it emerges from an a priori Christological viewpoint. Hence, Eichelberger's stance is not founded on an inquiry into the historical formation of Christianity — that is, how in historical terms Christianity can be seen apart from the transgressions of putatively white Christology. In fact, Biblical texts contradict the substance of this distinction.[39]

What the reader must keep in mind is that Black Christologists—such as Eichelberger—are in an ideological battle over Christianity in the attempt to forge it as an instrument for Black liberation. The charges against white Christology correspond with the efforts to shore up Christianity as a viable weapon against oppression and for Black liberation. For many among the Black Christological group, this entails the belief that Jesus was a Black Messiah, accordingly they are accenting the relevancy of Christianity for Black people.

Yet, how do we know if white Christology is a distortion of "authentic" Christianity? What theological analysis can ground this claim? Why must we presume that white Christology—if based on Western Christianity—is a deviation from "true" Christianity? Are Church doctrines from Nicene and Chalcedon inauthentic white declarations? Evidently, the premise that Western Christianity is white undercuts a considerable amount of conventional beliefs held by Black Christologists. If Nicene and Chalcedon dogma are ultimately white, then quite a few Black Christologists have embarked on a journey headed in the wrong direction. The idea of the Holy Trinity formula and Jesus's place within the Godhead—which are based on the Nicene and Chalcedon declarations—often appear in Black Christological pronouncements. This becomes most apparent in the next chapter with our treatment of Major Jones.[40]

Therefore, how should we consider the biblical canon? Is it essentially the nonwhite and authentic rendering of both Christianity and Christology? In contrast, does the process of canonization, which took place within the Western Christian church offer white—inauthentic—texts with the New Testament?[41] Subsequently, how would biblical Scriptures provide us with the needed sources to make the required differentiation?

Up till now, we discover that biblical texts in no way challenge the institution of slavery. The Hebrew Bible/Old Testament sanctions the institution of slavery. The same can be said of Paul's conception of Christology and the reality of slavery during his time. Even the slave parables of the Matthean Jesus, for instance, point us toward the affirmation of slavery.[42]

Therefore, in view of this biblical impasse, how we answer the question, "What would Jesus do today?" lacks definitive theological/biblical grounds for our recourse in opposition to slavery. In more general terms, all forms of exploitation and oppression as systemic relations are problematic from the biblical perspective on Jesus in ancient history. The typical Christological appeal to various ethical principles—embodied in the New Testament—is not rendered as a critique of political and economic institutions and social systems.[43]

Improved personal relations, in abstraction of social institutions and structures, often prevail as the primary biblical focus on Jesus's ethical teachings. If Jesus is a social reformer, then biblical texts give us very little to go on. Hence, the Matthean Jesus can accordingly magnify the virtue of forgiveness and simultaneously speak about slavery without any criticism. From the New Testament, very little can be deduced about Jesus as a foe of slavery and other institutions of oppression.[44] Changing attitudes and ethical ideals rather than social structures become paramount in biblical texts. In this regard, about biblical texts, theologian Josiah U. Young offers a perceptive insight:

> Without the *irrefutable* presence of the Christ in the midst of history, like a force field invulnerable to transience and corruption, anti-racist Christology is a waning candle in the dark. As I see it, the reason for this is not just the fact that racism persists in some white North American churches and has the power of a pro-white history behind it. The paradoxical character of the Bible is also a problem. Since the Bible is the church's sacred text, one has to deal with the paradoxes until Christ comes to clear things up.[45]

Since Black Christology is an antiracist Christology, then perhaps it is what Young describes as "a waning candle in the dark." Hence, from Young's outlook, we cannot conclude whether it is genuine Christology until Jesus reappears on earth. Consequently, it all theologically reduces to faith in the return of Jesus from heaven. Anchoring the solution on the faith claim that Jesus is returning to earth takes us beyond any rational means for justifying that Black Christology directs us toward authentic Christology. Black Christology has nothing to tangibly offer—concerning this theological conundrum—besides our persistence at "keeping the faith."

Nevertheless, the adherence to Christology continues as a rather tenacious historical presence among Black Christians. This has been decisive respecting their interpretation of the secular world and the subsequent viewpoint regarding the African American presence in it. Anthony Pinn astutely notes, "Christology has been a mainstay of African American Christian thought; in fact, it has been the central theological category used to frame the nature and meaning of human engagement with/in the world. However, this has come at a cost."[46] Successively, we must inquire into the very meaning of Christology to better amplify and clarify its connection to whiteness.

Although, Yancy's "objective was neither to argue for the historical reality of Jesus nor for his metaphysical status as divine," we submit, however, they cannot be brushed to the side. Both the historical reality of Jesus and his metaphysical status as divine are fundamental tenets of Christology and vital aspects in any Christological investigation. Precisely because these notions are core issues surrounding Christology, whether one supports or disagrees with them, there remains the overriding mandate for an evaluation. We argue this mandate is pivotal for answering the question, "Who was Jesus?"[47]

Yancy's premise about "the perspective of Christology" that requires no more than "a point of narrative embarkation, a place woven out of *hope, love, and desire*" stands as insufficient. What are the Christological foundations for narrative embarkation? Does it reside in the New Testament narrative? If it does, then critical inspection of such documents must come into play. As F. F. Bruce astutely notes,

> [T]he character of Jesus can be known only from the New Testament records: the influence of His character is therefore tantamount to the influence of the New Testament records. Would it not, then, be paradoxical if the records which, on the testimony of a rationalist historian, produced such results were devoid of historical truth. . . . Whether our approach is theological or historical, it does matter whether the New Testament documents are reliable or not.[48]

We contend that the very meaning of Christology—as an investigatory framework—must be addressed and not presumed. Without critical review of Christology, we are left with an idealist presumption concerning Christianity as free from any oppressive features and thus suitable as a framework to investigate whiteness as hegemonic in character.

In this regard—except for Albert Cleage—Black Christologists do not deviate from the present (orthodox) Christological position contained within Western Church dogma, which is prominently represented by the Nicene and Chalcedon creeds. With Black Christology, the previously established Christian (Western Church) dogma assumes what amounts to a Black veneer. What cannot be overlooked, such creeds uphold both the historical reality of Jesus and his metaphysical status as divine. Subsequently, these church doctrines serve as the chief presumptive context of Christology and consequently they facilitate our answering, not only "Who was Jesus?" but also "What would Jesus do?"[49]

However, what if we assume and demonstrate that Jesus is neither a historical person nor divine entity? Jesus would become a mythic figure of no real material presence or, for that matter, even so-called spiritual existence. We would have to disclose that the idea of Jesus takes us on the road toward a fictive account. It would follow that Christology is a rather vacuous approach to the problem of whiteness, whatever whiteness may be, let alone support the position that Jesus's racial identification is theologically meaningful. The aim of Blackening the supposed historical Jesus, in turn, becomes irrelevant as a Christological position.

The concern of this observation is not simply about Black Christologists advocating a false proposition—regarding the racial identity of Jesus—rather their Christological proposal becomes meaningless. Such thinking—on the theological significance—regarding Jesus's identity amounts to being conceptually misdirected or false consciousness. From this critical viewpoint, Jesus is no more than a mythic character. We must point out that there is a considerable body of research supporting the thesis that Jesus is ultimately a mythic representation.[50]

To date, very few African American scholars have attempted to broach the topic of the Christ myth. With his *Pagan Origins of the Christ Myth*—originally published in 1941—African American historian John G. Jackson became the pioneering—if not remaining the solitary—Black scholar within this genre.[51] However, while it is uncommon to find African American religion scholars who support the notion regarding the mythic character of the person of Jesus, contemporary religion scholar William David Hart conveys critical sentiments about the historical Jesus. Hart insightfully states,

> Jesus is virtually a fictional character, an artifact of the many ways that we have imagined him. Our knowledge of him is even less reliable than the knowledge we acquire from an autobiography, with its fictive narratives. Indeed, on the fictional-factual continuum, our knowledge of Jesus is closer to novelistic than to biographical. Apart from various Eros-driven interpretations. . . . And insofar as there is evidence at all, there is nothing special about Jesus practices that speaks to the issue of whiteness.[52]

Hart's conclusion, "insofar as there is evidence at all, there is nothing special about Jesus practices that speaks to the issue of whiteness," explicitly indicates what Jesus *has not done*, which could relate to concerns about whiteness. In effect, we have a moot question with the query "What would Jesus do?" about whiteness. Furthermore, Hart's comments serve as the critical marker on the epistemological limits concerning the historical Jesus as well as the notion of divine placement.

On Hart's account, following from the biblical conception of Jesus's life and work, Christology obviously becomes a useless instrument for examining whiteness. Hence, faced with this challenge, how do we determine what is Christology? Previously, it was stated that by Christology we mean, "[T]hat part of Christian doctrine concerned with the revelation of God in Jesus Christ. Traditionally, this has been expressed in the doctrine of incarnation, the doctrine of the union divine and human natures and the one person."[53]

We also added that the notion of Jesus as *the Christ* or *Messiah* has profound theological implications. What is the meaning of Christ/Messiah? Does not the notion of Messiah have Jewish roots that really precede Christianity? Was not Jesus a Jew? How and when did Jesus become a Christian?[54] What is expected of the Christ? Was he to liberate Jews of his time or save the entire world for Christianity? Was Jesus's mission one of religious salvation or political and economic liberation? Does the Messiah/Christ perform supernatural miracles or serve as the leader of a social and secular movement?[55]

Accordingly, we query, How does the New Testament depict Christ? Is there a singular or multiple depictions? Does it occur that conflicting depictions consume biblical accounts? Does Jesus have divine status? Is he a deity on par with God? How did Jesus become God? Such questions are the subject matter of Christology.[56] On the New Testament, Christopher Tuckett explains:

> We are now more than ever aware of the enormous variety within the collection of texts we call the New Testament and the variety within primitive Christianity. Older reconstructions of the development of Christian thinking or theology had perhaps worked with a rather monolithic model of an original, pristine and unified tradition of orthodoxy only branching out into ("heretical") offshoots rather later, perhaps second century. We are now much more conscious of the tremendous variety that characterizes the earliest period in Christian history to which we have access. . . . The conflict element is not always so evident in relationship to Christology, though one wonders if Paul's passing reference to some people in Corinth who were apparently preaching another Jesus (2 Cor. 11:4) is not a reference to Christology?[57]

The preceding questions and insights help set the stage about whiteness in Christological terms. The subject matter of Christology is both varied and ever-changing. Thus, Christological perspectives on whiteness do not admit to an easy consensus. Indeed, this is indicative of the fact that Christology is also an academic inquiry with extensive research in the form of books and scholarly articles. The conflicting scholarly viewpoints on Christology is indirectly linked to ideas about the racial identity—or lack therein—of Jesus as the Messiah.[58]

Thus, while Eichelberger emphasizes "white Christology is a vehicle of enslavement," Anthony Pinn observes how Christology among African Americans slaves truly played itself out in that brutal context:

> Early discussions and depictions of Jesus Christ within the African American imagination did not necessarily fix on the physical presentation of Christ as similar to that of enslaved Africans. . . . Little attention in this early Christology is given to the biological reality of Jesus the Christ; instead, enslaved Africans emphasize his relationship to suffering humanity and the consequential demand for justice. In general, the color of Jesus was of less importance, a lesser marker of the value of black (enslaved) bodies than was a shared relationship to God.[59]

Transparently, the African American Christological perspective, during slavery, did not presume that the Black racial identification of Jesus theologically mattered. Despite Pinn's historical observations, Eichelberger accents that Jesus's racial identity theologically matters to African Americans. Eichelberger is not alone in this belief that not only is there a

Black Messiah but also that Black Christians should adopt this dogma. For most in the Black Christology school this is the prevailing viewpoint.

Often without historical research, Black Christologists resort to biblical theology to buttress the notion of the Black Messiah. They assume that if Jesus was the Black Messiah, then embracing Christianity is far from adherence to white ideology, which assumes the form of white Christology. Given this viewpoint, the idea of the Black Messiah portends that not only is the Black Jesus theologically meaningful, it is also central to the accurate adoption and interpretation of Christianity.

Our previous discussion on Albert Cleage and Gayraud Wilmore, in chapter 4, demonstrated that proponents of the Black Messiah can be separated on the grounds of the literal and symbolic notions about Blackness. Nonetheless, all within this Black Messiah school, in different ways, maintain that the Blackness of Jesus is theologically significant. In part, the claim of theological significance is based on the presupposition that white Christology is harmful to Black Christians and the aim of true salvation and liberation. In line with Albert Cleage, James Cone, Gayraud Wilmore, Major Jones, and others, Eichelberger steadfastly asserts:

> Some opponents of the concept of the Black Messiah declare that any argument which consist of the blackness of Jesus of Nazareth is invalid because it reduces the universality of Jesus in the appeal to a particular constituency, Black people.... Some of the white Christians who make the argument above insists that the color of Jesus is not important; therefore, Black people must not insist on the blackness of the Messiah, because this shuts out all nonblack peoples. Unfortunately, the same people fail to note that they have developed their theologies, Christologies, and ideologies regarding Jesus the Christ on a subtly unstated, but very real, presumption of his whiteness.[60]

What is translucent is that Eichelberger's claim for the Black Messiah, when deemed historical in character, demands the relevant analysis of the complex of social relations regarding race, ethnicity, religion, and class during the period of antiquity in which it is presumed Jesus lived. If not, we are saddled with an anachronistic reading, which distorts the historical facts. We covered many of those points in the last chapter and will not repeat them at this juncture.[61] Nevertheless, it is important to note, the challenge with addressing the matter of whiteness—or rather white racism—and its incompatibility with Christology is not limited to the Black Christological claimants.

Indeed, some African American theologians—not just white Christians—affirm the universality joined to Christology and nevertheless simultaneously offer a critique of the racism that resides within the body of the white Christian church. In chapter 3, we observed that this criticism of white racism was entailed in Richard I. McKinney's critique of Black Theology.

There are others such as George D. Kelsey who belong to this camp and are critical of white racist Christianity. Yet, they do not appeal to any form of Black Christology and its attendant antiwhiteness. For McKinney and Kelsey, whiteness is not within the same categorical realm as white racism. What Jesus *would not do*, on their interpretation, is to view whiteness as problematic to his task of bringing the Gospel message to the world. McKinney and Kelsey both embrace Christological universality and in so doing offer a different perspective on whiteness than we find with Black Christology.

THE TRADITION OF AFRICAN AMERICAN CHRISTOLOGICAL UNIVERSALITY: THE MATTER OF WHITENESS

For this group of Christological universalists, the theological perspective that whiteness is incompatible with Christology points to the fact that whiteness is only an indicator of a more fundamental problem. Namely that whiteness directs us on the path to the racialist viewpoint on Christology. The considered—elemental—problem, in this instance, is not whiteness as such, rather it is racialist forms of Christology. The underlying presumption is that racialist viewpoints obstruct the universality of the Christian message and thus impede the pivotal function of Christology. These theologians presuppose that Christology is neither Black nor white.

Hence, Black Christology as an alternative does not lead to authentic Christology because it fails to transcend racial designations.[62] Some of the most noted names among African American theologians belong to this camp. This universality rooted in Christology was well articulated by Martin Luther King Jr., Benjamin E. Mays, and Charles Leander Hill.

Now let us review how Dr. Benjamin E. Mays amplifies the Christological point about racialist ascriptions. "This universalism in the Gospel is climaxed and attested to by the fact that Christ died for all mankind.... In both the ancient and medieval church, the basis of membership was faith, in Jesus Christ, our Lord. The basis of membership was faith, not race; Christ, not color; creedal acceptance and not nationality."[63]

From this theological perspective, the question of what is the key disruptive factor respecting Christology, rather than whiteness per se, it is the view that Christian theology is tied to racial/national monikers. This follows because Mays believes the addition of racial qualifiers to Christology is antithetical to Christian articles of faith. Racial monikers attached to Christology, Mays assumes, effectively occlude the universal character of Christianity. Subsequently, the notion of Black Christology would also not be an applicable solution to the incompatibility problem of whiteness with Christology.

From Mays's vantage point, we can conclude that Black Christology only duplicates racialist ascriptions in Black form. Foundationally, on this account, the problems associated with whiteness—as well as any Black designation—that are pinned to Christology actually expedites the racialist subversion of Christian universality. Hence, whiteness is not a site that poses the problem of hegemony. Hegemonic influence of whiteness is manifest only when it is employed as racialist attributions onto the corpus of Christology. Mays thinks that Christology must stand above racial and national moorings, since he accepts as true that Christology, in its essence, is universal in character and believes that church doctrine has historically supported this belief.

When we look carefully at Dr. Martin Luther King Jr., and his perspective on the matter, it's clear that there is full agreement with the previously cited position of Mays. In some ways, King extends on Mays's pronouncement. In addition to transcending race and nationality, King considers transgressing beyond all forms of contradictory social conditions. Universalism in Christology is not bound by adhering to the critical analysis of conflicting social relations. The idea of Christ, for King, is one of a messenger that espouses the virtue of reframing from the ethical condemnation of sinners. Moreover, King's adherence to Jesus's principle of altruism fosters a kind of Christology that prohibits denouncing exploitative class contradictions. Christological universality, King argues, remains as all-encompassing ethic by advancing neighborly love as the solution to social ills. Let's now examine King's declaration.

> In our quest to make neighbourly love a reality, we have in addition to the inspiring example of the Good Samaritan, the magnanimous life of our Christ to guide us. His altruism was *universal, for he thought of all men, even publicans and sinners, as brothers.* His altruism was dangerous, for he willingly travelled hazardous roads in a cause he knew was right. His altruism was excessive, for he chose to die on Calvary, history's most magnificent expression of obedience to the unenforceable.[64] [Italics added]

King's universalism is deeply embedded in his notion of Christology. The life and work of Jesus, in King's estimation, extends beyond social designations and political location. From this theological position, the Christological mission does not propose that social groups, in any specified fashion, would become the focal point of Jesus's attention. Instead the global community of humanity—without respect to religious, ethnic, class, or racial differences—looms large on the Christological horizon. We believe it is not fortuitous that Dr. King is not an advocate of Black Christology. Thus, his universalism is antithetical to the particularistic nature of Black Christology.

We think that Jon M. Temme precisely offers the correct summation of Dr. King's Christological position and its relationship to Black Christology. Let's reexamine King's Christology through the critical lens of Temme.

> King's christology, emphasizing the humanity of Jesus and the liberating activity of the Christ within the traditional symbols of Western Christianity, offered nothing startlingly new. It could even be argued that his was not really a black christology at all. In terms of style or methodology there was little to identify King's theology with the black experience. King drew upon traditional, western sources in expressing his christology, and he presented it in a form or genre that was certainly not uniquely black.[65]

There are certain apposite philosophical questions affixed to Temme's declaration. First, granting Temme's estimation about King's adherence to "traditional symbols of Western Christianity," then King does not presume that "Western Christianity" is identical with white Christology. This is because King presupposes the universality of western Christianity in its fundamental makeup continues as non-racial. Furthermore, given that "it could even be argued that his [King's] was not really a black christology at all," therefore we conclude that he did not advance some form of particularistic theology. However, it is imperative that we query, Is there any justification for thinking that since King did not hold to Black Christology that he was not a liberation theologian?

Of necessity, should we surmise that Christological universalism nullifies overcoming oppression and specifically the oppression faced by African Americans? Only on the grounds of conflating Black Christology with liberation theology can we reach such a conclusion. Otherwise, what King's Christology presents is another lens—besides that of Black Christology—on the issue of whiteness and its compatibility/incompatibility status.

While the legacy of King was clearly antiracist, this does not entail that he held an antiwhiteness posture. In his appraisal, whiteness is not within the same categorical realm as white racism. In this regard, perhaps King deviates from Yancy's notion of whiteness as white privilege. For both King and Mays, nonetheless, the incompatibility of whiteness with Christology is not founded with an attack on whiteness. Rather, the focus is on racialist attributions which are attached to Christology. Importantly, they are not alone in this belief among African American theologians.

African American philosopher/theologian Charles Leander Hill's comments are a most appropriate response at this interval. Dr. Hill conveys why he makes Christianity his personal religious commitment. A commitment that reflects his Christological—universal—standpoint and how it specifically relates to the problems of race and racism. Therefore, in his Christological universality, Hill does not neglect racism, better yet he thinks universality is a vital response to all forms of racism. He adamantly states,

I am a Christian because *Christ's appeal is to all men, not to anyone race.* Herein is the true catholicity, the true internationality, the true ecumenicity, of the Christian religion. To a member of an oppressed minority in America, this aspect of Christianity makes a great appeal. Deprived of the full rights of citizenship, victims of segregation and racial discrimination, victims of violence to our person and property, taking the crumbs that fall from the table of a half-loaf democracy, we are saved from other despair only by the encouragement we get from the knowledge that at the altar of the Lord, all men born on a plane of equality.[66]

From King's, Mays's, and Hill's perspective, Christological universality is the vantage point for viewing whiteness. In no uncertain terms, they are opponents of all manner of racialist ascriptions fastened to Christology. In their view, the problem of whiteness is a contextual issue and not an autonomous concern entwined with hegemonic designs in association with white privilege. In turn, we can infer that they would claim that what Jesus would do—respecting whiteness in Christological terms—is to call for the allegiance to the universality of his message, what Hill describes as "the true catholicity, the true internationality, the true ecumenicity, of the Christian religion."

Such universality would successively become the hallmark of Christology. Blackness and whiteness would go out the Christological window, and universality would transcend all particularistic interests. With strong warrant, we think this is the collective hermeneutical lens of King, Mays, and Hill. This shared Christological viewpoint on Jesus (and the problem of whiteness) issues from the Christian mandate for universality.

In our view, whether Christological universality effectively addresses the problem of white racism and supremacy as a social and political economic reality is an open question. On the reexamination of King's Christological statement, "His [Christ's] altruism was universal, for he thought of all men, even publicans and sinners, as brothers. . . . His altruism was excessive, for he chose to die on Calvary, history's most magnificent expression of obedience to the unenforceable," clearly we uncover not only Christological universality but also "obedience to the unenforceable." What does King intend with the statement that Jesus's posture on Calvary was "obedience to the unenforceable?" Moreover, how does "obedience to the unenforceable" translate into actual sociopolitical practice in the world? What is its connection to universality?

Is this an apolitical response that upholds personal salvation (soteriology) rather than political liberation? If the point of King's statement is soteriological—about the notion of salvation—then spiritual conversion becomes paramount. Rather than a critical analysis on changing the material conditions of exploitation; Christology accents the personal concern of spiritual transformation. Here, we think, Victor Anderson's comments on Christology are most instructive:

> Christology is Christian discourse surrounding the person and work of Jesus the Christ. God's soteriological aim to reconcile not only all to God, but all to all, is mediated in and through the person and work of Jesus as the bearer of good news. For some, Christ's person and work perform a recapitulation of the promises, covenants, and buildings with biblical Israel as God's elect among the nations. Within this mimesis of recapitulation, "there is no longer Jew or Greek, there is no longer slave or free, there is no longer male or female; for all that you are one in Christ Jesus" (Galatians 3:28).[67]

Anderson continues,

> However, it appears the such a biblical universalism, as articulated by Paul, is more the work of Paul and his followers than an articulation of the scandalous gospel of Jesus, which analysis announces repetition of "otherness" and dissimilitude. However, Paul's mimesis of salvation levels all racial/ethnic distinctions within salvation history, for he preaches that "there is no distinction between Jew and Gentile; the same Lord is Lord of all and richly blesses all who call on him, for everyone who calls on the name of the Lord will be saved" (Romans 10:12–13).[68]

At the very least, if the universality of Christology is in accord with the Pauline—Christological—doctrine of transcendent universality, then the concrete material conditions of subjugation, the conflicting relationship between the oppressors and oppressed, exploiter and exploited, will be sorely neglected. We earlier observed—in chapter 3—this point respecting McKinney's claim on the matter of Christian universality.[69]

What is evident is that Christological universality of the Pauline variety is philosophically idealist in character. Hence, it is substantially removed from offering a practical guide for overcoming capitalist exploitation and Black oppression as material realities. Thus, we can conclude that this Christology fails to effectively confront the concrete reality of white racism. This Christology of universalism as a form of idealism is detached from changing the conditions of exploitation, degradation, and oppression. Theologian Josiah U. Young ably points out for our consideration the import of Pauline (Christological) universality:

> Of course, Paul, like Luke, was no revolutionary. His concern was the Kingdom of God. He wished to maintain proper church discipline, to hold the ecclesia together, until Christ's arrival. He tolerated a form of slavery, as is borne out by 1 Corinthians 7, and thus did not trouble the status quo. (Paul writes in 7:21, "Were you a slave when called? Do not be concerned about it.") He thought this age of sin and death was passing away. Why make waves over what had no future?[70]

The Pauline—Christological—doctrine of transcendent universality is a spiritual viewpoint on human equality, which surpasses changing the actual conditions of oppression, such as we find with slavery. Therefore, we note, the Pauline Christological doctrine of transcendent universality is a philosophically idealist approach to real material conditions of inequality and exploitation. In fact, Anthony Pinn amplifies our argument and thus warns: "Christology actually renders bodies docile—in line with the discourse of control and relationship generating the status quo—rather than encouraging the formation of embodied bodies to seek to bolster the dynamics of power and control."[71]

Pinn continues, "Christology is not concerned with the articulation of a relationship to this embodied body, but rather seeks to stem the tide and focus on the culturally/theologically constructed body—the one that gives itself and in process seeks to abandon our materiality."[72] Pinn's observation is no doubt a serious challenge to any form of Christological commitment. At root, the Christological allegiance to philosophical idealism—with its ancillary abandonment of our materiality—is obstructive to fighting the reality of the hegemonic power that stands in alignment with conditions of white racism and capitalist exploitation. In a nutshell, the question of power relationships is not directly reducible to the ethical concerns, which transpires as focusing on the Christological notions of hope, love, and desire.

Nonetheless, when we study the practical side of King's, Mays's, and Hill's applications of their Christology, it is quite evident that all were engaged—albeit in differing levels and manner—in the concrete struggle to end racism in its various forms. In fact, King's involvement in this practical movement compels M. Shawn Copeland to conclude, "Functionally, King's Christ was a black Christ, whose prophetic practice was committed to the banishment of segregation and discrimination."[73]

Whether one is in alignment with Temme's conception of King's formal Christology—one removed from the Black experience—or with Copeland's functional approach—which amplifies how King's social gospel is translatable into the notion of the Black Christ—the cardinal sustaining principle of Christological universality becomes the constant thread throughout. King's Christological position is clear, namely that Jesus's altruism was universal and transcended racialized antitheses such as found with the dichotomous notion of Black versus white Christology.

Given this fact about universality, perhaps Copeland's claim reaches a stumbling block, particularly if asked to go outside of her generalization about King's adoption of a "Black Christ." Thus, there is the need for further specifications on her viewpoint respecting the content of Black Christology vis-à-vis King's Christology. If the idea that King's opposition to segregation and discrimination constitutes the sufficient basis for King assuming the status of Black Christologist; this would in turn locate not only him, but also Mays, Hill, McKinney, and Kelsey, to name only a few, within the Black Christology camp.

Yet, we have concretely established that the particularistic starting point of Black Christology—Jesus as the Black Messiah—entails a host of theologically attendant ideas, which stand as adversative to Christological universality. Without any further investigation into the Christology of King, Mays, and Hill, the fact remains they all agree that Jesus's mission was one of universal magnitude.

It follows that for these theologians, the understanding of Jesus as the "very embodiment of caritas" requires grasping the universal scope of his deeds. In response to Yancy's question, "What would Jesus do?" King, Mays, and Hill could readily respond that given Jesus's universal pronouncement respecting his mission in the world, Jesus would jettison whiteness as a racialist ascription that restricts the true meaning of Christology. Yet, he would not resort to antiwhiteness. We contend that this is a charitable treatment of King's, Mays's, and Hill's positions regarding how Christology is relevant to the problem of whiteness. Although, Yancy could perhaps disagree with their evaluation, we do not think that he would have any fundamental disagreement on our assessment of the above.

What we can gather from the preceding is that Christological perspectives on whiteness tremendously vary in both substance and form. Thus, Yancy's assumption about his text as "specifically designed to address the problem of whiteness from *the perspective* of Christology" could be read as collapsing Christology into a uniform framework of a single lens. At this interval in our discussion, it is clear we cannot presume that there is any individual perspective founding Christology, and this remains true even among African American theologians.

The scope of diversity is not restricted to the Black versus white Christology polemic nor the theological meaning attached to the race of Jesus Christ. Hence, on the question "Why does the racial identity of Jesus theologically matter?" one cannot with justification claim that there is a singular "Black" answer. In fact, both the proponents of African American slave Christology and the African American tradition of Christological universality, we unearthed, do not adhere to the notion that the racial identity of Jesus is of theological import.

Furthermore, white Christology, Black Christology, African American slave Christology, and the African American tradition of Christological universality each present a different take on the subject matter of whiteness. For example, the very definition of whiteness—respecting Christological perspective—remains entangled within disparate conceptual moorings. On the one hand, theologians attached to the Black Christology camp (Johnson and Eichelberger) conflate whiteness with white privilege/racism and thus propose the Christological position of antiwhiteness. On the other hand, the Christological universality school—Mays, King, and Hill—is also stringently opposed to white racism; however, the adoption of antiwhiteness is not on its Christological agenda.

CONCLUSION

Up to this moment, we have not attempted to establish which Christological position is the authentic—fitting—option for the treatment of the whiteness problem. From the standpoint of our philosophical critique, the appropriately suited Christological viewpoint for interrogating whiteness remains an exterior question. We think this is because the question of authenticity—or determining the appropriately suited Christological viewpoint—for advancing the interrogation of whiteness is fundamentally theological in character rather than a philosophical concern. Therefore, theologically establishing the authenticity of Christology—regarding whiteness—stands outside of our philosophical purview as well as the fact that it remains historically moot.

The theological and historic Christian nexus of orthodoxy versus heresy is an insufficient marker for establishing authentic Christology. One Christian's orthodoxy is another Christian's heresy. It stands to reason that Black Christology is intractably bound in this theological conundrum. The theological option as to what Christology is suitable continues on as unsupported in any rational manner.

However, concerning the philosophical investigation of theological claims about representing genuine Christology, we submit that what remains must pertain to the theoretical and logical adequacy of the justifications provided. Therefore, our observation is that the theological quest for Christological authenticity continues as a matter ensnared in the net of philosophical idealism, which is of no minor consequences. Especially if authentic Christology is thought to be liberatory in some manner and hence related to the material conditions of Black oppression and capitalist exploitation, then idealism proves to be disastrous as a solution to these problems.

Consequently, our philosophical objective centered on the limits of theological methodology vis-à-vis authentic Christology. Specifically, we had the task of explicating how the pursuit of Christological authenticity—given its ahistorical method—must address the plurality of Christologies and the adjoining conflicts over orthodoxy. The main philosophical conclusion, about the methods employed, we have already sufficiently confirmed—namely, that the pursuit of authenticity stands on ambiguous logical grounds and ahistorical assumptions, which ultimately points to philosophical idealism. It becomes evident that, philosophically speaking, idealism emerges as the chief stumbling block.

If this is the case, then extending beyond the notion of an appeal to ethical ideals—supposedly embodied in Christological principles—becomes pivotal. Claiming that Jesus is the embodiment of caritas is not the same as the view that Jesus was a foe of institutional structures such as slavery—the latter position of which the New Testament not only fails to confirm but also demonstrates the contrary stance, explicitly, Jesus affirming slavery as a legitimate institution.

Therefore, we must conclude that the quest for Christological authenticity is an ideological ruse replete with impenetrable theological contradictions such as the historic polemics on orthodoxy and heresy, not to mention the historical fact that the presence of multiple Christianities undermines the idealist notion of authenticity. Subsequently, Christological authenticity has ultimately proven to be a red herring, a ploy beyond the reach of historical substantiation and philosophical coherency.

Moreover, we markedly confirmed that restricting the critical focus on white Christology alone—and not Christology more generally—indeed proves insufficient. Therefore, the choice does not reside in discovering Christological alternatives to confront whiteness. Consequently, the inadequacy of Christological perspectives—respecting the problem of whiteness—crucially mandates establishing what are the general limitations of Christology as such. Thus, the overriding question becomes, What kind of investigative framework do we have in the exercise of Christological inquiry?

Accordingly, in answering this question, we must not overlook Hart's and Pinn's conclusions—namely that the entirety of Christology is an inadequate—and in fact irrelevant—basis for judging whiteness. Given this penetrating insight, it therefore requires that one must stand outside the parameters of Christology. It follows that all efforts at racializing Christology and subsequently the notion of Black Christology fall short of the mark for rendering that whiteness is incompatible with Christology. In the wake of the general inadequacy of Christology, then Christology itself becomes our foremost theoretical problem.

At this juncture in our deliberations, we have a conceptual shift from the problem of whiteness to the problem of how effective are the tools of Christology itself. Hence, our theoretical framework transpires as philosophical inquiry into the very limitations of Christology. We submit that we have decidedly demonstrated that the very efforts to define white Christology cannot be removed from the very nature of Christology as such.

This critique of Christology importantly entails that we cannot overlook the significant matter of Christology in its historical function as religious ideology. This function, we found, vitally buttresses the persistent realities of oppression and exploitation, extending back to antiquity on to our contemporary times of the capitalist system and its accompanying racism, national oppression, and class exploitation—all of which are formidable problems faced by African Americans from slavery until today.

What cannot be neglected, considering these conditions, is that there are many Black Christians still locked in the captivity of Christian dogma. The long influence of Christianity on African American culture is a concrete manifestation of Christianity's ideological function in the material circumstances of Black life. Perhaps this explains why Black Christology—despite its limitations—continues to have a strong appeal for some Black Christians. The immediate problems attached to racism and national oppression spark the fervent quest for solutions. Philosophical scrutiny on the proposal for the Christological solution to such problems remains the primary aim of our deliberations in this chapter.

Another key aspect—in our philosophical evaluation—is in explicating the difference between an actual argument with the relevant justification versus assertions that go without any rational support or accompanying empirical evidence. The latter is often the case with faith claims that occur within Christological discourse, whether Black or white. We will discover in the next chapter that resorting to faith claims becomes a stopgap measure when reasoned argumentation proves futile.

If Black Christology is reducible to faith claims, then the critique of white Christology is merely rendered as a conflicting matter of faith claims on the subject. Thus, when the air is taken out of the balloon, the flight to majestic heights of authenticity rapidly crashes to the ground because we have no more than a theological illusion. When all is said and done, we simply have contending positions on "the will to believe."

Therefore, the aim of carrying out this task of philosophical inquiry into the very limitations of Christology is also the objective of our next chapter on Black Theologian Dr. Major J. Jones. Jones offers up his Black Theology, which views Christology in terms of God's presence in the world via both the divine character and humanity of Jesus. For Jones, the Christological issue of Jesus as historical person and divine entity is affirmed by means of a series of theological arguments supplemented with ancillary faith claims. Our task is to philosophically appraise such theological arguments and then uncover the adjoining pitfalls of his faith claims. Hence, we now turn to our final chapter, "The Color of God and Jesus's Divinity: A Philosophical Assessment."

NOTES

1. George Yancy, ed., *Christology and Whiteness: What Would Jesus Do?* (New York: Routledge, 2012), 27.
2. Yancy, *Christology and Whiteness*, 36.
3. N. T. Wright, *Who Was Jesus?* (Grand Rapids, MI: William B. Eerdmans Publishing Co., 2001). Kamal S. Salibi, *Who Was Jesus?: Conspiracy in Jerusalem* (London: Tauris Parke Paperbacks, 2007). Marcus Borg, *Jesus in Contemporary Scholarship* (Harrisburg, PA: Trinity Press International, 1994).
4. James Papandrea, *The Earliest Christologies: Five Images of Christ in the Postapostolic Age* (Downers Grove, IL: Inter Varsity Press, 2016). Simon Gathercole, *The Preexistent Son: Recovering the Christologies of Matthew, Mark, and Luke* (Grand Rapids, MI: William B. Eerdmans Publishing Co., 2006).
5. Chigor Chike, "Black Christology for the Twenty-First Century," *Black Theology* 8(3) (April 2015): 357–78. Diane Hayes, "Christology in African American Theology,"

in Katie G. Cannon and Anthony B. Pinn, eds., *The Oxford Handbook on African American Theology* (New York: Oxford University, 2014).

6. Justin Meggitt, "Popular Mythology of the Early Empire and the Multiplicity of Jesus Traditions," in R. Joseph Hoffmann, *Sources of the Jesus Tradition: Separating History from Myth* (Amherst, NY: Prometheus Books, 2010). Don Schweitzer, *Contemporary Christologies* (Minneapolis: Fortress Press, 2010). Craig A. Evans, "The Misplaced Jesus: Interpreting Jesus in a Judaic Context," in Bruce Chilton, Craig A. Evans, and Jacob Neusner, eds., *The Missing Jesus: Rabbinic Judaism and the New Testament* (Leiden: Brill Academic Publishers, 2002).

7. Joseph A. Johnson Jr., "Jesus, The Liberator," in James H. Cone and Gayraud S. Wilmore, eds., *Black Theology: A Documentary History, Volume One, 1966–1979* (Ossining, NY: Orbis Books, 1993): 208.

8. Bart D. Ehrman, *Lost Christianities: The Battles for Scripture and the Faiths We Never Knew* (New York: Oxford University Press, 2003). Veli-Matti Kärkkäinen, *Christology: A Global Introduction* (Grand Rapids, MI: Baker Academic, 2003). Papandrea, *The Earliest Christologies*.

9. Papandrea, *The Earliest Christologies*. Schweitzer, *Contemporary Christologies*. Geza Vermes, *The Changing Faces of Jesus* (New York: Penguin Compass, 2002). Walter Bauer, *Orthodoxy and Heresy in Earliest Christianity* (Philadelphia: Fortress Press, 1971).

10. Maghan Keita, *Race and the Writing of History: Riddling the Sphinx* (New York: Oxford University Press, 2000). Denise Eileen McCoskey, *Race: Antiquity and Its Legacy* (New York: I. B. Tauris, 2012). For race-based notions of civilization, see Clarence J. Munford, *Race and Civilization: Rebirth of Black Centrality* (Trenton, NJ: Africa World Press, 2001). Arthur Kemp, *AWAKENING: The Rise of Western Civilization* (Burlington, VT: Ostara Publications, 2009). For a critical interpretation, read Silvia Federici, "The God That Never Failed: The Origins and Crises of Western Civilization," in Silvia Federici, ed., *Enduring Western Civilization: The Construction of the Concept of Western Civilization and Its Others* (Westport, CT: Praeger Publishers, 1995), 63–89. Willie James Jennings, *The Christian Imagination: Theology and the Origins of Race* (New Haven, CT: Yale University Press, 2010). Bruce Chilton, "Christianity: What It Is and How It Defines Western Civilization," in Jacob Neusner, *Religious Foundations of Western Civilization: Judaism, Christianity, and Islam* (Nashville: Abingdon Press, 2006).

11. For a critical assessment on ancient Greece as the cradle of Western/world civilization, consult David Livingstone, *The Dying God: The Hidden History of Western Civilization* (Lincoln, NE: The Writers Club, 2002). Cheikh Anta Diop, *The African Origin of Civilization: Myth or Reality* (Chicago: Lawrence Hill Books, 1974). Henry Olela, *From Ancient Africa to Ancient Greece: An Introduction to the History of Philosophy* (Atlanta: Select Publications Corp., 1981). Ali Mazrui, *Ancient Greece in African Political Thought* (Nairobi: Afropress, Ltd., 1967).

12. Hannaford correctly argues that to think of ancient Greece in racial terms—for example, as "white" culture—is an anachronistic reading. Consult Ivan Hannaford, *Race: The History of an Idea in the West* (Washington, DC: Woodrow Wilson Center Press, 1996). Silvia Federici, ed., *Enduring Western Civilization: The Construction of the Concept of Western Civilization and Its Others*, (Westport, CT: Praeger Publishers, 1995). McCoskey, *Race: Antiquity and Its Legacy*.

13. Morrison offers a critical evaluation of the Eurocentric nature of the philosophy of religion regarding Western culture in Roy D. Morrison II, "Black Enlightenment: The Issues of Pluralism, Priorities and Empirical Correlation," *Journal of the American Academy of Religion* 46(2) (1978); and consult Robert E. Hood, *Must God Remain Greek?: Afro-Cultures and God-Talk* (Minneapolis: Fortress Press, 1990). Also read, Nick Hostettler, *Eurocentrism: A Marxian Critical Realist Critique* (New York: Routledge, 2012), and Martin Bernal, *Black Athena: The Fabrication of Ancient Greece, 1785–1985, Volume 1* (New Brunswick, NJ: Rutgers University Press, 1987).

14. Hegel states, "[T]he knowledge of Spirit for itself or actually, as it is itself or potentiality, is the being in-and-for itself of Spirit as exercising knowledge, the perfect, absolute religion, in which it is revealed what Spirit, what God is; that is the Christian

religion." (*Lectures on the Philosophy of Religion*, E. B. Speirs, ed. and trans., volume 3 [London: Kegan Paul, 1895], 83–84). Teshale Tibebu, *Hegel and the Third World: The Making of Eurocentrism in World History* (Syracuse, NY: Syracuse University Press, 2011), and Rocío Zambrana, "Hegel, History, and Race," in Naomi Zack, ed., *The Oxford Handbook of Philosophy and Race* (New York: Oxford University Press, 2017). Also consult Michael H. Hoffheimer, "Race and Law in Hegel's Philosophy of Religion," in Andrew Valls, ed., *Race and Racism in Modern Philosophy* (Ithaca, NY: Cornell University Press, 2005), and Olufemi Taiwo, "Exorcising Hegel's Ghost: Africa's Challenge to Philosophy," *African Studies Quarterly* 1(4) (1998).

15. Eric Osborn, *Tertullian, First Theologian of the West* (New York: Cambridge University Press, 1997). Miles Hollingworth states, "Augustine ranks as one of the major sights of Western late antiquity" (*Saint Augustine of Hippo* [New York: Oxford University Press, 2013], ix). Leonard Elliott-Binns, *The Beginnings of Western Christendom* (Cambridge: James Clark & Co., 2002), see especially chapter IV, "North Africa." Kossi Adiavu Ayedze, "Tertullian, Cyprian and Augustine on Patience" (Doctoral dissertation, Princeton University, 2000).

16. William Scott Green, "What Do We Mean by 'Religion' and 'Western Civilization,'" in Jacob Neusner, ed., *Religious Foundations of Western Civilization: Judaism, Christianity, and Islam* (Nashville: Abingdon Press, 2006). Sampie Terreblanche, *Western Empires, Christianity and the Inequalities between the West and the Rest 1500–2010* (Johannesburg: Penguin Books, 2014). Yosef Ben-Jochannan, *African Origins of the "Major" Western Religions* (New York: Alkebu-lan Book Associates, 1970). Mark Ellingsen, *African Christian Mothers and Fathers* (Eugene, OR: Cascade Books, 2015).

17. Walter Homolka, *Jewish Jesus Research and Its Challenge to Christology Today* (Leiden: Brill, 2016), 111.

18. Jacob Neusner, ed., *Religious Foundations of Western Civilization: Judaism, Christianity, and Islam* (Nashville: Abingdon Press, 2006). Daniel B. Lee, "The Great Racial Commission: Religion and the Construction of White America," in Henry Goldschmidt and Elizabeth McAlister, eds., *Race, Nation, and Religion in the Americas* (New York: Oxford University Press, 2004).

19. Dana L. Robert, *Christian Mission: How Christianity Became a World Religion* (Malden, MA: Wiley-Blackwell, 2009), consult especially Part 1. Emily Conroy-Krutz, *Christian Imperialism: Converting the World in the Early American Republic* (Ithaca, NY: Cornell University Press, 2015).

20. Paul Harvey, *Through the Storm, Through the Night: A History of African American Christianity* (Lanham, MD: Rowman & Littlefield, 2011), 5. Terreblanche, *Western Empires*. For a historical treatment of the topic by a Black Theologian, consult Robinson A. Milwood, *Western European and British Barbarity, Savagery, and Brutality in the Transatlantic Slave Trade: A Critical Study* (Bloomington, IN: Xlibris Corporation, 2013).

21. Ramsay MacMullen, *Christianity and Paganism in the Fourth to Eighth Centuries* (New Haven, CT: Yale University Press, 1997). Robert E. Hood, *Begrimed and Black: Christian Traditions on Blacks and Blackness* (Minneapolis: Fortress Press, 1994), 23–34, 45–71.

22. Ehrman, *Lost Christianities*. Bauer, *Orthodoxy and Heresy in Earliest Christianity*. For a critical review of Bauer and Ehrman, see Andreas J. Köstenberger and Michael J. Kruger, *The Heresy of Orthodoxy* (Wheaton, IL: Crossway, 2010). Also consult Meggitt, "Popular Mythology of the Early Empire."

23. Bauer, *Orthodoxy and Heresy in Earliest Christianity*. Bauer's original text is published in German (1934). Also consult Paul A. Hartog, ed., *Orthodoxy and Heresy in Early Christian Contexts: Reconsidering the Bauer Thesis* (Eugene, OR: Pickwick Publications, 2015). Joseph Hammond, *Heterodox Christologies* (Morrisville, NC: Lulu Press, 2016).

24. Otto Friedrich August Meinardus, *Two Thousand Years of Coptic Christianity* (New York: The American University Press in Cairo, 2002). Philip Jenkins, *Jesus Wars* (New York: HarperCollins Publishers, 2010). James Hitchcock, *The History of the Catholic Church: From the Apostolic Age to the Third Millennium* (San Francisco: Ignatius Press,

2012). For an overall treatment of Eastern European Christianity, consult Ken Parry, ed., *The Blackwell Companion to Eastern Christianity* (Malden, MA: Wiley-Blackwell, 2010). Janet A. Timbie, "Coptic Christianity," in Ken Parry, ed., *The Blackwell Companion to Eastern Christianity* (Malden, MA: Wiley-Blackwell, 2010). David Appleyard, "Ethiopian Christianity," in Ken Parry, ed., *The Blackwell Companion to Eastern Christianity* (Malden, MA: Wiley-Blackwell, 2010).

25. Robinson A. Milwood, *European Christianity and the African Slave Trade: A Black Hermeneutical Study* (Bloomington, IN: AuthorHouse, 2007).

26. Eric C. Williams, *Capitalism and Slavery* (Chapel Hill: University of North Carolina Press, 1994), 136. Harry Kelsey, *Sir John Hawkins: Queen Elizabeth's Slave Trader* (New Haven, CT: Yale University Press, 2003), 20, 88. John Hawkins, *The Third Troublesome Voyage Made with the Jesus of Lubec, 1567–1568* (Madison: Wisconsin Historical Society, 2003).

27. Harvey, *Through the Storm, Through the Night*, 5. Daniel B. Lee, "The Great Racial Commission." Katie Geneva Cannon, "Racism and Economics: The Perspective of Oliver C. Cox," in Katie Geneva Cannon, Emilie Maureen Townes, and Angela D. Sims, eds., *Womanist Theological* Ethics (Louisville, KY: Westminster John Knox Press, 2011). Terreblanche, *Western Empires*.

28. Moni McIntyre, "The Black Church and Whiteness: Looking for Jesus in Strange Places," in George Yancy, ed., *Christology and Whiteness: What Would Jesus Do?* (New York: Routledge, 2012), 127.

29. Jennifer A. Glancy, *Slavery in Early Christianity* (New York: Oxford University Press, 2002). David M. Gwynn, *Christianity in the Later Roman Empire: A Sourcebook* (New York: Bloomsbury Academic, 2015). Chris L. de Wet, *Preaching Bondage: John Chrysostom and the Discourse of Slavery in Early Christianity* (Oakland: University of California Press, 2015). Hector Avalos, *Slavery, Abolitionism, and the Ethics of Biblical Scholarship* (Sheffield: Sheffield Phoenix Press, 2013).

30. Junius P. Rodriquez, "Introduction: Slavery in Human History," in Junius P. Rodriquez, General Editor, *The Historical Encyclopedia of World Slavery*, Volume 1 (Santa Barbara: ABC-CLIO, 1997), xvii.

31. Cannon, "Racism and Economics," 11–12.

32. M. Shawn Copeland, "The (Black) Jesus of Detroit: Reflections on Black Power and the (White) American Christ," in George Yancy, ed., *Christology and Whiteness: What Would Jesus Do?* (New York: Routledge, 2012), 273.

33. George Raymond Beasley-Murray, *Baptism in the New Testament* (Grand Rapids, MI: William B. Eerdmans Publishing Co., 1973), 90–91.

34. Robinson A. Milwood, *White Christianity Is Fraudulent* (Bloomington, IN: Author House, 2015).

35. For a substantive treatment of Black Christology, consult Hayes, "Christology in African American Theology." Chike, "Black Christology for the Twenty-First Century," 357–78. W. H. Becker, "Black Power in Christological Perspective," *Religion in Life* 38(3) (1969). Kelly Brown Douglas, *The Black Christ* (Ossining, NY: Orbis Books, 1994). Jacquelyn Grant, *White Women's Christ, Black Women's Jesus* (Atlanta: Scholars Press, 1989). Thomas Bohache, *Christology from the Margins* (London: SCM Press, 2008), see especially chapter 4, "A Savior Just Like Me: Black, African, and Asian Christologies." Also consult the South African notion of Black Christology in Takatso Mofokeng, *The Crucified Among the Crossbearers: Towards a Black Christology* (Kampen: J. H. Kok, 1983).

36. David Eller, "Love Your Enemy, Kill Your Enemy: Crusades, Inquisitions, and Centuries of Christian Violence," in John W. Loftus, ed., *Christianity Is Not Great* (Prometheus Books, 2014). Hector Avalos, *Fighting Words: The Origins of Religious Violence* (Amherst, NY: Prometheus Books, 2005).

37. William L. Eichelberger, "A Mytho-Historical Approach to the Black Messiah" *The Journal of Religious Thought* 33(1) (April 1976): 64–65. Also read Joseph A. Johnson Jr., "The Need for a Black Christian Theology," *The Journal of Interdenominational Theological Center* 2(1) (Fall 1974).

38. Avalos, *Fighting Words*.

39. Avalos, *Slavery, Abolitionism, and the Ethics of Biblical Scholarship*.

40. Khaled Anatolios, *Retrieving Nicaea: The Development and Meaning of Trinitarian Doctrine* (Grand Rapids, MI: Baker Academic, 2011). Ted A. Campbell, *The Gospel in Christian Traditions* (New York: Oxford University Press, 2009). David M. Gwynn, "The Council of Chalcedon and the Definition of Christian Tradition," in Richard Price and Mary Whitby, eds., *Chalcedon in Context: Church Councils 400–700* (New York: Oxford University Press, 2004).

41. Lee Martin McDonald and James A. Sanders, eds., *The Canon Debate* (Grand Rapids, MI: Baker Academic, 2002). Adam Nicolson, *God's Secretaries: The Making of the King James Bible* (New York: HarperCollins, 2005).

42. Jennifer A. Glancy, "Slaves and Slavery in Matthean Parables," *Journal of Biblical Literature* V.119, n.1 (2000): 67–90. D. B. Martin, *Slavery as Salvation: The Metaphor of Slavery in Pauline Christianity* (New Haven, CT: Yale University Press, 1990). Ilaria Ramelli, *Social Justice and the Legitimacy of Slavery: The Role of Philosophical Asceticism from Ancient Judaism to Late Antiquity* (New York: Oxford University Press, 2016).

43. Hector Avalos, *The Bad Jesus: The Ethics of New Testament Ethics* (Sheffield: Sheffield Phoenix Press, 2015). David M. Goldenberg, *The Curse of Ham: Race and Slavery in Early Judaism, Christianity, and Islam* (Princeton, NJ: Princeton University Press, 2003).

44. Glancy, *Slavery in Early Christianity*. Avalos, *The Bad Jesus*. James Albert Harrill, *Slaves in the New Testament: Literary, Social, and Moral Dimensions* (Minneapolis: Fortress Press, 2010).

45. Josiah U. Young, "Who Belongs to Christ?," in George Yancy, ed., *Christology and Whiteness: What Would Jesus Do?* (New York: Routledge, 2012), 197.

46. Anthony Pinn, "Looking like Me?: Jesus Images, Christology, and the Limitations of Theological Blackness," in George Yancy, ed., *Christology and Whiteness: What Would Jesus Do?* (New York: Routledge, 2012).

47. John McIntyre, *Shape of Christology: Studies in the Doctrine of the Person of Christ* (Edinburgh: T&T Clark, 1998).

48. F. F. Bruce, *The New Testament Documents: Are They Reliable?* (Grand Rapids, MI: Wm. B. Eerdmans Publishing Company, 1981), 3. Also consult Robert M. Price, *Incredible Shrinking Son of Man: How Reliable Is the Gospel Tradition?* (Amherst, NY: Prometheus Books, 2003).

49. There is an ecumenical version of both the Nicene and Apostles' Creed, the former written in 1975 under the auspices of International Consultation on English Texts (ICET), published in the book *Prayers We Have in Common*, while the latter is the ecumenical version of the English Language Liturgical Consultation (ELLC). Consult JoHannah Reardon, "The Nicene and Apostles' Creeds: A Close Look at These Two Creeds Helps Define What Christians Believe," http://www.christianitytoday.com/biblestudies/articles/churchhomeleadership/nicene-apostles-creeds.html [accessed September 14, 2015]. Lewis Ayres, *Nicaea and Its Legacy: An Approach to Fourth-Century Trinitarian Theology*, Volume 13 (New York: Oxford University Press, 2004). Gwynn, "The Council of Chalcedon."

50. David Fitzgerald, *Nailed: Ten Christian Myths That Show Jesus Never Existed at All* (Morrisville, NC: Lulu Press, 2010); *Jesus: Mything in Action, Vol. II* (Seattle: Amazon/CreateSpace, 2017). Robert M. Price, *Jesus Is Dead* (Cranford: American Atheist Press, 2007). Richard Carrier, *On the Historicity of Jesus: Why We Might Have Reason for Doubt* (Sheffield: Sheffield Phoenix Press, 2014). David Friedrich Strauss, *A New Life of Jesus*, Volume I (London: Williams and Norgate, 1865). Arthur Drews, *The Christ Myth* (Amherst, NY: Prometheus Books, 1998) (originally published in 1910). John M. Robertson, *Christianity and Mythology* (London: Watts, 1910). Earl Doherty, *Jesus: Neither God Nor Man—The Case for a Mythical Jesus* (Ottawa: Age of Reason Publications, 2009). George Albert Wells, *Did Jesus Exist?* (Amherst, NY: Prometheus Books, 1992). D. M. Murdock, *Who Was Jesus?: Fingerprints of the Christ* (Seattle: Stellar House Publishing, 2011). Burton L. Mack, *Who Wrote the New Testament?: The Making of the Christian Myth* (New York: HarperCollins, 1996). R. Joseph Hoffmann, *Jesus Outside of the Gospels* (Amherst,

NY: Prometheus Books, 1986). Robert M. Price, *Deconstructing Jesus* (Amherst, NY: Prometheus Books, 2000). Meggitt, "Popular Mythology of the Early Empire."

51. John G. Jackson, *Pagan Origins of the Christ Myth* (Austin: The Atheist Press, 1991). Also consult John G. Jackson, *Man, God, and Civilization* (New York: Citadel Press, 1972).

52. William David Hart, "Jesus, Whiteness, and the Disinherited," in George Yancy, ed., *Christology and Whiteness: What Would Jesus Do?* (New York: Routledge, 2012), 254. It is constructive to compare Hart's remarks to Wilhelm Bousett's comments before the Fifth International Congress on Free Christianity and Free Thought in Berlin (1910). Bousett states, "Our knowledge of the real facts of His life is of so little that it could be written on a slip of paper. The teaching or the Gospel of Jesus is a web not often to be disentangled, woven in the tradition of His community, and of possibility true words of the Master. What the Gospels tell us about the peculiar self-consciousness of Jesus, and its forms and therefore about His innermost, is overshadowed by the dogma of his community" (*On the Significance of the Personality of Jesus for Belief*, cited in Walter P. Weaver, *The Historical Jesus in the Twentieth Century: 1900–1950* [Harrisburg, PA: Trinity Press International, 1999], 64).

53. Van A. Harvey, *A Handbook of Theological Terms* (New York: Simon & Schuster, 1992), 48.

54. Peter Gomes states, "It still shocks some Christians that Jesus was not a Christian, that he did not know our Bible, and what he preached was substantially at odds with his biblical culture, as with ours as well" (*The Scandalous Gospel of Jesus: What's So Good About the Good News?* [New York: Harper One, 2007], 14). Also read Geza Vermes, *Jesus the Jew: A Historian's Reading of the Gospels* (Minneapolis: Fortress Press, 1981), and Craig A. Evans, "The Misplaced Jesus."

55. Homolka, *Jewish Jesus Research*. L. Michael White, *Scripting Jesus: The Gospels in Rewrite* (New York: HarperOne, 2010). Hyam Maccoby, *Jesus the Pharisee* (London: SCM Press, 2003).

56. Bart Ehrman, *How Jesus Became God: The Exultation of a Jewish Preacher from Galilee* (New York: HarperCollins, 2014). Gathercole, *The Preexistent Son*. Norman Russell, *The Doctrine of Deification in the Greek Patristic Tradition* (New York: Oxford University Press, 2004).

57. Christopher Mark Tuckett, *Christology and the New Testament: Jesus and His Earliest Followers* (Louisville, KY: Westminster John Knox Press, 2001), 6. Also read Helmut Koester, *From Jesus to the Gospels: Interpreting the New Testament in Its Context* (Minneapolis: Fortress Press, 2007).

58. For a brief overview of scholarly works, consult the following: Hayes, "Christology in African American Theology." Ehrman, *How Jesus Became God*. Raymond E. Brown, *An Introduction to New Testament Christology* (New York: Paulist Press, 1994). Köester, *From Jesus to the Gospels*. Bart Ehrman, *Jesus, Interrupted: Revealing the Hidden Contradictions in the Bible and Why We Don't Know about Them* (New York: HarperOne, 2009). Maccoby, *Jesus the Pharisee*. Craig A. Evans, "The Misplaced Jesus." James H. Evans, *We Have Been Believers: An African-American Systematic Theology* (Minneapolis: Fortress Press, 1992). Eichelberger, "A Mytho-Historical Approach to the Black Messiah." Jon M. Temme, "Jesus as Trailblazer: The Christology of Martin Luther King, Jr.," *The Journal of Religious Thought* 42(1) (April 1985). Becker, "Black Power in Christological Perspective."

59. Pinn, "Looking like Me?," 259.

60. Eichelberger, "A Mytho-Historical Approach to the Black Messiah," 72.

61. Hayim Lapin, "The Law of Moses and the Jews: Rabbis, Ethnic Marking, and Romanization," in Natalie B. Dohrmann and Annette Yoshiko Reed, eds., *Jews, Christians, and the Roman Empire* (Philadelphia: University of Pennsylvania Press, 2013). Lloyd A. Thompson, *Romans and Blacks* (New York: Routledge, 2015). David C. Sim. "Jews, Gentiles, and Ethnic Identity in Matthew," in Geoffrey Dunn and Wendy Mayer , eds., *Christians Shaping Identity from the Roman Empire to Byzantium* (Leiden: Brill, 2015).

62. For another work in this tradition, consult Tom Skinner, *How Black Is the Gospel?* (New York: J. B. Lippincott, 1970).

63. Freddie C. Colston, *Dr. Benjamin E. Mays Speaks: Representative Speeches of a Great American Orator* (Lanham, MD: University Press of America, 2002), 217–18.

64. Martin Luther King Jr., *Strength to Love* (Philadelphia: Fortress Press, 1981), 35. [Special note to the reader: The publicans were tax collectors who worked in conjunction with the tax farmers and Roman rulers. See John L. Mckenzie, *The Dictionary of the Bible* (New York: Simon & Schuster, 1995), 707.] Hence, King argues that in terms of Christology, Jesus did not condemn anyone based on class exploitation. Rather class conciliation was a key component of the Christological message of universality.

65. Temme, "Jesus as Trailblazer," *The Journal of Religious Thought* V. 42, n. 1 (April 1985): 79.

66. Charles Leander Hill, *The Evangel in Ebony* (Boston: Meador Publishing Company, 1960), 57.

67. Victor Anderson, "The Mimesis of Salvation and Dissimilitude in the Scandalous Gospel of Jesus," in George Yancy, ed., *Christology and Whiteness: What Would Jesus Do?* (New York: Routledge, 2012), 295. Also consult Robert C. Williams, critical book review, "Amos Jones Jr., *Paul's Message of Freedom: What Does It Mean to the Black Church?*" *Horizons* 12(2) (Fall 1985); and for an affirmative stance on Paul's Christology, read Amos Jones, Jr., *Paul's Message of Freedom: What Does It Mean to the Black Church?* (Valley Forge, PA: Judson Press, 1984).

68. Anderson, "The Mimesis of Salvation and Dissimilitude in the Scandalous Gospel of Jesus," in George Yancy, ed., *Christology and Whiteness: What Would Jesus Do?* (New York: Routledge, 2012), 295. Anderson's distinction between Paul's Christological universalism and the "scandalous" Gospel of Jesus draws on Gomes, *The Scandalous Gospel of Jesus*.

69. For a critical reading on Paul, consult Leon Edward Wright, "Paul Revisited: From Cult to Cosmos," *The Journal of Religious Thought* 32(1) (Spring–Summer 1975).

70. Young, "Who Belongs to Christ?," 204. For a contrasting (apologetic) reading on Paul, read Brad Ronnell Braxton, *No Longer Slaves: Galatians and African American Experience* (Collegeville, MN: The Liturgical Press, 2002).

71. Pinn, "Looking like Me?," 268.

72. Pinn, "Looking like Me?," 268.

73. Copeland, "The (Black) Jesus of Detroit," 279.

SIX

The Color of God and Jesus's Divinity

A Philosophical Assessment

This chapter is a critical—philosophical—examination of African American theologian Dr. Major J. Jones's approach to the question of the color of God and how it relates to the belief in Jesus's divinity. In his text, *The Color of God: The Concept of God in Afro-American Thought*, Jones seeks to develop a summary methodological approach to the notion of Black Theology. Published in 1987 (with a third printing in 1990), Jones grapples with pivotal issues of systematic theology, with particular reference to the manner by which systematic theology can contribute to the development of Black Theology—as a school of thought—and its concomitant insights on the racialized concept of "Black God."

With respect to the racialized God-concept, Jones remarks, "In this book I have sought to express a true and authentic Afro-Americanized concept of God. This God-concept can best reveal itself to minds free of alien distortions that becloud God's efforts at self-disclosure to a people in the relevance of their particular existence."[1]

Two presumptions are pregnant in this declaration. First, Jones believes that the Afro-Americanized God-concept is authentic and reveals itself principally to Black human beings. Second, Black minds must be receptive to such revelations. Thus, we can presume the failure to receive God's self-disclosure is not due to any fault with God's capacities. Rather, we understand that it is minds that are beclouded by alien distortions that prohibit the truth about the God-concept, namely, it must assume an Afro-Americanized form.

Jones does not shy away from the fact that he considers Christian theology as relevant to the particularity of Black existence. Jones is forthright and candid about what he seeks to achieve in his book. Of prime significance, he argues that there is a vital conceptual distinction between the white God-concept and the Afro-American concept of God. This Afro-Americanized God-concept is especially important for African Americans and particularly for Black Christians to embrace as their own religious outlook. Given his alternative theology, Jones thinks that his fellow African American Christians can effectively liberate themselves from the white God-concept.

In Jones's assessment, the white God-concept is essentially an alien distortion of God, and this specifically pertains to Black Christians and their respective need for a relevant Black Godhead. Jones observes, "Black consciousness, indeed, demands liberation and purification of the God-concept itself. We will free it from the many alien connotations that denied the full affirmation of Black humanity, merely because one is Black and not White."[2]

The centrality of Black consciousness pertaining to the liberation and purification of the God-concept itself should not be lost on the reader. It seems Jones's call for "liberation and purification" fundamentally amounts to his Afro-Americanization of the God-concept. In concert with A. M. E. Bishop Henry M. Turner, Jones staunchly believes that the white God-concept has been instrumental in African American spiritual oppression as well as maintaining control over the general thinking of Black people. For illustration, we observe the theological connection between the two men, when Turner strongly argues,

> We have as much right biblically and otherwise to believe that God is a Negro, as you buckra, or white people have to believe that God is a fine looking symmetrical and ornamented man. For the bulk of you and all the fool Negroes of the country, believe that God is white-skinned, blue-eyes, straight-haired, projecting-nosed compressed lipped and finely-robed white gentleman sitting upon a throne somewhere in the heavens. . . . We do not believe that there is any hope for a race of people who do not believe that they look like God.[3]

Therefore, in Turner's opinion—in close approximation with Jones—the problem of the color of God has tremendous importance regarding the development of Black (rhetorical) theology as a liberation project.[4] For Turner, white Christians are culprits in advancing the ethnocentric idea that God is white, which subsequently continues as detrimental to Black aspirations for freedom. Turner once described the United States with the statement, "This land of lynchers, this nation of color prejudice, this white man's heaven and the black man's hell."[5] Consecutively, Turner argues that the belief in the Black God-concept offers substantial hope in the fight for liberation. Turner fervently believed that he had a mission to advance a counter-theology to white racist Christianity. It was Turner's contention that white Christians were persistently aiming for ideological hegemony over Black life. Historian John Dittmer explains,

Turner viewed this mission with a great sense of urgency and began to develop a Black theology of liberation grounded in the basic tenets of Christianity. To achieve this end, Turner realized, blacks must reject all teachings of the white church that confirm their inferior status. He was particularly sensitive to the symbolic significance of "whiteness" in Christian teachings and discouraged singing of such verses as, "now wash me and I shall be whiter than the snow," explaining that the purpose of washing was to make clean, not white.[6]

Sequentially and in step with Turner, Jones offers the following comment about the color of God and how God becomes Black in concrete theological terms. Jones adamantly proclaims:

> If we are Black, must not God's self-address to us be related to the blackness of the persons being addressed? God's address to Black people includes his knowledge of Black awareness, Black pride, Black self-respect, and the deep desire for a full, Black self-determination. God's self-address to Black people includes their political desire to be free and the aspiration to be equal in every way. If God needs to become Black in his self-address to Black persons, then God becomes Black. In this sense, God's self-address to the Black person takes on a particular form and conveys a particular message. It is personal, yet it is to a whole people.[7]

"If God needs to become Black in his self-address to Black persons, then God becomes Black." On this accounting, the Black God-concept is a signifier indicating that God needs to communicate to Black people. Thus, we can presume that God cannot effectively communicate with Black people when other than assuming Black form. Essentially God's Blackness as signifier is all about relating to Black persons. It appears we can assume—following from his aforementioned claim—that Jones's idea of Black God is at root relational and situational rather than referencing an absolute existence in any ontological (ultimately real) sense of the term. We can plausibly reach this conclusion since the meaning of Blackness (as it resides in his Black God-concept) derives from how it is related to the Black experience.

In glaring contrast, the ontological question of God's absolute existence, in fact, points us toward the universal transcendence of the God-concept. Herein, this theological view boldly affirms that God's absolute being is without limitations or restrictions of any particular type. Respecting Jones's standpoint, what we uncover is that God's absolute being logically and ironically emerges as a significant limitation and primary restriction on his capacity to communicate with Black people. This is because God's self-address to Black people must be considered in terms of a particularized attribute—Blackness—rather than any universal/absolute characteristics. What becomes abundantly clear—with Jones's claim—God in his self-address to Black people develops into something other than absolute in makeup and character.

We believe this summation is a charitable reading of Jones's claim. For it is Jones's premise that God needs to relate with Black people and therefore manifest himself as relevant to their concerns. This position of relevancy stands in conflict with Jones's own initial assertion. Expressly, the failure to receive God's self-disclosure is not due to any fault in God's capacities. Rather, we discover that it is Black minds that are beclouded by alien distortions that prohibit the truth about the God-concept, which Jones declared assumes an Afro-Americanized form. Now, we have instead the declaration that God must become relevant to Black people. Subsequently, it is our conclusion that Jones's Black God-concept transforms into a perceived need for relevancy, which is attached to God's absolute being.

Of course, the idea of an absolute God that stands in need—in any fashion—is theologically problematic. It is a theological claim that requires philosophical assessment. Any assertion about the attribution of need is a clear indicator of limits and restriction placed on absolute being. Thus, the prevailing Christian theological presupposition is that an absolute God, unlike finite beings, has no limitations and hence remains bereft of needs. In short, Jones's Black God-concept—derivative of the need to communicate to Black people—stands in counterposition to the prevailing Christian theological presupposition as well as his first proclamation about the impact of alien distortions on Black minds which critically misrepresent God's message to African Americans.

Jones's latter claim has some definitive complications regarding the concept of the Black God. If it is that "God's self-address to the Black person," actually establishes the anchor for the Black God-concept, then relational and situational determinations are the key existential rudiments instead of the absolute existence of God as foundational. Even on the premise that God's will grounds his self-address, the conclusion is quite evident that the Black God-concept primarily exists as the key means for communicating with Black persons.

Yet we find that Jones proffers, "God relates to the person and to the people in the light of who he or she is and in light of who a people might be. God's *absolute being* becomes relevant to the individual or to the people address, color included"[8] [italics added]. We contend that Jones's idea that the absolute being of God is in concert with relational and situational determinations—which are actually human characteristics and circumstances—effectively undermines the presumption that God's absolute existence and transcendent reality should ground the Black God-concept. This results precisely because the concept of Blackness results from the context of comprehending the Black experience, which is a very human endeavor.

Jones is an astute Christian theologian, and he should know that the notion of God's absolute being should not change for any human circumstances. For instance, Christian theological anthropology posits that humans are finite and imbued with sin, thus correspondingly in need of redemption. In this regard, African American philosopher/theologian George D. Kelsey brings to our attention: "Man is finite. He is but a creature. He is therefore limited in his capacity. By the very nature of his being he is incapable of achieving the absolute ideal. Moreover, man does not possess the complete potential strength of his finitude. For his nature has been polluted by the Fall. He is, as a result of the Fall, essentially a sinner. The impact of the Fall operates profoundly upon us all."[9]

While at this juncture in his text Jones seems to discount the sinful and finite character attached to the African American experience. In contrast, he is quite aware of this absolutist theological viewpoint—concerning the God-concept—stands as decisive for Christian thought and is especially prevalent in Black religious thinking. Without any criticism of this belief, Jones unequivocally states,

> Most Black Christians have agreed with Western theology that limitations on the essential attributes of God are derogatory and unthinkable. Popular Black religious thought has generally agreed with the dominant formal theology on this point: If God is not the Almighty, then he is not truly God. In Black religious belief as with most Christian theology, Black or White, God's infinity includes much more than absolute power, knowledge, and goodness; omnipresence for example, is "all, everything." In summary, a popular idea of God affirms the divine nature as Perfect Being, "all," "everything," and all-inclusive attribution of perfection implying the co-inherence of all other attributes.[10]

Jones does not inquire into how the absolute conception of God functions in real social terms. Why is it that the absolute being of God has material consequences in social life? It's noteworthy that the idea of absolute God—as supernatural ends—found its worldly expression with the Christian church specifically regarding its institutionalization and attendant social functions. In this regard, the observation of Dr. George D. Kelsey is most helpful in providing a historical context for how Christian theology was instrumental for church authority. Kelsey argues that the immutability of an absolute God is translatable into the absolute power inextricably vested in church authority. This doctrine on the matter of Church authority was particularly apparent during the medieval age.

Kelsey remarks, "In the medieval world the controlling ideal was the unity of civilization under the guidance and protection of the church. The function of all individuals and groups was to render their proper service in a great hierarchy of value and being. All values were finally made serviceable to supernatural ends, as interpreted by the church."[11]

However, Jones argues that God's absolute being assumes the form of Blackness and thus this absolute being must change, that is, *become* something different than absolute in character. Significantly, the notion of *becoming* entails the status of both being and not-being, thus, we have both the ontological presence and absence of a given entity. Most assuredly, Jones is aware that an absolute entity (of perfection) cannot become other than what it is. Hence, the notion of *absolute being* necessarily excludes—by way of deduction—any existential possibility of *not-being*. As Parmenides noted long ago, change entails both *being* and *not-being*, that is, becoming; hence, becoming or change contradicts the impression of absolute being as immutable and hence perfect in character.

The Christian notion of the absolute being of God means that God is everywhere at all times and therefore cannot be absent from anywhere at any time. It follows that the ontological premise of an infinite God means that he ought not to be conceived of in any other manner. All conclusions about the attributes of God must be consistent with this premise. In other words, Christian theology presumes that God's existence is omnipresent and immutable, which does not permit conceiving him to become anything other than what he is thought to already be—a perfect being.

Along these lines, Jones contradicts himself when he says, on the one hand, "In summary, a popular idea of God affirms the divine nature as Perfect Being, 'all,' 'everything,' and all-inclusive attribution of perfection implying the co-inherence of all other attributes." On the other hand, Jones still insists upon God's self-address as relational and situational. Hence, Jones's Black God-concept is based on the Black (human) experience. We think that there are three key reasons why it's the Christian case that the absolute being of God's existence contradicts Jones's Black God-concept and the contention about relational and situational determinations rooted in their connection to the Black experience.

First, logically God's transcendent and absolute character must stand independently of all human existence including Black people. Second, the hallmark of God's absolute being is immutability. Therefore, the very notion of transcendent absolute being stands in contradiction with the capacity to change. Expressly it is presumed—as an absolute being—that God's substance and manifested form are one and the same. Consequently, we must conclude that God's self-disclosure cannot be on human terms. Third, this explicitly means God's existence is not subject to the changing circumstances of Black existence.

Nonetheless, we know that Black existence is always dynamic and subject to change. This propensity for the ever-changing Black experience—along with its transformative context—results from how Black existence is fundamentally material in its makeup. In contradistinction, any claim to God's absolute existence must be founded on the belief that God is an immaterial (spiritual) entity of infinite dimension. We will shortly observe that Jones does not disagree with our assessment. We only contend that he fails to completely garner its logical ramifications respecting his Black God-concept as the self-disclosure of an absolute being to finite beings.

It is precisely the limited character of material existence—its determinate composition—which is at the crux of why all things of the world are in motion, change, and development. Therefore, both nature and society are subject to definitive laws of motion. Nevertheless, the concept of the unchanging character of God as absolute being implies that he stands outside of such dialectical laws of motion. This presumption about God's absolute being overtly locates him as a transcendent entity, an entity not subject to either the laws of nature or society. This remains true even when it is thought that God is immanent in the world. This is because when God—as absolute being—is said to be in the world, it is presupposed that he (ontologically) stands apart from it. God is in the world but not part of it.

Jones, we think, overlooks the logical implications ancillary with God's absolute being, which subsequently relates to the specific concern about how the dimensions of relational and situational context forged the Black God-concept. Nevertheless, Jones is very clear on this last point concerning God's immanent existence in the world. Therefore, let us examine how Jones tackles the issue of the immanent existence of God in the world and its relationship to the idea of absolute being. Jones articulates:

> Although God is in the world, he should not be conceived as being merely in the world, nor "at one" with the world. God's full reality can only be known or realize within the world only partly. . . . God transcends the world and all human existence; and is conceived ontologically by Black religious experience as a personal being whose entity is more than the total of either the natural order or human existence. God is both historical and trans-historical, immanent in the world, and, yet, not at one with the world.[12]

Moreover, Jones acknowledges, "God alone is self-existent, free from all dependence on any other external being and from any limitations by other forces. This means that the ground of the ultimate explanation of God's being is within his radically free, wholly independent, self-existing self. This can be said of no other ontological being; for, all others—only God excepted—are in some way dependent on another."[13]

The idea regarding "God's being is within his radically free, wholly independent, self-existing self" has a certain Aristotelian ring to it. For Aristotle's "Unmoved Mover" remains in a state of self-contemplation since movement and change involves engagement with others and contemplation of objects outside of God's "self-existing self." In Aristotle's view, after the initial push to start the universe in motion, the "Unmoved Mover" is entirely transcendent and does not intervene in the world.

In concert, Jones's claim that "God alone is self-existent, free from all dependence on any other external being and from any limitations by other forces." When this is with the view that "This can be said of no other ontological being" there are immediate ramifications of an ontological sort. First, since God alone is self-existent, then God cannot be dependent in any manner. Logically, this would include dependent on communicating to Black people in any specified manner derivative of the Black experience. Second, the ontological status of Black people—as creatures of God—is one of dependency and foremost dependence on God. It follows that Black people are not in any way ontologically independent of God.

Yet, the process of change affixed to the Black concept of God—as Jones outlined on God's self-address—is predicated upon God *becoming* relevant to human beings. Nevertheless, if "God's full reality can only be known or realized within the world only partly" the conclusion must be that the Black God-concept is only a partial reflection of God's reality. However, with Jones's account, God's self-address to Black people mandates that God must demonstrate his relevancy to the Black experience.

We ask, Why is it that God's relevancy—to Black people—must be rendered in terms of a mandate? Given this line of reasoning, how do mandates for relevancy apply to an absolute being? Granting that such mandates are applicable, it follows that God must change from an absolute being to manifestly finite status—that is assume the form of the Black persona—thus becoming relevant for Black people.

Simply put, it is God's responsibility to relate his message to Black people's experience. This presupposition in fact subverts the notion that God is an absolute being and thus erodes any notion about the ontological dependence of human beings—in particular Black people—on God. What becomes primary is the relevancy of God's self-address to Black people. This relevancy requirement overrides that Black people, through Jones's Black God-concept, learning somehow to communicate with God in view of his absolute status.

In other words, God must change from an absolute being and assume the characteristics embodied in the given group to which he seeks to communicate. Nonetheless, Jones must suppose that God's divine message actually concerns what are absolute principles, which are embedded in what is accepted as his divine existence as absolute being. Given all the above, Jones has created for himself a logical snare, for he insists that God's absolute being is consistent with human relational and situational identities such as being Black. Based on Jones's entire argument, there would be no Black God-concept if there were no Black people.

When Jones argues that God's self-address of necessity must relate to Black people or any other social group (such as women) for that matter, his argument actually becomes the basis for a logical trap.[14] This is because we expressly have a concrete logical inference, namely that the Black God-concept is ontologically dependent upon the existence of Black people. Why God becomes Black is based on the solitary imperative of relating to the Black experience. In effect, we observe rather than the idea that Blackness resides within the absolute context of God's existence, it is derivative of God's divine concerns about Black reality.

Therein, Jones's notion of Black God is straightforwardly relational and ontologically dependent on connecting with the Black experience. Instead of Black people depending upon an absolute God, this absolute deity penultimately depends on the configuration of the Black experience and thus morphs into Jones's Black God-concept. With Jones's Black God-concept what transpires is an ontological reversal. We are sure that this ontological reversal—where his Black God-concept becomes penultimately dependent on Black realities—is not Jones's chief aim or primary intention, rather it is a formidable logical implication issuing from his claim. Indeed, he later remarks, "God may well have ontological being over and above and quite apart from how humans project the divine nature, character, and personhood; nevertheless, God as personal being is always conceived or conceptualized, to a greater degree, in anthropomorphic terms derived from the ways human beings view themselves."[15] Jones continues,

> Theologians of every stripe who have agreed that God has personhood have also agreed that a full and complete understanding of God is beyond all human comprehension. All mere human attempts to speak of God are related to one's own humanness.... Here, because I want to talk about God's color only in relation to Black people, I discussed God's blackness and his moral character. If one were White, God would look White.[16]

Clearly Jones's latter argument is a fundamental shift from the former one of God's self-address to Black people that previously served as the catalyst for his theological construct—Black God. Transparently, the first Black God-concept amounts to a revelation or self-disclosure from God. With Jones's second claim, rather than God acting as the facilitator for demonstrating his relevancy for Black people, the Black God-concept results from human efforts, based on attendant limitations about envisioning God. This issues from the epistemological difficulties surrounding the complex notion of absolute being. Hence, it requires humans apprehending God in anthropomorphic fashion. The idea of the Black God becomes directly a matter of how Black human beings are incapable of grasping the absolute being of God and hereafter resort to viewing God in Black (human) terms.

This second idea of Black God does not begin with God's self-disclosure or self-address, rather it starts with Black (human) theological construction. Instead, it is something which Black people resort to thus humanly comprehending God in view of his absolute being. At this juncture, Jones makes it clear that the Black God-concept is an inadequate one but also a very human way of wrestling with the limits of human comprehension respecting the absolute nature of God's being.

Now the Black God-concept becomes a theological (human) construction or projection about God in racial terms instead of an ontological inquiry into the actual nature of God's existence. Importantly, it does not begin on the grounds—which is critical to the first claim—of how God himself is at the foundation for the Black God-concept. With this second claim, respecting the Black God-concept, Jones is fully aware of the persistent problem concerning God as absolute being.

Now Jones acknowledges that the Black God-concept is a subjectively human, more precisely an epistemological response—on the part of Black people—to capture, however limited, the meaning of God. Accordingly, all talk of God in racial terms whether it be Black or white is a matter of theological construction and human projection and surely not based on ontological considerations. Hereafter, this Black God-idea as theological construct intentionally disregards God as ultimate reality—specifically the thorny question of ontological status—and thus it consciously sidesteps the problem of absolute existence as an object of inquiry. Jones is content to presume that God's absolute existence is notably beyond this particular theological construction on the Black God-concept.

Here we find that Jones is consistent with African American philosopher Dr. Thomas Nelson Baker. "The great [artistic] masters all show their religious devotion to their own race types, and the very countenance of the 'Mother of God' is that of the nationality and race of the artist."[17] In unison, Baker argues for a Black aesthetic. "Until the American Negro is restored to himself aesthetically, both the Negro man and Negro woman will be easy prey to designing members of the Caucasian type, and wealth accumulated by Negro enterprise and brain will be in more cases than one left in the hands of the white race."[18]

Of note respecting Baker's assessment, the racialized conception of God results from precise human viewpoints. However, Baker makes perfectly clear that God is independent of the universe, yet we can only know God by means of his manifestation in the world. He states, "No one would say that God cannot exist without the universe; but for us being who we are, the universe is a condition for a knowledge of God. It is through his works that we see and know God."[19]

As with Baker, Jones's idea of a racialized God-concept derives from specified human relations. Consequently, we have antithetical theological propositions which attempt to explain how we come to the Black God-concept. This is a glaring contradiction in Jones's presentation, which stands without resolution. In effect, Jones is caught in a nagging contradiction based on mutually exclusive proposals for the origins of his Black God-concept. Either God is Black, which is based on the manner of his self-addressed communication to Black people, or the Black God-concept is a human projection formatted as a Black theological construct.

THE BLACK GOD-CONCEPT: A SNARE OF ANTITHETICAL PROPOSITIONS

There is a considerable ontological separation between the theological construct and human projection of the Black God-concept from how this same conception is a matter of God's will—God's self-address—which at least putatively stands on absolute ontological grounds. The latter argument is sustained by the presumption of God's ontological primacy, which serves as the epistemological foundation for God knowing with complete certainty the complexity of the Black experience, while the former argument is based on the view that Black people—given their place in the world—cannot truly know who God is, particularly in terms of his absolute existence.

The ontological gap—the vast distance between the ultimate grounds of God's being and conditional human existence—separating the two propositions therein involves fundamentally different notions about knowledge or in philosophical terms—epistemology. In the first proposal God's complete—absolute—knowledge is said to support the Black God-concept, while the second position is based on the limited knowledge of Black human beings, which serves as the basis for the equivalent Black God-concept.

Therefore, we discern, Jones's latter argument is rooted in the perspective that the Black God-concept is the restricted lens on the actual (absolute) existence of God. In this instance, the Black God-concept is only Black humanity's attempt to fathom what the unknowable God is. The Black God-concept is a human projection, subsequently of human proportion rather than divine inspiration. Unfortunately, we discover, Jones is completely oblivious to the contradiction he created with his antithetical claims supporting the Black God-concept.

However, despite qualitative differences on epistemological points of derivation, we have two arguments based on the common assumption that while God is personal in character, he is also an absolute being. The idea that God is personal in character presumes that God has something of a personality or personhood. Yet, the very idea of personhood mandates determinate features, which identify unique characteristics and special qualities prototypically exhibited by means of the human personality.

For example, when references are made to God as jealous, loving, caring, or forgiving, all these characteristics only make sense from the standpoint of the human personality and attendant social relations. From a critical—logical—viewpoint, absolute being mandates an indeterminate characteristic respecting God's existence. This is because, in principle, God is removed from mutually determined social relations, which serve as the grounds for the formation of personality traits or personhood. We cannot overlook that Jones argued that God is self-subsistent and does not rely on any other being. Nevertheless, the Christian theological detachment of God's personality traits—personhood—from any definitive social context for their formation issues forth an incoherent conception of personality or personhood. As a result, when referring to God as absolutely loving or caring, such references add up to essentially absolutizing human personal traits without the necessary and decisive social relationships, which are foundational for such characteristics.

Subsequently, we discover that this theological presumption—God's capacity to display personal characteristics within the orbit of absolute existence—becomes an insurmountable roadblock to an intelligible conception of what amounts to the Black God-concept. This is a dilemma that Jones is not fully cognizant of and remains a logical snare of major proportions. Jones proceeds as if there is no rational hurdle that stands in the way of his Black God formulations. Anyhow, he insists, "Black people need a God who can make the difference, if they are to have *faith in God* as the subject of their religious quest, liberation, freedom, salvation, and *the ultimate salvation of more than just the Black world. God must be worthy of Black worship"* [20] [italics added]. He further adds,

> Help from God is surely more needed than human assistance, especially from a powerless people. Black theologians dare not conclude upon a God who is less than personal and all-powerful: There must be no doubt about the outcome of the Black struggle for justice. An absolute God must equal the difference between Black power and Black hope. With or without the help of human beings, God is our absolute assurance of ultimate success.[21]

First, we ask: Given the multitude of Black denominations and persons of various religious beliefs, how can it be certain that one has found the God of the ultimate salvation, with dominion extending beyond the Black world? Besides, what does it mean to obtain the *ultimate salvation*? How does this notion of *ultimate salvation* stand in concrete relation to Black liberation? In what way does salvation differ from liberation? Is ultimate salvation equivalent with the achieved spiritual (sacred) status conferred by God? [22]

What we do know—Jones fails to make clear given his conflated formulation—is that Black liberation constitutes a determinate material condition in sharp contrast to ultimate salvation. Foremost, Black liberation is a secular issue, while ultimate salvation is religious or spiritual (philosophically idealist) in substance. Nonetheless, one's religious commitment could be what amounts to a sacred (apolitical) stance on God's salvation sans adopting some type of theology with an adjoining posture on Black liberation.

If a given Black person finds satisfaction with a specific God-concept that differs from Jones, are we to conclude they have what amounts to an alien conception of God? What if a Black Christian devotee thinks that

God transcends racial monikers, then could not one worship God with the aim of praising him? Would it not follow that this action would be immediately in concert with personal salvation and separate from the secular realm? Furthermore, if Black people are to make such a choice (about what God-concept to worship), then it is strictly a human choice and not a divine commandment. It all boils down to a matter of theological preference on the part of humans. Whatever the God-concept in play—in functional terms—it is ultimately a human decision. This is what Black theologian/philosopher William R. Jones technically terms as "functional ultimacy."[23]

Accordingly, we could have the resultant viewpoint that the secular concern of liberation is strictly a matter of human endeavor. For such a person, God would not be relevant to the issue of Black liberation. Hence, one would dispense with God altogether respecting this secular concern and yet concurrently believe that God is the wellspring of universal and personal salvation, that is, salvation beyond the Black world. Given Jones's conflation of spiritual with secular concerns, we must especially highlight the matter of worshipping God is intimately related to the operational God-concept.

For instance, how do we discern the process for determining what God-concept must be worthy of Black worship? Is the act of African Americans worshipping God a matter of personal salvation or collective liberation? If it is the former, one could claim that the delegated God-concept of commitment proves to be satisfactory as a matter of gaining personal salvation. If it is the latter—as we found earlier with our discussion on Albert Cleage—Black liberation is far from our present reality.[24]

Hence, for Jones, we must depend and wait on God in obtaining the goal of Black liberation. This leads directly to our second point, Why believe that "Help from God is surely more needed than human assistance?" Clearly, this assumption chiefly depends on the precise God-concept in play. As Frederick Douglass concluded, powerless people should not depend upon the "makeshift of theology and superstition" but rather of their own human initiative to gain power and liberation. The denigration of human action inevitably points to quietism, not power and liberation. Douglass astutely observes,

> A contest had in fact been going on in my mind for a long time, between the clear consciousness of right and the plausible makeshift of theology and superstition. The one held me an abject slave—a prisoner for life, punished for some transgressions in which I had no lot or part; the other counsel me to manly endeavor to secure my freedom. This contest was now ended; my chains were broken, and the victory brought me unspeakable joy.[25]

In sharp contrast to Major Jones's call for dependence on God—"Help from God is surely more needed than human assistance, especially from a powerless people"—Frederick Douglass challenges such dependency and accents the priority of human initiative. Douglass's remarks are most penetrating and perceptive, he emphatically concludes:

> I found that God never began to hear my prayer for liberty until I began to run. Then you ought to have seen the dusk rise behind me in answer to my prayer.... It is idle, a hollow mockery, for us to pray to God to break the oppressor's power, while we neglect the means of knowledge which will give us the ability to break this power.[26]

Notice that Douglass emphasizes the power of *human knowledge* for actions leading to freedom instead of *faith in prayer for God's deliverance*. Arguably, Douglass's standpoint is one of religious humanism, if not completely secular in character.[27] The same cannot be said of Jones's God-dependent theology (theism) where "Black people need a God who can make the difference."

Crucially, in Jones's statement, he makes the leap from how "Black people need a God who can make the difference" to the conclusion that there actually exists such a God that can meet this need. However, the presence of such a need does not logically entail that there must be an existent absolute entity with the capacity to guarantee such needs are met. Jones's belief that "God is our absolute assurance of ultimate success" rests not on any demonstrated proof that such a God exists, rather it amounts to no more than wishful thinking and blind belief.

In summation, Jones argues that if Black people have such material needs for power and liberation, then they must theologically construct the requisite God-concept, which guarantees they can meet their needs. Hence, we obtain and maintain an anthropocentric conception of Black God because it derives from a felt human need. Correspondingly, Jones insists it is just a matter of believing in the appropriately suited and hence constructed God-concept for the "absolute assurance of ultimate success."

What Jones suggests is that the security of eventual Black victory over oppression ultimately rests on building the appropriate God-concept. Douglass, in turn, recommends that rather than makeshift theology offering any guarantees, we need to act on our own. Liberation is a matter of the human struggle and fight against oppression. It is fundamentally a material process within the real world of oppression. For Jones, makeshift theology fostering the Black God-concept is the path to spiritual liberation.

Hence, when we return to Jones's claims, apparently the outcome of the struggle remains at best a mystery. By mystery we mean beyond the pale of rational thinking and coherent discourse. For instance, when we come to translate the notion that God is a personal entity—which at the same time possesses absolute existence and is all-powerful—it is impossible to put such an idea into intelligible terms. The unintelligibility of

Jones's concept is due to his embrace of irrationalism. There is no rational basis or empirical indicator for his idea that "an absolute God must equal the difference between Black power and Black hope." In contradistinction, Douglass advocates we utilize our human capacities and thus we cast aside superstition. Indeed, it follows that all forms of superstition remain rooted in irrationalism.

Regarding Jones's proposition about God, what becomes transparent is that his key premise stands beyond the scope of rational justification. In other words, what we have is a species of irrationalism. Consequently, Jones's proposition about God is not far removed from superstition and makeshift theology. We must say that although Jones is responsible for creating this theological puzzle, he is not completely oblivious to his own irrationalism. He forthrightly tells us:

> The divine unreality becomes the reality of God when a community of faith responds to the reality of divine unreality. Because God is not direct in his approach to human beings—because God is silent and hides himself—God is sometimes presumed to be nonexistent. Absolute proof of God's existence is beyond the scope of mere human reason. This is why Black Theology is written for a church who simply assume God to be. This does not mean, of course, that the quest for the true knowledge of God's existence is unnecessary. . . . Black theology knows that what God does for us in faith is greater than what God does for us in knowledge.[28]

The idea that "absolute proof of God's existence is beyond the scope of mere human reason" directly indicates that Jones is committed to irrationalism and unintelligible thinking. Jones's convoluted notion of the "divine unreality becomes the reality of God" does very little to facilitate rectifying the problem of unintelligibility; yet he is most transparent that faith has primacy over any knowledge one may have about God. Successively, Jones's assertion about faith evokes a very significant question, Does it follow that the Black God-concept is essentially a faith claim? If this is the case, then Jones could respond to this dilemma—respecting the unintelligibility of his God-concept—with the assertion that it all rides on faith and not rational demonstration.

If what "God does for us in faith is greater than what God does for us in knowledge," from a pragmatic standpoint why bother with knowledge at all? The overriding principle of faith—for the belief in Jones's Black God-concept—in effect points to what amounts to abandoning any coherent principle for grounding this belief in the idea of Black God. Since belief in the Black God-concept is one and the same as the belief in God as such, then the notion of belief in God as such cannot be affirmed on a rational basis, and consequently we have only faith to depend on as our foundation.

Furthermore, if "God is not direct in his approach to human beings" and in fact "God is silent and hides himself," how can God *directly* become involved in the Black liberation struggle? When Jones suggests that God is *not direct* in his approach to humans and in fact *hides himself*, it follows there is no rational basis for uncovering this feature of God's existence. Therefore, Jones's assumption that his Black God-concept is immediately consistent with Black liberation is actually a contradiction in terms. Since God is indirect in his approach and hidden from view, then we have no way of directly knowing what God is doing, one way or the other.

The logical implication about an indirect deity is clear: explicitly, we cannot reasonably know what side God is aligned with vis-à-vis the matter of African American struggle. Hence, the statement that God is on the side of Black liberation reduces to dismissing reason and embracing faith. In Jones's estimation, the very existence of God—not to mention his relevancy to African American liberation—is all about faith. The reduction of the belief in God to a faith claim simply means that Jones resorts to obscurantism respecting God's connection to Black liberation not to mention the very belief in the existence of God.

The fact that God is unknowable—in principle—is a sufficient condition to nullify any pretense of an epistemological—knowledge-based—approach to the meaning of God, with its ancillary Black God-concept. Fundamentally, Jones's notion of the Black God-concept rests principally on fideism. Harvey explains, "Fideism is derived from the basic Latin root meaning faith, and refers generally to the doctrine and the Christian assertion of matters of blind belief and cannot be known or demonstrated to be true."[29]

Unlike Augustine, Anselm, Gaunilo, Aquinas, Paley, Leibniz, and even Isaac Newton, among others, Jones is willing to scrap any proof for demonstrating the existence of God. In a nutshell, the Black God-concept is a faith claim founded on blind belief and therefore not in any manner a justified belief or demonstrated (epistemologically based) truth. Hence, Jones asserts, "Absolute proof of God's existence is beyond the scope of mere human reason. Therefore, Black Theology is written for a church who simply assume God to be."

Given that the Black church tradition, according to Jones, has never bothered to develop formal proofs for the existence of God, then he concludes that it follows that Black systematic theology should forgo such an exercise. While this is a questionable line of argumentation—given the normative/critical dimension of systematic theology versus traditional beliefs about the existence of God—Jones nevertheless anchors his exploration into systematic theology on such grounds.

It is apparent that for Jones the function of Black systematic theology is less a matter of providing a critical assessment of conventional beliefs in African American religious thought. Instead, we observe that Jones aims to deliver a justification for conventional theological thinking among Black Christians. In sum, Black systematic theology collapses into an apologetic framework that offers pragmatic utility for (rather than critique of) the prevailing beliefs in Black Christian thought. In concurrence with this conclusion, Jones further accents his commitment to fideism, when he explains what transpires as the first criterion—for the belief in God—thus functioning within the framework of Black Theology.

> The first criterion for belief in a God who is usable within the Afro-American religious experience is the need to be able to say that "God is." To say "God is" is to assert *without any rationality or otherwise supportive argument* that there is a God. Because God's ontological is-ness is God's very nature, everything else exist in relation to God. God is the Being itself of all other beings: God is our reality. God's is-ness is ultimate, because God is the beginning and the end.[30] [Italics added]

Whatever the basis for the unintelligibility of Jones's Black God-concept, his solution is not predicated on any reasonably based supportive argumentation. The mere assertion that "God is" suffices as an explanation because it solely rests on Black (traditional) Christian faith. Clearly, this assertion, in lieu of an argument, is no more than a subjective response enmeshed in irrationalism. On this point, Jones uncritically accepts Black Christian commonplace beliefs as the substance of Black Theology. Consecutively, what transpires is a theology of fideism dressed in Black attire. Although it may be convenient in day-to-day African American religious encounters to simply proclaim "God is," such assertions do not adequately address the logical trap affixed to Jones's Black God-concept.

We submit that what may be "usable within the Afro-American religious experience" is far from sufficient for a systematic theological inquiry, not to mention a philosophical assessment of theological claims. Jones's Black Theology considerably departs from modern-day (critical) notions on systematic theological reflection. In stark contrast to Jones's indiscriminating position, African American theologian Dr. J. W. E. Bowen argues:

> When we come to the modern period in the construction of theology, we find the rubrics of philosophy properly utilized; and while there is due respect for the continuity of truth formerly arrived at, we find an independent position taken by all theologians. Criticism has arisen in its lower and higher forms, which insist that all facts be tested by criteria and only those allowed to pass into permanent existence capable of satisfying "the law of sufficient reason."[31]

Far from the "principle of sufficient reason," Jones ends up relying on the description of the orthodox beliefs among Black Christians for grounding his Black Theology.[32] Thus, he effectively relinquishes his role to critically engage African American Christian thought. Accordingly, the question before us becomes, Must the Black Theologian simply affirm the viewpoints of Black Christians or should the Black Theologian bring critique to bear on common-day beliefs and persistently ungrounded theological assumptions? In his preface to *The Color of God*, Jones already declared:

> The Black Theologian—let it be said—must be an iconoclast of his or her own justifications, reductions, and accommodations, less we commit the equal and opposite idolatry of White Theology. Black Theology, theological feminism, and any other liberation theology or any human ideological captivity of God's purity and freedom can be as much a distortion of God as the White God of oppression has been, rendering God less than God, creating God in the human image rather than the other way around. To make the God-concept pure is to free it up and lifted up, so that it may transcend all narrow, merely human points of view.[33]

We contend it has been confirmed that Jones is far from the mark on what he thinks is the vital role for the Black Theologian. Jones asserts that the role of iconoclast is to guard against the tendency toward anthropomorphism, although in fact, his second argument for the Black God-concept, we explained and demonstrated, is decidedly a human projection and theological construction. Clearly with the second argument (and implicitly respecting the first) the Black God-concept becomes a makeshift measure born of human considerations as pivotal to the ensuing proposal as to how we must view God.

For example, Jones is transparent about the fact that his Black God-concept remains anthropomorphic at base. He states, "All mere human attempts to speak of God are related to one's own humanness. . . . Here, because I want to talk about God's color only in relation to Black people, I discussed God's blackness and his moral character. If one were White, God would look White."[34]

Consequently, what we observe with this statement is exactly the act of "creating God in the human image rather than the other way around." Paradoxically, this is precisely what Jones warns Black Theologians against doing. Jones becomes trapped in the very dilemma that he cautions is the bane of misdirected theological thinking. Could it be that Jones's quandary is inherent in the very project of identifying the Black God-concept? Is he caught in the captivity of Christian dogma? Does offering up the Black God-concept in any way release Jones from the perils of Christian theology and its attendant dogma? The answer to these questions is manifest in Jones's commitment to the dogma of the Holy Trinity.[35]

At this juncture, it is instructive to review African American philosopher Dr. Carleton L. Lee's astute observation on the relationship between theology and dogma. Lee conveys, "[M]y over-weaning [is] to be suspicious of all theology because theology, it seems to me, tends toward dogmatism. This is one of its functions—to serve the body of dogma which any believing group regards as essential to the furtherance of its faith."[36]

In this respect, Jones unabashedly says that "faithfulness to the Holy Trinity is one motivation underlying this book; faithfulness to my human color is the other."[37] Therefore, Jones in no manner expects on departing from the classical notion of the Christian Trinitarian dogma. Subsequently, his accent on the Black God-concept in no way leaves from this (white?) tradition of Christianity as embodied in the church and its history. As to the point about this pivotal Christian tradition/dogma, Altizer's remarks are instructive.

> The dogma of the Trinity is truly the axis of all orthodox Christianity, and perhaps a refusal or reversal of that dogma is the axial center of all truly are deeply heterodox Christianity. Yet the doctrine of the Trinity was not fully evolved until the last quarter of the fourth century of the Christian era, and then only as a consequence of the most bitter dogmatic war that Christianity has ever undergone—one primarily centered on Christology—and it was the dogmatic victory of a new orthodox Christology that decisively generated and sealed the dogma of the Trinity.[38]

Jones's treatment on the Christian dogma of the Trinity is expressed in two contradictory statements. On the one hand he states, "We must conclude that whether one attempts a Christology and heavenly terms or a Christology in earthly terms, the question of how Jesus was related to God is central to any adequate understanding of them both. Especially for Black Theology, the historical reality of Jesus must be made fruitful and relevant in our minds."[39] Jones continues in his presentation of Christology. He additionally remarks,

> God's presence in Jesus Christ is not always been understood fully as to Jesus's unity with God. Understanding of that relationship has undergone a long development. The difficult debates of the ancient church about Jesus' divinity were necessary to grasp the full meaning of God's presence in Jesus and if some *rational understanding* of Jesus's unity with God was to prevail.[40] [Italics added]

On the other hand, he contradicts himself by stating that the correct understanding about Jesus vis-a-vis God virtually emerges in the early stages of Christianity. What becomes problematic centers on what Jones means by the *early Christian experience*. He indicates:

> In Black Theology, we neither separate Jesus and God and see them as apart, nor do we empty God out or subject him to Jesus Christ. . . . The proper introduction to an understanding of Black Theology's view of God's presence in Christ as Creator, Redeemer, and continuing presence in the Holy Spirit is, I contend an accurate historical understanding of the early Christian experience.[41]

Jones's contention that he has "an accurate historical understanding of the early Christian experience" is not supported by the facts of history, not to mention that this contradicts his earlier statement—namely, the idea that the Trinitarian Godhead is the product of a long struggle, on the part of the Christian church. On Altizer's account, it was not until the last quarter of the fourth century CE when this notion became the dominant view about the Trinity—as a cardinal component of Christian dogma—and this remains something that can be established on historical grounds with concrete research. In fact, the very general idea of Christian orthodoxy is the historical product of continuous theological polemics within the church.[42]

Subsequently, Jones's idea that the Trinity is part and parcel of the *early* Christian experience is factually questionable. This emerges as transparent with his first statement, this happened several decades—in fact almost three centuries—into the development of Christianity. We will not address the details of this long debate on Christian dogma.[43] What comes to light as significant, for our review, is that we can gather how Jones views the matter of Jesus's status as human and divine.

Given that this statement gives us an initial view into how Jones conceives the relationship between Jesus and God, we will now embark upon the second part of this chapter and explore the theological problem on the divinity of Jesus. We discovered in our previous chapters that a number of those who belong to the Black Theology school of thought advocated for the idea of the Black Messiah. For some the notion of the Black Messiah was literal, and for others the idea of Black Christ was figurative and symbolic. Sequentially, there were those who argue that Jesus was merely a man, while others claimed the divinity of Jesus. At this juncture in our review of his text, Jones has yet to show very little of his hand on this very provocative topic of the Black Messiah or the divinity of Jesus.

Jones consciously directed his attention in the first five chapters (of his book) without any detailed discussion of Jesus. Yet, the relative silence about Jesus was not a matter of benign neglect or the sin of omission. Jones makes this point clear in chapter 6 of his text. In this chapter, he explains why he made this conceptual distinction within the very structure of his text. The reader comes to understand why he delays extensive commentary on Jesus. Jones states,

> In discussing the God-concept, I have said very little about Jesus Christ. My emphasis has been on God, the creator. The discussion has centered on God, because we must first see God in the fullness of his being in order to see Jesus Christ's as the second person in the Godhead. This is especially true in view of the many attempts currently to reinterpret Jesus in light of contemporary religion and life. When we speak of Jesus Christ in these pages, we are not talking about a different God or some person other than the God of our discussion. To con-

ceive of Jesus Christ separately from God would be to miss the meaning and purpose of the divine advent in human history.[44]

In the next part of our chapter, we explore in what way the ramifications attendant with the host of problems adjoined to Jones's Black God-concept will ultimately have an impact on how he establishes the theological locus for Jesus's divinity and humanity. With the adoption of the Trinity formula, Jones aims at clarifying how Jesus in concrete theological terms is related to God. This is the substance of the problems associated with Christology. In light of the fact that Jones is attempting to tackle this issue from the standpoint of Black Theology, we must embark upon the subsidiary question of Black Christology.

In summary, we must return to the Christian notion of the Trinitarian God-head and the ancillary issues respecting the idea of the Holy Spirit, along with its connection to Jesus as Christ. The adjoining multitude of issues, we contend, becomes crystallized in the question: Does Major J. Jones fall into alignment with the movement for Black Christology and the quest for authenticity? In partial answer to the above question, we have the following commentary from Jones:

> Black Christology is not a mere writing of another life of Christ; it is, rather, a liberating reflection upon an interpretation of the Black religious experience. It aims to lead the believer to encounter the risen Redeemer who is the Liberator of both the oppressor and the oppressed. Black Christology fuses the "Jesus of history" together with the "Christ of faith" into a third, new man—the Black Messiah of liberation.[45]

Notably, despite Jones's effort at elaborating a distinctively Black Liberation Theology and its corresponding Black Christology, he nonetheless submits the Black Christ as "Liberator of both the oppressor and the oppressed." However, we must inquire, Why does the oppressor need liberation? Is not Black liberation precisely liberation from such oppressors? How does liberating oppressors work itself out in practical terms? Do we have in substance the rearticulation of some form of universal soteriology masquerading as Black Liberation Theology? Transparently, Jones's Black Christology is unclear and ambiguous when it comes to the practical agenda of Black liberation.

We will undertake an extended inquiry into this deliberation on Black Christology and Jones's conception of the Black Messiah shortly in the next section. For now, we should note that a considerable number of the Black Theology School axiomatically hold to the presupposition that Jesus is both human and divine. Hence, this is manifested in the direct relationship between the historical Jesus and the Jesus of faith.

Arguably this belief becomes the most salient feature of Black Christology. This unique representation of combining mutually exclusive categories—such as human characteristics with divine status—is one of the primary theological riddles of Black Christology. Now let us proceed to a more detailed analysis of how Jones captures the Black Christology viewpoint on the divinity of Jesus.

THE DIVINITY OF JESUS: A PHILOSOPHICAL ASSESSMENT

In our prior discussion, we unearthed that Jones proposed what constituted antithetical propositions respecting the very notion of the Black God-concept. Accordingly, we found that Jones conflated the distinction between the Black God-concept as divine in origin contra the idea that this concept pertained to a theological construction founded on human efforts. Additionally, we addressed the problem of conceptualizing God with respect to absolute being and how this transcendent status proved to be problematic respecting its relevance to the world and precisely the Black experience. God—as immanent being—was considered to be in the world but not of the world. Thus, how a transcendent or even immanent God would intervene into the Black struggle for liberation—which is material in substance—all amounted to residing as a matter of faith. In a nutshell, we concluded that Jones created a logical snare based upon antithetical proposals for the Black God-concept.

Pivotal to the issue of antithetical propositions was the ontological and epistemological divide separating the idea of God as absolute being with complete knowledge (omniscience), while Black human beings were constrained by their incomplete knowledge of God. This constraint led to the containment of the Black God-concept within anthropomorphism. If the Black God-concept was no more than a human creation and at the same time this concept resulted from God's self-address to Black people, then it is clear that Jones is faced with an unanswerable dilemma beyond the pale of a rational solution.

Consequently, the result was a nagging contradiction that remained unresolved. We unveiled this persistent contradiction continues on, despite Jones's attempt to embrace fideism as an explanation and solution to the problems of antithetical propositions and the unintelligibility of the God-concept. The resort to fideism meant that faith in God was the key solution—to his contradictory propositions about God's transcendence—which Jones offered as a guarantee for Black liberation. Jones's God-dependent theology directly points us toward a heavenly solution regarding earthly problems—specifically, faith in God is the path for securing Black liberation. We offer this summation as an introduction into how it provides a context for Jones's treatment of Jesus as historical person and divine entity.

We submit that Jones's treatment of Jesus is another approach to the initial problems at hand. At root, there persists the troublesome problem of the translation from an absolute being (divine entity) to the concrete particularities and material existence of the Black experience. Jones presumes that his treatment of Jesus Christ effectively ushers in a resolution to the contradiction between the absolute existence of God and the material context of human history and specifically the Black experience. This is because Jones presumes that Jesus enters human history as both divine and human.

Nevertheless, what we should not miss is the fact that this presumption is theological in substance and hence it is a theological claim on history and decisively not historical in its makeup. Though, we should note, the process of how *the belief* that Jesus became God, subsequently, is in fact a historical matter subject to review.[46] In divergence, Jones is under the impression that he is dealing with human history and offers the following recommendation:

> For the Black theologian, whatever is said about God and his relation to human beings must be related to actual human history. The whole message of Jesus was the proclamation of God, his nature, his power, and his purpose for humanity. The center of attraction was not simply Jesus as man, but the revelation of God through and by Jesus. Jesus Christ, both human and divine, was therefore representative both of God's involvement with his people and of his people in their liberation struggle. No other motive suffices. The quest for salvation must be understood as God's involvement with his people in the world, if it is to be relevant for Blacks.[47]

While we agree that the real test respecting God's existence is manifestly "his relation to human beings must be related to actual human history," the theological presumption that Jesus entered human history in such a manner—human and divine—is open to critical philosophical review. Indeed, Jones also states, "In the person and work of Jesus, God entered into human history and took upon himself the limitations and difficulties of human existence (John 1:4; Phil. 2:6–8)." This declaration does not provide a historical study; however, Jones elects to uncritically rely on biblical texts for a depiction of human history during the time of Jesus. The above statement amounts to an assertion within the framework of biblical theology.[48]

Consequently, what we have is a theological proposition respecting the fact that the person and work of Jesus is identical with God's entrance into history. Earlier we found that the question of God's entrance into history as finite material being was problematic because God as an absolute being—existing in the spiritual realm—had to undergo the specified process of transformation into the particularity of material existence with its corresponding laws of motion.

Now, we have the view that Jesus can make such a transformation because he is both human and divine. Therefore, it follows that Jesus enters human history and encounters the limitations and difficulties affixed to human existence yet remains a divine being. This statement cannot stand as historical in character. The notion that Jesus and God are one and the same is at the core of the issue, and the issue is entirely one of Christological perspective on Jesus as divine and human.[49]

Jones's reliance on biblical texts does not in any way suffice as a historical inquiry into the question of the historical Jesus. As we've seen in our earlier chapters, the conflation of Jesus of faith with the historical Jesus is a theological problem quite attendant with several Black Theologians. We uncover that Jones follows along this tradition without any acute reflection on the distinction between the historical Jesus and the Jesus of faith. Indeed, Jones goes on to say:

> There seems, however, to a been sufficient proof of the historical Jesus—in the New Testament history, his remembered teachings, records of his exceptional deeds, expressions of faith in the early church, and the comments of those who knew him in the flesh—enough to know that his life cannot be doubted. The Jesus of history ought never to be taken lightly. Without him there is no adequate example of what human life ought to be. Those who knew him then—just as those who know him now—were legion.[50]

We must caution that the proof there was a historical Jesus does not entail that the details presented in the New Testament are reliable as a historical source. In fact, critical examination of biblical texts, we have earlier found, point us in the opposite direction. Hence, this requires that we critically review Jones's above-mentioned proclamation in some detail. In that way, we can better grasp the significance of claims regarding the historical Jesus and the associated notions about his divinity.[51]

The idea of his divinity which is more in tune with theology than it is with history. This is an important distinction, we think, Jones overlooks precisely because of his prior theological commitments to the Trinitarian conception in Christian thought. Subsequently, we submit that Jones speaks more as a theologian instead of a historian that carefully weighs the details of historical reconstruction based on the relevant sources. At foundation, this is adjoined to how Jones is uncritical of biblical texts, which chiefly contain ahistorical elements rooted in myth.[52]

Be this as it may, any discussion of the historical Jesus is a question about history and not theology. In our inspection, we must be cognizant of how Jones attempts to find a resolution to his prior dualism. It could very well be that given that he understands Jesus is both historical and divine that the dualism which we previously encountered is now embodied in Jones's notion of Jesus as both historical person and divine entity.[53]

If this is the case, it follows that Jones has not resolved the problems resultant with his earlier antithetical proposals concerning the Black God-concept. Therein, rather than a resolution and solution to the problem—with the addition of Jesus as an integral part of the Trinitarian Godhead—we have the real possibility of amplifying this problem in a more convoluted fashion. Once more, we must emphasize that the question of the divinity of Jesus is a theological issue which extends beyond the boundaries affixed to rigorous historical inquiry into the idea of the historical Jesus. In contradistinction, the belief in the divinity of Jesus stands on the foundation of faith. Thus, we suggest that historical criticism is an appropriate method to employ about our analysis of Jones's proposition about the historical Jesus as divine person.[54]

Herein it becomes evident that the questions posed in our introduction and chapter 1 are most pertinent. Among them were the following inquiries: How does the New Testament depict Christ? Is there a singular or multiple depictions? Does he have divine status? Is he a deity on par with God? Additionally, we can ask, Did the earliest followers of Jesus presume that he was God? Here we are pointing to the followers of Jesus before the advent of the Christian church.[55]

How Jones approaches such questions will frame the remainder of this chapter. It is not inconsequential that Jones asserts, "The Jesus of history ought never to be taken lightly. Without him there is no adequate example of what human life ought to be. Those who knew him then—just as those who know him now—were legion." Yet, it is evident that Jones's assertion rests on a particular view—namely, that biblical texts are historical accounts that derive from direct testimony from those who knew Jesus. The theological implications of such an interpretation are significant for the relevance of biblical texts for the Black liberation movement. The supposition is that biblical texts serve as historical reference for Black liberation.[56]

Black biblical scholar Ron Liburd comments, "[T]he black community with other Christians in general harbors the notion that the Bible in its entirety constitutes absolute authority for ethical conduct; it is the 'Word of God.' With this presumption, African Americans, I argue, have placed gross restrictions on their ability to forge a truly liberation hermeneutic for our black religious community."[57]

The fact remains, however, that the writers of the New Testament and particularly the Gospels were not people who directly knew Jesus and they wrote several decades after his death. In a substantive manner, the Gospel texts consist of divergent theological claims on the life of Jesus than an accurate historical explanation. Moreover, we discover conflicting interpretations respecting the life of Jesus, which at base are differences reflecting inconsistent theological perspectives instead of historical inaccuracies relating to a biographical accounting.[58]

Now let us return to how Jones treats the Christian Trinitarian formula with detail to Black Christology. It is important to note that in Jones's formulation of this theological problem, he again relies on establishing this issue by framing it within the conventional forms of African American beliefs, specifically held by the Black church. Jones makes the following observation:

> God himself, not the Trinitarian God-concept or any other particular theory about the divine nature, is the central focus of the Black church. God is One and God is triune—these are theological givens, taken for granted in Black theology. . . . Black theology has spent little energy debating "how" the personal and holy God made his presence known in Jesus Christ. Rather, Black theological talk is about our faith that God was doing something in Christ for our redemption.[59]

Jones continues,

> Again, a rich assortment of related terms is taken for granted in the Black church: the life, death, and resurrection of Jesus; the offices of Jesus's prophet, priest, and King; and much more. But, as with our understanding of God, the person and work of Christ as the Redeemer is taken more seriously when we consider Jesus Christ not only as the Savior of souls but also as the Liberator of his people. We are chiefly interested in Christology in this narrower sense: what is God attempting to achieve for Black people through Jesus Christ?[60]

With this declaration, Jones effectively identifies the position of Black Theology with the ideas predominant in the Black church. Again, we find that Jones neglects to provide critical evaluation of conventional African American Christian thinking and beliefs, especially those found in the Black church. For Jones, Black Theology—as systematic theology—is no more than formal repetition of how the Black church usually understands the life, death, and resurrection of Jesus. On Jones's view, the function of Black Theology once more becomes no more than apologetic in character.

Although Jones previously claimed, "The difficult debates of the ancient church about Jesus' divinity were necessary to grasp the full meaning of God's presence in Jesus and if some *rational understanding* of Jesus's unity with God was to prevail"[61] [italics added]. The fact remains that political differences centered on theology were crucial to what became the orthodox position. Instead of *rational understanding* on the matter, we have the descent into fideism. Hence, Jones's position on the life, death, and resurrection of Jesus saddles Black Theology and pushes it into the camp of supernaturalism, superstition, and irrationalism instead of historical investigation.[62] Such a posture stands in stark contrast to Black philosopher/theologian Dr. Roy D. Morrison II. Morrison unabashedly states:

> For epistemological reasons, I do not believe in any form of supernaturalism. I do not think that it matters very much whether Jesus arose from the grave. The only thing that really matters is what he did or did not do after he allegedly arose from the dead. I do not believe there is any such thing as a holy spirit. I regard that as an ancient superstition, beyond that disbelief, however, I have some solid knowledge. I know that no spirit of any kind has supernaturally intervened to remove America's racial caste system under which Christianity has so impotently and comfortably prostituted itself.[63]

In Morrison's view, the belief in the resurrection of Jesus and the Christian Trinitarian dogma about a holy spirit are forms of supernaturalism. He rejects such notions because as forms of supernaturalism, they fail the test of epistemological scrutiny. Although Morrison is a proponent of Black Theology, he does not advocate the Christian variety of which Jones prominently holds a place of distinction. While Morrison rejects the Trinity, Jones fully embraces it as an integral part of Black Theology. In contradistinction, Morrison casts aside faith as a nonviable epistemological option and sequentially Jones believes that faith is an overriding principle grounding Black Christian theology as belief system. This is why Jones openly supports the notion of the Trinity despite its unintelligibility and lack of rational support.

ON THE UNITY OF GOD AND JESUS AND FAITH IN THE HOLY TRINITY

We uncover that Jones offers contradictory statements about the issue of the Trinity. For example, Jones says the Black church is focused on "God himself, not the Trinitarian God-concept" and yet, he also argues that the Black church believes "God is one and God is triune." What we have with these two statements is a contradiction in terms. Clearly, if God is triune, then it stands that the Trinitarian God-concept is most applicable in this instance. The Trinitarian formula is operative whenever it is said that God is triune.

What remains absent with the Black church's belief that "God is triune" is not the Trinitarian dogma, more precisely it is the adjoining sustained argumentation for the belief. This is because the Black church's notion of the triune God functions as "theological given" rather than the *conclusion* resulting from the process of theological reasoning. The triune God is axiomatic and stands without rational demonstration. Jones admits as much but fails to understand how this axiomatic status of a triune God is conceptually adjoined to the formal notion of the Trinitarian God-concept.

Jones also makes transparent that the work of Jesus as Christ involves not only the role of Savior of souls but also the Liberator of his people. Thus, the relation of the secular and sacred are merged into a singular theological perspective on the role of Jesus. Nevertheless, what constituted this liberation process, who required the act of liberation as well as identifying those engaged in the role of oppressor—in this historical/biblical moment—are not concretely identified by Jones.[64]

Despite the lack of specification of historical details, Jones, however, makes the leap to conclude that Jesus in turn is analogously connected with Black people as an agent for God. Therefore, Black people can have faith in the fact that Jesus will be on the side of the African American liberation struggle. Yet, it becomes most apparent that Jones—due to his conflation of secular and sacred—enters on the path of salvation on the assumption that material liberation can be achieved. Jones posits:

> For the Black Christian, the great love a personal responsive holy God for human beings becomes real only to the degree that by the power of such a love, God overcomes human beings and incites them to corresponding love. This way, the people secure forgiveness of their sins. Through his passion, Christ becomes important to the Black Christian because he reconciles human beings to God and wins from God for the people an immunity from punishment and guilt, a guilt derived from our not having been what we were meant to be. With these two achievements—love and release—Jesus Christ delivers human beings from the powers of this evil world and opens the door to a new life.[65]

First, it is starkly apparent that Jones's proclamation—"Through his passion, Christ becomes important to the Black Christian because he reconciles human beings to God and wins from God for the people an immunity from punishment and guilt; a guilt derived from our not having been what we were meant to be"—gives sanction to the very notion that Frederick Douglass disclaimed. "A contest had in fact been going on in my mind for a long time, between the clear consciousness of right and the plausible makeshift of theology and superstition. The one held me an abject slave—a prisoner for life, punished for some transgressions in which I had no lot or part." God's punishment for original sin and the adjoining guilt complex plays no part in Douglass's self-identity as a person seeking liberation.

Moreover, what becomes clear in the above is that Jones does not offer a tangible analysis of how political, social, economic, and constituent worldly (material) conditions should be addressed. This is especially since the secular concern with Black liberation, for Jones, amounts to God's atonement for sin. Of course, we can see that this theologically speaks to the character of salvation as grounded on atonement for sins. Up till now, Jones says very little about concrete realities and social institutions with respect to liberation. All we get is the vacuous summary statement, "Jesus Christ delivers human beings from the powers of this evil world and opens the door to a new life." Yet, Jones points out:

> Jesus is "real" for Black people because what he does for them is "real." They look to him for eternal inheritance, to be sure; that is a Christological given of traditional theology. But they put particular stress on the social, political, and this-worldly spiritual liberation that Jesus is affecting among them now. On this account, Moyd reasons that the balanced reception of Jesus as the Savior from sin and guilt and the Liberator from oppression recommends Black Theology as offering a balanced Christology.[66]

It is apparent that Jones is content to describe how Black Christians and the Black church view Christology that allows for the belief in Jesus Christ as an integral part of their day-to-day secular encounters. What Jones has not demonstrated is how Jesus managed to make an impact on those secular concerns and particularly the Black liberation struggle. Biblical examples, for Jones, suffice as evidence for how God through Jesus Christ enters the Black experience. What is most glaring in Jones's theological perspective—about Black Christians and the Black church—is that systematic theological presentations must be consistent with the beliefs fostered by the Black religious experience. This results in the virtual identification of Jones's Black (systematic) Theology with his description of the Black religious experience.

Within the framework of his systematic theology, Jones provides what he designates as "An Afro-American Interpretation of God's Human Experience in Jesus Christ." In this discussion, Jones makes the bold proclamation that God is subject to change. He tenders,

> To identify God with Jesus Christ is not the same as equating the Father with Jesus. Neither is it to suggest that God was at one personally with Jesus Christ but with no one else. Rather, it is to say that something took place radically, in the very root of the personhood of God, when God expressed himself in the person and work of Jesus Christ. . . . How could God have undergone a birth like ours, the divine coming forth a human being, and still remain the same?[67]

There is a lot to unpack relating to the above proclamation. If previously Jones made the mistake of making God unintelligible by fostering antithetical propositions, now we encounter another group of nonintelligible propositions. For example, why is it that "to identify God with Jesus Christ is not the same as equating the Father with Jesus." For Jones clearly maintains in the same instance that "God expressed himself in the person and work of Jesus Christ." This identification was to such an extent that Jones even raises the question, "How could God have undergone a birth like ours, the divine coming forth a human being, and still remain the same?"

Quite obviously, if it was God who was born—and not someone else—it follows then God must be both father and son. What Jones seeks to do is to provide theological justification for mythic thinking. In this respect, we must acknowledge what Susan Ackerman significantly notes, "While . . . the term 'myth' is used in New Testament literature with negative connotations, much in the New Testament is in fact mythic in character."[68] Thus, we find instead of critically addressing the mythology that underlies the incarnation myth, Jones resorts to the fact that this is an integral part of Black Christian thinking. Consequently, in Jones's mind, when mythic biblical elements support Christian dogma, they suitably function as the appropriate subject matter for Black Christology.[69]

The unintelligibility of Jones's proposition is further compounded when he states, "when we say that he [God] truly became a human person by the assumption of human mind and soul, flesh and blood, we also believe that God still remain truly God in nature and person."[70] It follows that if one could accept such propositions, then one must abandon rational thought. Hence logic goes out the window and the embrace of faith emerges as mandatory. Where before faith was the stopgap measure for the reconciliation of antithetical propositions about the Black God-concept, at this juncture, now faith becomes the only way to accept Jones's notions about the Holy Trinity.

This is because Jones advocates the reconciliation of mutually exclusive categories such as God being born human and yet "still remain truly God in nature and person." If God's true nature is absolute being, then being born with flesh and blood is not only logically a muddled statement but materially impossible. God cannot exist as a natural being and at the same time remain supernatural, possess an absolute mind and simultaneously be saddled with the capacity of the human mind. Alas, Jones has not progressed any further along the lines of clarity and intelligibility. Rather he falls deeper into the abyss of irrationalism in his efforts to bring Jesus Christ into the picture as historical (human) person with the status of deity.

We think that Jones is quite aware of the fact that he's embarked on the road of unintelligibility. The contradiction between God as absolute being and the question of change as material in character continues as a mounting question. To assert that God changes—even through the person of Jesus Christ—is to acknowledge that change is principally a process, and this proves to be a formidable theological problem for a supposed absolute being. Thus, to solve this dilemma, Jones makes a distinction between external causes and self-change to explain how change is related to God through Jesus Christ. Jones posits, "[T]he response of relationship and holiness of the Father with the Son and the Holy Spirit is not subject to changes wrought upon God by external events. This does not, however, preclude God's freedom and ability to determine upon self-change."[71]

In brief, Jones's explanation for God's capacity for change hangs on the distinction between the impact of external events and the idea of self-change. Nevertheless, if God is an absolute being, which includes perfection, then the need for change logically becomes nonexistent. So, therefore, we ask, Why would God find it necessary to think in terms of changing from his status of absolute perfection? Jones's response to this question is quite intriguing yet perplexing. For God to even consider self-change, there must be a need for transformation in the very composition of absolute being and the attendant characteristics that shape such an entity. Jones explains:

> The content of God's consciousness is not so fixed that it cannot—if God willed it—be constantly changing to include future events, as yet unknown in their non-being. We believe human actions to be truly free, says that whereas God's knowledge of the past this total and absolute, *God's knowledge of the future events is not yet complete, particularly so far as acts of human freedom are concern*. The perfection of divine omniscience, then, must be construed to be God's always perfect increasing knowledge taking in, with the passage of time, all mobile reality as it expands. Not to know as real and sure what it is, as yet, neither sure nor real, it is not imperfection; to know the unreal and the unsure as uncertain and still forming is to know perfectly whatever is to be known.[72]
> [Italics added]

There are several points of consideration that we must address. Earlier in this chapter we found that Jones argued that human beings could not know God in his complete absolute being. Therefore, we inquire, How does Jones know about these features regarding God's consciousness and precisely that it is not fixed? Is this simply a faith claim? If it is the case, it follows that Jones's explanation is not subject to public scrutiny. Jones's belief is no more than his own projected guess based on faith. The assumption that God has fixed consciousness as absolute being has equal warrant from the Christian standpoint. What is before us is not differences in knowledge but matters of faith.

Next, we find that very idea of divine omniscience—God as all-knowing—is open to qualification and limitations, although Jones had previously warned us that any limitations put on God were inconsistent with Black Theology and Black Christian thinking. This was brought to our attention earlier with the following remarks:

> Most Black Christians have agreed with Western theology that limitations on the essential attributes of God are derogatory and unthinkable. Popular Black religious thought has generally agreed with the dominant formal theology on this point: If God is not the Almighty, then he is not truly God. In Black religious belief as with most Christian theology, Black or White, God's infinity includes much more than absolute power, *knowledge*, and goodness; omnipresence for example, is "all, everything." In summary, a popular idea of God affirms the divine nature as Perfect Being, "all," "everything," and all-inclusive attribution of perfection implying the co-inherence of all other attributes.[73]
> [Italics added]

Clearly, in the above statement, knowledge is included as an all-inclusive attribution of perfection, which we can only find in God. Now we discover that Jones is actually contradicting himself by saying that God's omniscience is qualified by human freedom and the future of human action. Again, Jones is trapped in the snare of trying to explain real human action and its material reality in view of the presumption of an absolute (all-knowing) God. For if Jesus is human, then human action and material reality confines what Jesus—as human being—can do. Consequently, God/Jesus as human being is restricted in his absolute being. This, of course, is the logical contradiction that emerges from the combined status of human and divine.

As stated previously, the social world and its material makeup is inherently bound by the process of the materialist dialectical laws of motion, change, and development. Jones is compelled to explain how such change can take place in social reality and at the same time affirm the existence of an absolute being which logically implies an unchanging (permanent) character, although the world of material reality—unlike the presupposition about God—is in constant change and therefore knowledge of the world must be dynamic and ever-changing in character. The idea of absolute knowledge apart from change and transformative features is something that is not constituent with the world of nature or society. On the presumption that God is transhistorical and transcendent, it follows that knowledge is absolute and unchanging.

Jones is forced to reconcile the absolute nature of Jesus/God's knowledge with the fact that human knowledge is always bound within the framework of the process of cognition instead of the static circumstances of being as such. This fact emerges from the human condition, and it is the only way that human beings can comprehend what it means to be knowledgeable. Could it be that Jones is returning to anthropomorphism with his qualification respecting the omniscient (all-knowing) attribute of God? This is most translucent with his statement, "The perfection of divine omniscience, then, must be construed to be God's always perfect increasing knowledge taking in, with the passage of time, all mobile reality as it expands. Not to know as real and sure what it is, as yet, neither sure nor real, it is not imperfection; to know the unreal and the unsure as uncertain and still forming is to know perfectly whatever is to be known."[74]

This clearly indicates that Jones's conclusion amounts to no more than wordplay and muddled logic. For not knowing is not reducible to knowledge, rather not knowing is ignorance. To say that God—even as Jesus—is ignorant yet omniscient is a contradiction in terms of which there is no real resolution or solution. What remains is unintelligibility, which is based on nonsensical propositions. Therefore, Morrison rejects such propositions on epistemological grounds. With Jones's analysis, we have fideism masquerading as a treatise on God's knowledge.

No amount of faith can be a substitute for real knowledge. This is the cardinal problem Jones confronts when inserting Jesus into the pantheon of the Holy Trinity. What Jones wants us to believe is predicated on supernaturalism and irrationalism. Penultimately, we are back at the question of the relevancy issue. In this instance, how relevant is it for Jesus to act as a deity on behalf of Black people? The issue of Jesus assuming human and divine forms and thus entering human history is one part of the theological puzzle.

The other part of the relevancy puzzle is in explaining how Jesus — who enters history two-thousand years ago — remains relevant for Black people today. Jones is adamant on this point, and he argues it is the task of Black Christology to make Jesus Christ and Christianity's relevance front and center. In unequivocal terms, Jones states:

> For the Black community of faith, the results of any adequate Black Christological formulations must present Jesus in the light of the Black religious experience. No conclusions will suffice that do not describe who Jesus was, what he did, and what he said as the direct expression and implementation of God in action, doing "divine things humanly," among Black people in on their behalf. We are concerned here with whether it can be said of Jesus' life, teachings, and death that God was experiencing in Jesus what it was like to be human the same way we Black humans have experience that condition.[75]

Since the demonstration of Jesus's relevancy to Black people is the cardinal problem facing Black Christology, it follows that Jones would conclude in no uncertain terms, "We are concerned here with whether it can be said of Jesus' life, teachings, and death that God was experiencing in Jesus what it was like to be human the same way we Black humans have experience that condition." We think it would be a reasonable inference to say that Jones's notion of Black Messiah is more a matter of symbolism than a literal identity. The relevance of the symbolic relationship of Jesus to the Black experience then becomes for Jones the overriding issue in Black Christology.

Unlike Albert Cleage who insists that Jesus is literally Black and therefore we can point to ancient Black history as an indicator for Black people today, Jones decides on convincing us about the relevancy of the Holy Trinity. Nonetheless, we submit, the Trinity formulation obstructs really knowing Jesus as human being. In a nutshell, humans are not affixed to any absolute characteristics.

It is mandatory, Jones thinks, that Black Christology embrace that Jesus was both human and divine. Consequently, the antithetical propositions, which we earlier uncovered, remained without resolution; unfortunately they are not resolved with the conception of the holy Trinity and the historical entry of God as Jesus Christ. Jones in advancing the dogma of the Holy Trinity only complicated and confused what was already in unintelligible proposition.

Specifically, we have an absolute being — God — who changes from an absolute existence (of the spiritual sort) to finite status of material character, in the person of Jesus. This proposal, Jesus as both human and God, ultimately remains a mystery and accordingly outside our rational comprehension. It is not a historical matter of empirical bearing, instead it is ultimately a theological issue of faith.

We penultimately conclude this chapter with an appropriate citation from Jones that amplifies this point. Jones elaborates on the mystery of God's incarnation as Jesus. Without any critical assessment of this mythic characterization, Jones accepts Jesus's incarnation as God in the flesh. He proclaims:

> The mystery of Jesus Christ is revealed in the incarnation of God, the incarnation of eternal, original, unchangeable being brought into this sphere of temporal, it came, transitory existence, where we humans live in must die. Because in Jesus Christ the eternal presence of God among human beings is encountered, the salvation of the world is found in him. . . . In God's act of becoming human, something happened to him and something also happen to his creation.[76]

Given that Jesus's entry into human history is a matter of God's incarnation, then all this transforms into a mystery which extends beyond the reach of rational deliberation and demonstration. Since any attempt to affirm the belief that Jesus Christ was the incarnation of God is humanly unknowable, then it continues as an ongoing mystery. We are only left with faith as the final summit of appeal. Unfortunately, faith is not knowledge, it persists as the foundational commitment to blind belief. In other words, Jones's Black Christology is ultimately anchored in fideism rather than any form of intelligible epistemology. What should not be lost on the reader is that Jones's conception of Black Christology and the ancillary embrace of fideism does not exhaust the scope of Black Theology, not to mention send us on the road toward the philosophy of religion, where philosophy of religion is directed toward a critical inspection of theological claims.

Dr. Roy D. Morrison II, concerning matters about knowledge, reason, and faith, provides a significant alternative. Dr. Morrison's critical perspective stands as our summary philosophical critique on Major J. Jones's treatment of Jesus as deity and the Trinitarian dogma—constituting the Black Godhead. Now for Morrison's concluding remark:

> For epistemological reasons, I do not believe in any form of supernaturalism. I do not think that it matters very much whether Jesus arose from the grave. The only thing that really matters is what he did or did not do after he allegedly arose from the dead. I do not believe there is any such thing as a holy spirit. I regard that as an ancient superstition, beyond that disbelief, however, I have some solid knowledge. I know that no spirit of any kind has supernaturally intervened to remove America's racial caste system under which Christianity has so impotently and comfortably prostituted itself.[77]

NOTES

1. Major J. Jones, *The Color of God: The Concept of God in Afro-American Thought* (Macon, GA: Mercer University Press, 1987). Major J. Jones was born in Rome, Georgia (1918). He received his BA from Clark College (Atlanta), earned his BD from Gammon Theological Seminary, his STM from Oberlin College, and his Doctor of Theology from Boston University in 1957, where he was a classmate of Martin Luther King Jr. Jones served as clergy to several churches as well as holding several academic appointments at higher educational institutions. He was president of Gammon Theological Seminary from 1967 to 1985. Jones died January 22, 1993, in Atlanta, Georgia. Anthony Pinn provides a substantive biographical sketch of Dr. Jones in John R. Shook, ed., *The Bloomsbury Encyclopedia of Philosophers in America: From 1600 to the Present* (New York: Bloomsbury Publishing, 2016), 512–14.

2. Major J. Jones, *The Color of God*, viii.

3. Edwin Redkey, *Respect Black: The Speeches and Writings of Henry McNeal Turner* (New York: Arno Press, 1971), 176–77.

4. Andre E. Johnson, "God Is a Negro: The (Rhetorical) Black Theology of Bishop Henry McNeal Turner," *Black Theology—An International Journal* 13(1) (April 2015): 29–40. Mungo Ponton, *The Life and Times of Henry McNeal Turner* (Atlanta: A. B. Caldwell, 1917). Stephen Ward Angell, *Bishop Henry McNeal Turner and African-American Religion in the South* (Knoxville: University of Tennessee Press, 1992).

5. Consult *Voice of Missions* 7 (October 7, 1899): 2. Elijah Muhammed and the Nation of Islam later popularized Turner's idea about "this white man's heaven and the black man's hell."

6. John Dittmer, "Education of Henry McNeal Turner," in Leon Litwack and August Meier, eds., *Black Leaders of the Nineteenth Century* (Urbana: University of Illinois Press, 1988), 260. Also consult, Andre E. Johnson, *The Forgotten Prophet: Bishop Henry McNeal Turner and the African American Prophetic Tradition* (Lanham, MD: Lexington Books, 2012).

7. Major J. Jones, *The Color of God*, 32.

8. Major J. Jones, *The Color of God* 33.

9. George D. Kelsey, "The Nature of the Christian Ethic," *The Journal of Religious Thought* 2(1) (January 1945): 16.

10. Major J. Jones, *The Color of God*, 63.

11. George D. Kelsey, "The Churches and Freedom," *Journal of Religious Thought* (1956): 17.

12. Major J. Jones, *The Color of God: The Concept of God in Afro-American Thought*, 23.

13. Major J. Jones, *The Color of God*, 46.

14. Major J. Jones argues, "God addresses a man in his maleness and a woman in her femaleness; God becomes 'at one' with her or him. God has a personal word in relation to who he or she is at the level of their gender. Because God is 'everything in every one,' we need not belabor the question as to whether God is male or female" (*The Color of God*, 33).

15. Major J. Jones, *The Color of God*, 38.

16. Major J. Jones, *The Color of God*, 38.

17. Thomas Nelson Baker, "Ideals," Part 2, *Alexander's Magazine* (October 1906): 40.

18. Baker, "Ideals," Part 2, 40. Thomas Nelson Baker was the first Black person to receive a PhD in philosophy from an institution in the United States, Yale University in 1903. For a substantial treatment of Baker both with respect to his biography and philosophical perspective on Black aesthetics, consult George Yancey, "On the Power of Black Aesthetic Ideals: Thomas Nelson Baker as Preacher and Philosopher," *The A.M.E. Church Review* 117 (384) (October–December 2001): 50–67.

19. Thomas Nelson Baker, *The Ethical Significance on the Connection between Mind and Body* (Doctoral Dissertation: Yale University, 1903): 4. Baker's dissertation is copyrighted by Thomas Nelson Baker III, 1996.

20. Major J. Jones, *The Color of God*, 73.

21. Major J. Jones, *The Color of God*, 73.

22. James T. Murphy, *Defining Salvation in the Context of Black Theology* (Bloomington, IN: Xlibris Corp, 2012).

23. "I regard the principal of functional ultimacy to be the acknowledged norm of humanism and the unacknowledged standard for theism. The principle is another way of stating Protagoras' dictum, 'Man is the measure of all things.' I interpret this to mean that man can only act as if he were ultimate in the realm of values or history or both. It may well be the case that, ontologically speaking, he is not ultimate, but nonetheless it is necessary for him to choose, evaluate, regardless of the character of the rest of reality. This situation of man does not change, whether God exists or not. My own approaching universalizes this principal and interprets it as the consequence of man's freedom" (*Is God a White Racist? A Preamble to Black Theology* [Boston: Beacon Press, 1998], 243).

24. Cleage argues, "The fantasies of Christianity are very important to black people and they prove one thing—that theology is important to black people. We will never get free as black people until we change our theology. We got to forget the fantastic mythological element and we got to forget the idea that Jesus on Calvary freed black people. We were not saved by anything Jesus did on Calvary. If Jesus freed white people on Calvary that's for them to figure out. But certainly black people were not freed on Calvary, because we're still not yet free" ("Black Religion and Black Revolution" Item ID: daams 01023030 Box 1, Folder 23 Black Religion Symposium, 1972, Department of African and African American Studies records, 1966–1981).

25. Frederick Douglass, *The Life and Times of Frederick Douglass* (New York: Pathway Press, 1941), 225.

26. Cited in Reginald Davis, *Frederick Douglass: A Precursor of Liberation Theology* (Macon, GA: Mercer University Press, 2005), 73.

27. Davis, *Frederick Douglass*. William R. Jones, "Religious Humanism: Its Problems and Prospects in Black Religion and Culture," *Journal of Interdenominational Theological Center* 7(2) (1980): 169–86.

28. Major J. Jones, *The Color of God*, 26.

29. Van A. Harvey, *A Handbook of Theological Terms* (New York: Simon & Schuster, 1992), 99.

30. Major J. Jones, *The Color of God*, 46.

31. J. W. E. Bowen, "A Psychological Principle in Revelation," *The Methodist Review* 7(5) (September 1891): 736–37.

32. On the principle of sufficient reason, consult Alexander R. Pruss, *The Principle of Sufficient Reason: A Reassessment* (Cambridge: Cambridge University Press, 2006), and Gordon Belot, "The Principle of Sufficient Reason," *Journal of Philosophy* 97 (2001): 55–74.

33. Major J. Jones, *The Color of God*, x.

34. Major J. Jones, *The Color of God*, 38.

35. Thomas Altizer, *The Apocalyptic Trinity* (New York: Palgrave Macmillan, 2012).

36. Carleton L. Lee, "Black Religion and Black Revolution" Item ID: 01023143 daams Box 1, Folder 23 Black Religion Symposium, 1972 Department of African and African American Studies records, 1966–1981. On April 8, 1972, Duke University Black Studies under the direction of Prof. Walter W. Burford sponsored a symposium, "Black Religion and Black Revolution." The online record of this symposium is by courtesy of Duke University Libraries—Rubenstein Library—Guide to the Department of African and African American Studies records, 1966–1981. http://library.duke.edu/rubenstein/findingaids/uaafro/ Duke University Archives, David M. Rubenstein Rare Book & Manuscript Library, Duke University.

37. Major J. Jones, *The Color of God*, x.

38. Altizer, *The Apocalyptic Trinity*, 9.

39. Major J. Jones, *The Color of God*, 76.

40. Major J. Jones, *The Color of God*, 76. We note given Jones's commitment to fideism it is quite ironical that he concludes, "The difficult debates of the ancient church

about Jesus' divinity were necessary to grasp the full meaning of God's presence in Jesus and if some *rational understanding* of Jesus's unity with God was to prevail." What prevailed was not *"rational understanding"* rather to the victor gains the spoils. Consult Philip Jenkins, *Jesus Wars* (New York: HarperCollins Publishers, 2010), and Geza Vermes, *Christian Beginnings: From Nazareth to Nicaea* (New Haven, CT: Yale University Press, 2014).

41. Major J. Jones, *The Color of God*, 80–81.
42. Bart D. Ehrman, *The Orthodox Corruption of Scripture, The Effect of Early Christological Controversies on the Text of the New Testament* (New York: Oxford University Press, 1993). Helmut Koester, *Ancient Christian Gospels: Their History and Development* (Philadelphia: Trinity Press International, 1990). Peter J. Gomes, *The Scandalous Gospel of Jesus: What's So Good about the Good News* (New York: HarperCollins, 2007).
43. Bart D. Ehrman, *How Jesus Became God: The Exaltation of a Jewish Preacher from Galilee* (New York: HarperCollins, 2014). Helmut Köester, *From Jesus to the Gospels: Interpreting the New Testament in Its Context* (Minneapolis: Fortress Press, 2007).
44. Major J. Jones, *The Color of God*, 75.
45. Major J. Jones, *The Color of God*, 88.
46. For a historical treatment of the belief in Jesus's divinity, consult Ehrman, *How Jesus Became God*.
47. Major J. Jones, *The Color of God*, 76.
48. Major J. Jones, *The Color of God*, 76. For a critical treatment of the Gospel texts, consult Koester, *From Jesus to the Gospels*.
49. E. P. Sanders, *The Historical Figure of Jesus* (New York: Penguin Publishing Group, 1994).
50. Major J. Jones, *The Color of God*, 78.
51. Bart Ehrman, *Misquoting Jesus: The Story behind Who Changed the Bible and Why* (New York: HarperOne, 2005).
52. Lee Martin McDonald and James A. Sanders, eds., *The Canon Debate* (Grand Rapids, MI: Baker Academic, 2002). Burton Mack, *Who Wrote the New Testament?: The Making of the Christian Myth* (San Francisco: HarperCollins, 1995).
53. Ehrman, *How Jesus Became God*. Geza Vermes, *The Changing Faces of Jesus* (New York: Penguin Compass, 2002).
54. Christian Hartlich, "Historical-Critical Method: In Its Application to Statements Concerning Events in the Holy Scriptures," *Journal of Historical Criticism* 2(2) (1995): 122–39. Vermes, *Christian Beginnings*.
55. Bart D. Ehrman, *Lost Christianities: The Battles for Scripture and the Faiths We Never Knew* (New York: Oxford University Press, 2003). Vermes, *The Changing Faces of Jesus*. Jenkins, *Jesus Wars* . Burton L. Mack, *The Lost Gospel: The Book of Q and Christian Origins* (New York: HarperCollins, 1993).
56. Robert M. Price, *The Incredible Shrinking Son of Man: How Reliable Is the Gospel Tradition?* (Amherst, NY: Prometheus Books, 2003).
57. Ron Liburd, "Like a House on Sand: African American Biblical Hermeneutics in Perspective," *The Journal of the International Theological Center* 22(1) (1995): 71–91.
58. Mack, *The Lost Gospel*. Michael L. White, *Scripting Jesus: The Gospels in Rewrite* (New York: HarperOne, 2010). Ehrman, *The Orthodox Corruption of Scripture*.
59. Major J. Jones, *The Color of God*, 82–83.
60. Major J. Jones, *The Color of God*, 83.
61. Major J. Jones, *The Color of God*, 76.
62. Robert L. Calhoun and George A. Lindbeck (eds.), *Scripture, Creed, Theology: Lectures on the History of Christian Doctrine in the First Centuries* (Eugene, OR: Cascade Books, 2011). Gerd Lüdemann, *The Resurrection of Christ: A Historical Inquiry* (Amherst, NY: Prometheus Books, 2004). Helmut Koester, "Writings and the Spirit: Authority and Politics in Ancient Christianity," *Harvard Theological Review* 84(4) (1991).
63. Roy D. Morrison II, "Farewell to Wesley Theological Seminary: Reflections on Education, Theodicy, Justice and Human Fulfillment," Oxnam Chapel (April 21, 1993),

8. Document in possession of the author. Also read, Gerald Sigal, *The Resurrection Fantasy: Reinventing Jesus* (Bloomington, IN: Xlibris, 2012).

64. On this matter of a concrete analysis, consult Mary Marshall, *The Portrayals of the Pharisees in the Gospels and Acts* (Gottingen: Vandenhoeck & Ruprecht, 2015), and Joseph C. Webber Jr., "Jesus' Opponents in the Gospel of Mark," *Journal of Bible and Religion* 34(3) (July 1966).

65. Major J. Jones, *The Color of God*, 83.

66. Major J. Jones, *The Color of God*, 87. Jones refers to Olin P. Moyd, *Redemption in Black Theology* (Valley Forge, PA: Judson Press, 1974), 142.

67. Major J. Jones, *The Color of God*, 92.

68. Consult Susan Ackerman, "Myth," in Bruce M. Metzger and Michael D. Coogan, *The Oxford Companion to the Bible* (New York: Oxford University Press, 1993), 541. Robert M. Price, *Deconstructing Jesus* (Amherst, NY: Prometheus Books, 2000). Rudolf Karl Bultmann, *Jesus Christ and Mythology* (New York: Scribner, 1958).

69. Mack, *Who Wrote the New Testament?*. John M. Allegro, *Dead Sea Scrolls and the Christian Myth* (Amherst, NY: Prometheus Books, 1992). Hyam Maccoby, *The Mythmaker: Paul and the Invention of Christianity* (New York: Harper & Row, 1986).

70. Major J. Jones, *The Color of God*, 92.

71. Major J. Jones, *The Color of God*, 95.

72. Major J. Jones, *The Color of God*, 95.

73. Major J. Jones, *The Color of God*, 63.

74. Major J. Jones, *The Color of God*, 95.

75. Major J. Jones, *The Color of God*, 93.

76. Major J. Jones, *The Color of God*, 94.

77. Morrison, "Farewell to Wesley Theological Seminary," 8. Document in possession of the author.

Bibliography

Ackerman, Susan. "Myth." In *The Oxford Companion to the Bible*, edited by Bruce M. Metzger and Michael D. Coogan, 541. New York: Oxford University Press, 1993.
Allegro, John M. *Dead Sea Scrolls and the Christian Myth*. Amherst, NY: Prometheus Books, 1992.
Anatolios, Khaled. *Retrieving Nicaea: The Development and Meaning of Trinitarian Doctrine*. Grand Rapids, MI: Baker Academic, 2011.
Anderson, Victor. *Beyond Ontological Blackness: An Essay on African American Religious and Cultural Criticism*. New York: Continuum, 1995.
———. "The Mimesis of Salvation and Dissimilitude in the Scandalous Gospel of Jesus." In *Christology and Whiteness: What Would Jesus Do?*, edited by George Yancy, 196–211. New York: Routledge, 2012.
Andrews, Dale P. *Practical Theology for Black Churches: Bridging Black Theology and African American Folk Religion*. Louisville, KY: Westminster John Knox Press, 2002.
Angell, Stephen Ward. *Bishop Henry McNeal Turner and African-American Religion in the South*. Knoxville: University of Tennessee Press, 1992.
Appleyard, David. "Ethiopian Christianity." In *The Blackwell Companion to Eastern Christianity*, edited by Ken Parry, 117–36. Malden, MA: Wiley-Blackwell, 2010.
Ashanin, Charles B. "Afro-American Christianity: Challenge and Significance." *The Journal of Religious Thought* 16, no. 2 (Summer–Autumn 1959): 109–119.
Austin, Algernon. *Achieving Blackness: Race, Black Nationalism, and Afrocentrism in the Twentieth Century*. New York: NYU Press, 2006.
Avalos, Hector. *Fighting Words: The Origins of Religious Violence*. Amherst, NY: Prometheus Books, 2005.
———. *Slavery, Abolitionism, and the Ethics of Biblical Scholarship*. Sheffield, UK: Sheffield Phoenix Press, 2013.
———. *The Bad Jesus: The Ethics of New Testament Ethics*. Sheffield, UK: Sheffield Phoenix Press, 2015.
Ayedze, Kossi Adiavu. "Tertullian, Cyprian and Augustine on Patience." PhD dissertation, Princeton University, 2000.
Ayres, Lewis. *Nicaea and Its Legacy: An Approach to Fourth-Century Trinitarian Theology*, Vol. 13. New York: Oxford University Press, 2004.
Baker, Thomas Nelson. "Ideals, Part 2." *Alexander's Magazine* (1906): 37–42.
Banner, William A. "The Transmission of Our Religious Heritage: Christian Ideas of Human Equality and Social Justice." *The Journal of Religious Thought* 4, no. 2 (1947).
———. "Christian Ethics and the Moral Life." *The Journal of Religious Thought* 14 (1956): 7–16.
———. "Truth and Service." *The Journal of Religious Thought* 35, no. 2 (Fall 1978).
Barr, James. "Modern Biblical Criticism." In *The Oxford Companion to the Bible*, edited by Bruce M. Metzger and Michael D. Coogan, 319. New York: Oxford University Press, 1993.
Bascio, Patrick. *The Failure of White Theology: A Black Theological Perspective*. New York: P. Lang, 1994.
Bauer, Walter. *Orthodoxy and Heresy in Earliest Christianity*. Philadelphia: Fortress Press, 1971.
Beasley-Murray, George Raymond. *Baptism in the New Testament*. Grand Rapids, MI: William B. Eerdmans Publishing Co., 1973.

Becker, W. H. "Black Power in Christological Perspective." *Religion in Life* 38, no. 3 (1969): 404–14.

Beil, Gail K. "James Leonard Farmer: Texas' First African American PhD." *East Texas Historical Journal* 36, no. 1 (March 1998): 18–25.

Ben-Jochannan, Yosef. *African Origins of the "Major" Western Religions*. New York: Alkebu-lan Book Associates, 1970.

Bernal, Martin. *Black Athena: The Fabrication of Ancient Greece*, Vol. 1. New Brunswick, NJ: Rutgers University Press, 1987.

Blum, Edward J., and Paul Harvey. *The Color of Christ: The Son of God & the Saga of Race in America*. Chapel Hill: The University of North Carolina Press, 2012.

Bohache, Thomas. *Christology from the Margins*. London: SCM Press, 2008.

Borg, Marcus. *Jesus in Contemporary Scholarship*. Harrisburg, PA: Trinity Press International, 1994.

Bousset, Wilhelm. *On the Significance of the Personality of Jesus for Belief*. Cited in Walter P. Weaver, The Historical Jesus in the Twentieth Century, 1900–1950. Harrisburg, PA: Trinity Press International, 1999.

Bowen, J. W. E. "A Psychological Principle in Revelation." *The Methodist Review* 7, no. 5 (September 1891): 727–39.

Braxton, Ronnell. *No Longer Slaves: Galatians and African American Experience*. Collegeville, MN: The Liturgical Press, 2002.

Brown, Michael Joseph. *Blackening of the Bible: The Aims of African American Biblical Scholarship*. Harrisburg, PA: Trinity Press International, 2004.

Brown, Raymond E. *An Introduction to New Testament Christology*. New York: Paulist Press, 1994.

Bruce, F. F. *The New Testament Documents: Are They Reliable?* Grand Rapids, MI: Wm. B. Eerdmans Publishing Company, 1981.

Bruce, Calvin E., and William R. Jones. *Theology II: Essays on the Formation and Outreach of Contemporary Black Theology*. Lewisburg, PA: Bucknell University Press, 1978.

Brunner, Emil. *The Christian Doctrine of the Church, Faith, and the Consummation: Dogmatics, Vol. III*. Eugene, OR: Wipf and Stock Publishers, 2014.

Bultmann, Rudolf Karl. *Jesus Christ and Mythology*. New York: Scribner, 1958.

———. *Kerygma and Myth*. New York: Harper and Row, 1961.

———. *New Testament Mythology and Other Basic Writings*. Minneapolis: Fortress Press, 1989.

Bunnin, Nicholas, and Jiyuan Yu. *The Blackwell Dictionary of Western Philosophy*. Malden, MA: Blackwell Publishing, 2004.

Calhoun, Robert L., and George A. Lindbeck (eds.). *Scripture, Creed, Theology: Lectures on the History of Christian Doctrine in the First Centuries*. Eugene, OR: Cascade Books, 2011.

Camacho, Daniel José. "Why James H. Cone's Liberation Theology Matters More Than Ever." *Religious Dispatches* (June 2, 2015). religiondispatches.org/why-james-h-cones-liberation-theology-matters-more-than-ever/.

Campbell, Ted A. *The Gospel in Christian Traditions*. New York: Oxford University Press, 2009.

Cannon, Katie Geneva. "Racism and Economics: The Perspective of Oliver C. Cox." In *Womanist Theological Ethics*, edited by Katie Geneva Cannon, Emilie Maureen Townes, and Angela D. Sims, 3–20. Louisville, KY: Westminster John Knox Press, 2011.

Cannon, Katie, Emilie Townes, and Angela Sims. *Womanist Theological Ethics: A Reader*. Louisville, KY: Westminster: John Knox Press, 2011.

Carrier, Richard. *On the Historicity of Jesus: Why We Might Have Reason for Doubt*. Sheffield, UK: Sheffield Phoenix Press, 2014.

Cavin, Robert Greg. "Is There Sufficient Evidence to Establish the Resurrection of Jesus?" In *The Empty Tomb: Jesus beyond the Grave*, edited by Robert M. Price and Jeffery Jay Lowder, 19–42. Amherst, NY: Prometheus Books, 2005.

Chabot, Sean. "Framing, Transnational Diffusion, and African American Intellectuals in the Land of Gandhi." In *Popular Intellectuals and Social Movements*, edited by Michiel Baud and Rosanne Rutten, 19–40. New York: Cambridge University Press, 2004.

Chakravarty, Amiya. "A Tribute from a Friend." *The Journal of Religious Thought* 35, no. 2 (Fall–Winter 1978–1979): 58–60.

Chapman, Mark L. "Defending the Faith: Nascent Black Theology as an Apology for Christianity." *The Journal of the Interdenominational Theological Center* 20, no. 1–2 (Fall–Spring 1992–1993): 116–38.

———. *Christianity on Trial: African-American Religious Thought before and after Black Power*. Eugene, OR: Wipf and Stock Publishers, 2006.

Chike, Chigor. "Black Christology for the Twenty-First Century." *Black Theology* 8, no. 3 (April 2015): 357–78.

Chilton, Bruce. *Rabbi Jesus: An Intimate Biography*. New York: Doubleday, 2000.

———. "Christianity: What It Is and How It Defines Western Civilization." In *Religious Foundations of Western Civilization: Judaism, Christianity, and Islam*, edited by Jacob Neusner. Nashville: Abingdon Press, 2006.

Cleage, Albert B., Jr. *The Black Messiah*. New York: Sheed and Ward, 1968.

———. "Black Religion and Black Revolution," Item ID. Duke University Archives, David M. Rubenstein Rare Book & Manuscript, 1972. http://library.duke.edu/rubenstein/findingaids/uaafro/.

———. *Black Christian Nationalism: New Directions for the Black Church*. New York: Morrow, 1972.

Coggins, Richard. "Samaritan." In *The Oxford Companion to the Bible*, edited by Bruce M. Metzger and Michael D. Coogan, 671–73. New York: Oxford University Press, 1993.

Colston, Freddie C. *Dr. Benjamin E. Mays Speaks: Representative Speeches of a Great American Orator*. Lanham, MD: University Press of America, 2002.

Cone, James H. "Christianity and Black Power." In *Is Anybody Listening to Black America?*, edited by C. Eric Lincoln, 3–9. New York: The Seabury Press, 1968.

———. *Black Theology and Black Power*. New York: The Seabury Press, 1969.

———. "Black Theology and the Black Church: Where Do We Go from Here?" In *Afro-American Religious History: A Documentary Witness*, edited by Milton C. Sernett, 567–79. Durham, NC: Duke University Press, 1985.

———. "Biblical Revelation and Social Existence." In *Black Theology: A Documentary History*, edited by James H. Cone and Gayraud Wilmore, 159–76. Ossining, NY: Orbis Books, 1993.

Cone, James H., and Gayraud S. Wilmore. *Black Theology: A Documentary History, 1966–1979*. Ossining, NY: Orbis Books, 1993.

Conroy-Krutz, Emily. *Christian Imperialism: Converting the World in the Early American Republic*. Ithaca, NY: Cornell University Press, 2015.

Copeland, M. Shawn. "The (Black) Jesus of Detroit: Reflections on Black Power and the (White) American Christ." In *Christology and Whiteness: What Would Jesus Do?*, edited by George Yancy, 180–95. New York: Routledge, 2012.

Copher, Charles B. "Three Thousand Years of Biblical Interpretation with Reference to Black Peoples." In *African American Religious Studies: An Interdisciplinary Anthology*, edited by Gayraud S. Wilmore. Durham, NC: Duke University Press, 1989.

———. *Black Biblical Studies: Biblical and Theological Issues on the Black Presence in the Bible*. Chicago: Black Light Fellowship, 1993.

Davies, Everett F. S. "Negro Protest Movement: The Religious Way." *The Journal of Religious Thought* 24, no. 2 (1967): 13–25.

Davis, Reginald F. "African-American Interpretation of Scripture." *The Journal of Religious Thought* 57 (2005): 93–105.

———. *Frederick Douglass: A Precursor of Liberation Theology*. Macon, GA: Mercer University Press, 2005.

Dickerson, Dennis C. "African American Religious Intellectuals and the Theological Foundations of the Civil Rights Movement, 1930–55." *Church History* 74 (2005): 217–35.

———. "William Stuart Nelson and the Interfaith Origins of the Civil Rights Movement." In *Churches, Blackness, and Contested Multiculturalism*, edited by R. Drew Smith, William Ackah, and Anthony G. Reddie, 57–72. New York: Palgrave Macmillan, 2014.

Diop, Cheikh Anta. *The African Origin of Civilization: Myth or Reality*. Chicago: Lawrence Hill Books, 1974.

Dittmer, John. "Education of Henry McNeal Turner." In *Black Leaders of the Nineteenth Century*, edited by Leon Litwack and August Meier, 253–74. Urbana: University of Illinois Press, 1988.

Doherty, Earl. *Jesus: Neither God Nor Man—The Case for a Mythical Jesus*. Ottawa: Age of Reason Publications, 2009.

Douglas, Kelly Brown. "Teaching Womanist Theology: A Case Study." *Feminist Studies in Religion* 8 (Fall 1992): 133–38.

———. *The Black Christ*. Ossining, NY: Orbis Books, 1994.

Douglass, Frederick. *The Life and Times of Frederick Douglass*. New York: Pathway Press, 1941.

———. "Slaveholding Religion and the Christianity of Christ." In *Afro-American Religious History: A Documentary Witness*, edited by Milton C. Sernett, 102–11. Durham, NC: Duke University Press, 1985.

Drake, St. Clair. *Black Folk: Here and There, Vol. 2*. Los Angeles, CA: Center for Afro-American Studies University of California, 1990.

Drews, Arthur. *The Christ Myth*. Amherst, NY: Prometheus Books, 1998.

Dunn, Geoffrey, and Wendy Mayer. *Christians Shaping Identity from the Roman Empire to Byzantium*. Leiden: Brill, 2015.

Earl, Riggins R. *Toward a Black Christian Ethic: A Study of Alexander Crummell and Albert Cleage*. Nashville: Vanderbilt University, 1978.

Echols, Alice. "Nothing Distant about It: Women's Liberation and Sixties Radicalism." In *The Sixties: From Memory to History*, edited by David Farber, 149–74. Chapel Hill: UNC Press Books, 2012.

Ehrman, Bart D. *The Orthodox Corruption of Scripture, The Effect of Early Christological Controversies on the Text of the New Testament*. New York: Oxford University Press, 1993.

———. *Lost Christianities: The Battles for Scripture and the Faiths We Never Knew*. New York: Oxford University Press, 2003.

———. *Misquoting Jesus: The Story behind Who Changed the Bible and Why*. New York: HarperOne, 2005.

———. *Jesus, Interrupted: Revealing the Hidden Contradictions in the Bible and Why We Don't Know about Them*. New York: HarperOne, 2009.

———. *Forged: Writing in the Name of God—Why the Bible's Authors Are Not Who We Think They Are*. New York: HarperCollins, 2011.

———. *How Jesus Became God: The Exaltation of a Jewish Preacher from Galilee*. New York: HarperCollins, 2014.

Eichelberger, William L. "A Mytho-Historical Approach to the Black Messiah." *The Journal of Religious Thought* 33, no. 1 (April 1976): 63–74.

Eller, David. "Love Your Enemy, Kill Your Enemy: Crusades, Inquisitions, and Centuries of Christian Violence." In *Christianity Is Not Great*, edited by John W. Loftus, 25–46. Amherst, NY: Prometheus Books, 2014.

Ellingsen, Mark. *African Christian Mothers and Fathers*. Eugene, OR: Cascade Books, 2015.

Elliott-Binns, Leonard. *The Beginnings of Western Christendom*. Cambridge, UK: James Clark & Co., 2002.

Erskine, Noel Leo. *Black Theology and Pedagogy*. New York: Palgrave Macmillan, 2008.

Evans, Craig A. "The Misplaced Jesus: Interpreting Jesus in a Judaic Context." In *The Missing Jesus: Rabbinic Judaism and the New Testament*, edited by Bruce Chilton, Craig A. Evans, and Jacob Neusner, 11–40. Leiden: Brill Academic Publishers, 2002.
Evans, James. *We Have Been Believers: An African-American Systematic Theology*. Minneapolis: Fortress Press, 2012.
Farmer, J. Leonard. "Review." *The Journal of Religious Thought* 1, no. 2 (Spring–Summer 1944): 164.
———. *John and Jesus in Their Day and Ours: Social Studies in the Gospels*. New York: Psycho–Medical Library, Incorporated, 1956.
Farmer, James L. Jr. *Lay Bare the Heart: An Autobiography of the Civil Rights Movement*. Fort Worth: Texas Christian University Press, 1998.
Federici, Silvia. "The God That Never Failed: The Origins and Crises of Western Civilization." In *Enduring Western Civilization: The Construction of the Concept of Western Civilization and Its Others*, edited by Silvia Federici, 63–89. Westport, CT: Praeger Publishers, 1995.
Felder, Cain Hope. "Beyond Eurocentric Biblical Interpretation: Reshaping Racial and Cultural Lenses in Christian Education." *The Journal of the Interdenominational Theological Center* 40, no. 1 (2014): 5–20.
Ferguson, Stephen C., II. "Teaching Hurricane Katrina: Understanding Divine Racism and Theodicy." *APA Newsletter on Philosophy and the Black Experience* (2007): 1–5.
———. "King as Philosopher: An Examination of the Influences of Hegelian Dialectics on King's Political Thought and Practice." In *The Liberatory Thought of Martin Luther King Jr.: Critical Essays on the Philosopher King*, edited by Robert E. Birt, 87–108. Lanham, MD: Lexington Books, 2012.
Feuerbach, Ludwig. *The Essence of Christianity*. New York: Barnes & Noble Books, 2004.
Fitzgerald, David. *Nailed: Ten Christian Myths That Show Jesus Never Existed at All*. Morrisville, NC: Lulu Press, 2010.
———. *Jesus: Mything in Action, Vol . II*. Seattle: Amazon/CreateSpace, 2017.
Foner, Philip S. "From Slavery to Socialism: George Washington Woodbey, Black Socialist Preacher." In *Socialism and Christianity in Early 20th Century America*, edited by Jacob Henry Dorn, 65–92. Westport, CT: Greenwood: Press, 1998.
Fredriksen, Paula. *From Jesus to Christ: The Origins of the New Testament Images of Jesus*. New Haven, CT: Yale University Press, 1988.
Gallagher, Buell. "Conscience and Caste: Racism in the Light of the Christian Ethic." *Journal of Religious Thought* 2, no. 1 (1945): 20–29.
Gathercole, Simon. *The Preexistent Son: Recovering the Christologies of Mark, Matthew, and Luke*. Grand Rapids, MI: William B. Eerdmans Publishing Co., 2006.
Glancy, Jennifer A. *Slavery in Early Christianity*. New York: Oxford University Press, 2002.
Goldenberg, David M. *The Curse of Ham: Race and Slavery in Early Judaism, Christianity, and Islam*. Princeton, NJ: Princeton University Press, 2003.
Gomes, Peter J. *The Scandalous Gospel of Jesus: What's So Good about the Good News*. New York: Good News, 2007.
Grant, Carl A., and Shelby J. Grant. *The Moment: Barack Obama, Jeremiah Wright, and the Firestorm at Trinity United Church of Christ*. New York: Rowman & Littlefield, 2013.
Grant, Jacquelyn. "Womanist Theology: Black Women's Experience as a Source for Doing Theology, with Special Reference to Christology." *The Journal of the Interdenominational Theological Center* 13 (1986): 195–212.
———. *White Women's Christ and Black Women's Jesus: Feminist Christology and Womanist Response*. Scholars Press, 1989.
Grayling, A. C. *The God Argument: The Case against Religion and for Humanism*. London: Bloomsbury Publishing, 2014.
Green, William Scott. "What Do We Mean by 'Religion' and 'Western Civilization.'" In *Religious Foundations of Western Civilization: Judaism, Christianity, and Islam*, edited by Jacob Neusner. Nashville: Abingdon Press, 2006.

Greenberg, Gary. *The Bible Myth: The African Origins of the Jewish People.* New York: Kensington, 2003.
Gwynn, David M. "The Council of Chalcedon and the Definition of Christian Tradition." In *Chalcedon in Context: Church Councils, 400–700*, edited by Richard Price and Mary Whitby. New York: Oxford University Press, 2004.
———. *Christianity in the Later Roman Empire: A Sourcebook.* New York: Bloomsbury Academic, 2015.
Hagerty, Barbara Bradley. "A Closer Look at Black Liberation Theology." *NPR*, n.d. https://www.npr.org/templates/story/story.php.
Hammond, Joseph. *Heterodox Christologies.* Morrisville, NC: Lulu Press, 2016.
Hannaford, Ivan. *Race: The History of an Idea in the West.* Washington, DC: Woodrow Wilson Center Press, 1996.
Harding, Vincent. "Black Power and the American Christ." *Christian Century* (January 4, 1967): 10–13.
———. "The Religion of Black Power." In *Black Theology*, edited by James H. Cone and Gayraud Wilmore, 40–65. Ossining, NY: Orbis Books, 1993.
Harrill, James Albert. *Slaves in the New Testament: Literary, Social, and Moral Dimensions.* Minneapolis: Fortress Press, 2010.
Hart, William David. "Jesus, Whiteness, and the Disinherited." In *Christology and Whiteness*, edited by George Yancy, 156–68. New York: Routledge, 2012.
Hartlich, Christian. "Historical-Critical Method: In Its Application to Statements Concerning Events in the Holy Scriptures." *Journal of Historical Criticism* 2, no. 2 (1995): 122–39.
Hartog, Paul A. *Orthodoxy and Heresy in Early Christian Contexts: Reconsidering the Bauer Thesis.* Eugene, OR: Pickwick Publications, 2015.
Harvey, Paul. *Through the Storm, Through the Night: A History of African American Christianity.* Lanham, MD: Rowman & Littlefield, 2011.
Harvey, Van A. *A Handbook of Theological Terms.* New York: Simon & Schuster, 1992.
———. *The Historian and the Believer: The Morality of Historical Knowledge and Christian Belief.* Urbana: University of Illinois Press, 1996.
Hawkins, John. *The Third Troublesome Voyage Made with the Jesus of Lubec, 1567–1568.* Madison: Wisconsin Historical Society, 2003.
Hayes, Diana. "Christology in African American Theology." In *The Oxford Handbook of African American Theology*, edited by Katie G. Cannon and Anthony B. Pinn, 153–63. New York: Oxford University Press, 2014.
Hegel, George W. F. *Lectures on the Philosophy of Religion.* Translated by E. B. Speirs, Vol. 3. London: Kegan Paul, 1895.
Hildebrand, Reginald F. "Howard Thurman: Teacher of Teachers, Leader of Leaders, and Preacher of Preachers." *The News & Observer* 11 (February 14, 2007). http://www.unc.edu/depts/honors/docs/Food%20-%20Hildebrand.pdf.
Hill, Charles Leander. *The Evangel in Ebony.* Boston: Meador Publishing Company, 1960.
Hill, Markeva G. *Womanism against Socially Constructed Matriarchal Images.* New York: Palgrave Macmillan, 2012.
Hitchcock, James. *The History of the Catholic Church: From the Apostolic Age to the Third Millennium.* San Francisco: Ignatius Press, 2012.
Hoffheimer, Michael H. "Race and Law in Hegel's Philosophy of Religion." In *Race and Racism in Modern Philosophy*, edited by Andrew Valls, 194–216. Ithaca, NY: Cornell University Press, 2005.
Hoffmann, R. Joseph. *Jesus Outside of the Gospels.* Amherst, NY: Prometheus Books, 1986.
Hollingworth, Miles. *Saint Augustine of Hippo: An Intellectual Biography.* New York: Oxford University Press, 2013.
Homolka, Walter. *Jewish Jesus Research and Its Challenge to Christology Today.* Leiden: Brill, 2016.

Bibliography

Hood, Robert E. *Must God Remain Greek: Afro-Cultures and God-Talk*. Minneapolis: Fortress Press, 1990.

———. *Begrimed and Black: Christian Traditions on Blacks and Blackness*. Minneapolis: Fortress Press, 1994.

Hopkins, Dwight N. *Down, Up, and Over: Slave Religion and Black Theology*. Minneapolis: Fortress Press, 2000.

———. *Introducing Black Theology of Liberation*. Ossining, NY: Orbis Books, 2014.

Hostettler, Nick. *Eurocentrism: A Marxian Critical Realist Critique*. New York: Routledge, 2012.

Jackson, John G. *Man, God and Civilization*. New York: Citadel Press, 1972.

———. *Pagan Origins of the Christ Myth*. Austin: American Atheist Press, 1991.

———. *Christianity before Christ*. Austin: American Atheist Press, 2002.

Jeffers, James S. *The Greco-Roman World of the New Testament Era*. Downers Grove, IL: Inter Varsity Press, 2009.

Jenkins, Philip. *Jesus Wars*. New York: HarperCollins Publishers, 2010.

Jennings, Willie James. *The Christian Imagination: Theology and the Origins of Race*. New Haven, CT: Yale University Press, 2010.

Johnson, Andre E. *The Forgotten Prophet: Bishop Henry McNeal Turner and the African American Prophetic Tradition*. Lanham, MD: Lexington: Books, 2012.

———. "God Is a Negro: The (Rhetorical) Black Theology of Bishop Henry McNeal Turner." *Black Theology—An International Journal* 13, no. 1 (April 2015): 29–40.

Johnson, Joseph A., Jr. "The Need for a Black Christian Theology." *The Journal of Interdenominational Theological Center* 2, no. 1 (1974): 19–29.

———. "Jesus, The Liberator." In *Black Theology: A Documentary History, Volume One, 1966–1979*, edited by James H. Cone and Gayraud S. Wilmore, 193–203. Ossining, NY: Orbis Books, 1993.

Jones, Amos, Jr. *Paul's Message of Freedom: What Does It Mean to the Black Church?* Valley Forge, PA: Judson Press, 1984.

Jones, Major J. *The Color of God: The Concept of God in Afro-American Thought*. Macon, GA: Mercer, 1987.

Jones, Robert P. *The End of White Christian America*. New York: Simon & Schuster, 2016.

Jones, William R. "Theodicy and Methodology in Black Theology: A Critique of Washington, Cone and Cleage." *The Harvard Theological Review* 64, no. 4 (1971): 541–57.

———. "Towards an Interim Assessment of Black Theology." *The Christian Century* 89 (May 1972): 513–17.

———. "Religious Humanism: Its Problems and Prospects in Black Religion and Culture." *Journal of Interdenominational Theological Center* 7, no. 2 (1980): 169–86.

———. "Liberation Strategies in Black Theology: Mao, Martin, or Malcolm?" In Leonard Harris, ed., *Philosophy Born of Struggle, Anthology of Afro-American Philosophy from 1917*. Dubuque, IA: Kendall Hunt Publishing, 1983.

———. *Is God a White Racist? A Preamble to Black Theology*. Boston: Beacon Press, 1998.

Kärkkäinen, Veli-Matti. *Christology: A Global Introduction*. Grand Rapids, MI: Baker Academic, 2003.

Karveit, Magnar. *The Origin of the Samaritans*. Leiden: Brill, 2009.

Keita, Maghan. *Race and the Writing of History: Riddling the Sphinx*. New York: Oxford University Press, 2000.

Kelsey, George. "The Nature of the Christian Ethic." *The Journal of Religious Thought* 2, no. 1 (January 1945): 7–19.

———. *Racism: The Special Problem for Christianity*. Nashville: Christian Life Commission. SBC, 1964.

———. *Racism and the Christian Understanding of Man*. New York: Charles Scribner's Sons, 1965.

———. "The Racist Search for Self." *The Journal of Religious Ethics* 6, no. 1 (1978): 240–56.

———. "The Churches and Freedom." *The Journal of Religious Thought* 14, no. 1 (n.d.): 1956–57.

Kelsey, Harry. *John Hawkins: Queen Elizabeth's Slave Trader*. New Haven, CT: Yale University Press, 2003.
Kemp, Arthur. *AWAKENING: The Rise of Western Civilization*. Burlington, VT: Ostara Publications, 2009.
King, Martin Luther, Jr. *Strength to Love*. Philadelphia: Fortress Press, 1981.
Köester, Helmut. *Ancient Christian Gospels: Their History and Development*. Philadelphia: Trinity Press International, 1990.
———. "Writings and the Spirit: Authority and Politics in Ancient Christianity." *Harvard Theological Review* 84, no. 4 (1991): 353–72.
———. *From Jesus to the Gospels: Interpreting the New Testament in Its Context*. Minneapolis: Fortress Press, 2007.
Köstenberger, Andreas J. and Michael J. Kruger. *The Heresy of Orthodoxy*. Wheaton, IL: Crossway, 2010.
Krentz, Edgar. *The Historical-Critical Method*. Eugene, OR: Wipf and Stock, 2002.
Lapin, Hayim. "The Law of Moses and the Jews: Rabbis, Ethnic Marking, and Romanization." In *Jews, Christians, and the Roman Empire*, edited by Natalie B. Dohrmann and Annette Yoshiko Reed, 79–92. Philadelphia: University of Pennsylvania Press, 2013.
Lee, Carlton L. "'Black Religion and Black Revolution' Item ID: 01023143 Daams." Duke University Archives, David M. Rubenstein Rare Book & Manuscript, 1972. http://library.duke.edu/rubenstein/findingaids/uaafro/.
Lee, Daniel B. "The Great Racial Commission: Religion and the Construction of White America." In *Race, Nation, Religion in the Americas*, edited by Henry Goldschmidt and Elizabeth McAlister, 85–110. New York: Oxford University Press, 2004.
Liburd, Ron. "Like a House on Sand: African American Biblical Hermeneutics in Perspective." *The Journal of the Interdenominational Theological Center* 22, no. 1 (1995): 71–91.
Livingstone, David. *The Dying God: The Hidden History of Western Civilization*. Lincoln, NE: The Writers Club, 2002.
Logan, Rayford W. *Howard University: The First Hundred Years, 1867–1967*. New York: NYU Press, 1969.
———. "Reminiscences." *The Journal of Religious Thought* 35, no. 2 (Fall 1978): 61–62.
Lüdemann, Gerd. *The Great Deception: And What Jesus Really Said and Did*. Amherst, NY: Prometheus Books, 1999.
———. *The Resurrection of Christ: A Historical Inquiry*. Amherst, NY: Prometheus Books, 2004.
Maccoby, Hyam. *Jesus the Pharisee*. London: SCM Press, 2003.
Mack, Burton. *The Lost Gospel: The Book of Q and Christian Origins*. New York: HarperCollins, 1993.
———. *Who Wrote the New Testament?: The Making of the Christian Myth*. San Francisco: HarperCollins, 1995.
MacMullen, Ramsay. *Christianity and Paganism in the Fourth to Eighth Centuries*. New Haven, CT: Yale University Press, 1997.
Marbury, Herbert Robinson. *Pillars of Cloud and Fire: The Politics of Exodus in African American Biblical Interpretation*. New York: NYU Press, 2015.
Marcion of Sinope. *The Gospel of the Lord*. New York: AMS Press, 1980.
Martin, Michael. *Atheism: A Philosophical Justification*. Philadelphia: Temple University Press, 1990.
———. "The Resurrection as Initially Improbable." In *The Empty Tomb: Jesus beyond the Grave*, edited by Robert M. Price and Jeffery Jay Lowder. Amherst, NY: Prometheus Books, 2005.
Mays, Benjamin E. "Of One Blood: Scripture and Science Make No Race Description." *Presbyterian Life* 5 (February 1955): 7–8, 29.
———. "The New Social Order When Integrated." *Religious Education* 58, no. 2 (March 1963): 155–60.
Mazrui, Ali. *Ancient Greece in African Political Thought*. Nairobi: Afropress, Ltd., 1967.

McClendon, John H., III. "On the Nature of Whiteness and the Ontology of Race: Toward a Dialectical Materialist Analysis." In *What White Looks Like: African-American Philosophers on the Whiteness Question*, edited by George Yancy, 211–26. New York: Routledge, 2004.
———. "Act Your Age and Not Your Color: Blackness as Material Conditions, Presumptive Context, and Social Category." In *White on White, Black on Black*, edited by George Yancy, 275–96. Lanham, MD: Rowman & Littlefield, 2005.
———. "Dr. Richard Ishmael McKinney: Historical Summation on the Life of a Pioneering African American Philosopher." *American Philosophical Association Newsletter on Philosophy and the Black Experience* (2006): 1–4.
———. "Black/Blackness: Philosophical Considerations." In *Encyclopedia of the African Diaspora: Origins, Experiences, and Culture*, edited by Carol Boyce Davies, 198–203. Santa Barbara, CA: ABC-CLIO, 2008.
———. "Is Our Belief That Martin Luther King Jr. Is a Black Philosopher Justified?" In *The Liberatory Thought of Martin Luther King Jr.: Critical Essays on the Philosopher King*, edited by Robert E. Birt, 17–42. Lanham, MD: Lexington Books, 2012.
———. *Philosophy of Religion and the African American Experience: Conversations with My Christian Friends*. Leiden: Brill Academic Publishers, 2017.
McCoskey, Denise Eileen. *Race: Antiquity and Its Legacy*. New York: I. B. Tauris, 2012.
McDonald, Lee Martin, and James A. Sanders, eds. *The Canon Debate*. Grand Rapids, MI: Baker Academic, 2002.
McIntyre, John. *Shape of Christology: Studies in the Doctrine of the Person of Christ*. Edinburgh: T&T Clark, 1998.
Mcintyre, Moni. "The Black Church and Whiteness: Looking for Jesus in Strange Places." In *Christology and Whiteness*, edited by George Yancy, 75–83. New York: Routledge, 2012.
Mckenzie, John L. *The Dictionary of the Bible*. New York: Simon & Schuster, 1995.
McKinney, Richard I. "Reflections on the Concept of 'Black Theology.'" *The Journal of Religious Thought* 26, no. 2 (1969): 10–14.
———. "The Black Church: Its Development and Present Impact." *Harvard Theological Review* 64, no. 4 (October 1971): 452–81.
———. "Ethics of Dissent." *The Journal of Religious Thought* 29, no. 2 (1972): 68–79.
Meggitt, Justin. "Popular Mythology of the Early Empire and the Multiplicity of Jesus Traditions." In *Sources of the Jesus Tradition: Separating History from Myth*, edited by R. Joseph Hoffmann, 55–82. Amherst, NY: Prometheus Books, 2010.
Meinardus, Otto Friedrich August. *Two Thousand Years of Coptic Christianity*. New York: The American University Press, 2002.
Metzger, Bruce. *The Canon of the New Testament*. Oxford: Clarendon Press, 1987.
Milwood, Robinson A. *European Christianity and the African Slave Trade: A Black Hermeneutical Study*. Bloomington, IN: AuthorHouse, 2007.
———. *Western European and British Barbarity, and Savagery, and Brutality in the Transatlantic Slave Trade: A Critical Study*. Bloomington, IN: Xlibris Corporation, 2013.
———. *White Christianity Is Fraudulent*. Bloomington, IN: Author House, 2015.
Mitchell, Henry H. "Black Power and the Christian Church." *Foundations: A Baptist Journal of History and Theology* 11 (April–July 1968): 99–109.
Mofokeng, Takatso. *The Crucified among the Crossbearers: Towards a Black Christology*. Kampen: J. H. Kok, 1983.
Morgan, Joan. "Teaching the Young Keeps Him Young: 90 Year Old Dr. Richard McKinney of Morgan State Still Going Strong." In *Black Issues in Higher Education* (August 22, 1996): 42.
Morris, Calvin S. *Reverdy C. Ransom: Black Advocate of the Social Gospel*. Lanham, MD: University Press of America, 1990.
Morrison, Roy D., II. "Black Enlightenment: The Issues of Pluralism, Priorities and Empirical Correlation." *Journal of the American Academy of Religion* 46, no. 2 (1978): 217–40.

———. "The Emergence of Black Theology in America." *The A.M.E. Zion Quarterly Review* 94, no. 3 (1982): 2–17.

———. "Farewell to Wesley Theological Seminary: Reflections on Education, Theodicy, Justice and Human Fulfillment." Oxnam Chapel (April 21, 1993).

Munford, Clarence J. *Race and Civilization: Rebirth of Black Centrality*. Trenton, NJ: Africa World Press, 2001.

Murdoch, D. M. *Who Was Jesus?: Fingerprints of the Christ*. Seattle: Stellar House Publishing, 2011.

———. *Did Moses Exist?: The Myth of the Israelite Lawgiver*. Seattle: Stellar House Publishing, 2014.

Murphy, James T., Jr. *Defining Salvation in the Context of Black Theology*. Bloomington, IN: Xlibris Corporation, 2012.

Nelson, Blanche Wright. "A Tribute to My Husband." *The Journal of Religious Thought* 35, no. 2 (1978).

Nelson, William Stuart. "Religion and Racial Tension in America Today." *The Journal of Religious Thought* 2, no. 2 (1945): 164–78.

———. *The Christian Way in Race Relations*. New York: Harper and Brothers, 1948.

———. *Bases of World Understanding, An Inquiry into the Means of Resolving Racial, Religious, Class, and National Misapprehensions and Conflicts*. Calcutta: Calcutta University, 1949.

———. "Satyagraha: Gandhian Principles of Non-Violent Non-Cooperation." *The Journal of Religious Thought* 15, no. 1 (1957): 15–24.

Neusner, Jacob. *Religious Foundations of Western Civilization: Judaism, Christianity, and Islam*. Nashville: Abingdon: Press, 2006.

Nicolson, Adam. *God's Secretaries: The Making of the King James Bible*. New York: HarperCollins, 2005.

Olela, Henry. *From Ancient Africa to Ancient Greece: An Introduction to the History of Philosophy*. Atlanta: Select Publications Corp., 1981.

O'Neal, Brittany L. *Apologia for Black Liberation: The Concept of God in James H. Cone's Black Liberation Theology and William R. Jones' Humanocentric Theism*. Doctoral dissertation, Michigan State University, 2015.

Osborn, Eric. *Tertullian, First Theologian of the West*. New York: Cambridge University Press, 1997.

Papandrea, James. *The Earliest Christologies: Five Images of Christ in the Postapostolic Age*. Downers Grove, IL: Inter Varsity Press, 2016.

Parry, Ken. *The Blackwell Companion to Eastern Christianity*. Malden, MA: Wiley-Blackwell, 2010.

Perkinson, James W. *White Theology: Outing Supremacy in Modernity*. New York: Palgrave Macmillan, 2004.

Pinn, Anthony. "Looking like Me, Jesus Images, Christology, and the Limitations of Theological Blackness." In *Christology and Whiteness*, edited by George Yancy, 169–79. New York: Routledge, 2012.

———. "Major J. Jones." In *The Bloomsbury Encyclopedia of Philosophers in America: From 1600 to the Present*. New York: Bloomsbury Publishing, 2016.

Pojman, Louis P. *Philosophy of Religion: An Anthology*. Belmont, CA: Wadsworth, 2003.

Ponton, Mungo. *The Life and Times of Henry McNeal Turner*. Atlanta: A. B. Caldwell, 1917.

Prater, Eugene G. "Daniel Payne—Bishop Payne of African Methodism." *The Journal of Religious Thought* 15, no. 1 (1957): 59–70.

Price, Robert M. *Deconstructing Jesus*. Amherst, NY: Prometheus Books, 2000.

———. *The Incredible Shrinking Son of Man: How Reliable Is the Gospel Tradition?* Amherst, NY: Prometheus Books, 2003.

Rabow, Jerry. *50 Jewish Messiahs: The Untold Life Stories of 50 Jewish Messiahs since Jesus and How They Changed the Jewish, Christian, and Muslim Worlds*. Lynbrook: Gefen Books, 2002.

Reardon, JoHannah. "The Nicene and Apostles' Creeds: A Close Look at These Two Creeds Helps Define What Christians Believe." 2015. http://www.christianitytoday.com/biblestudies/articles/.
Redkey, Edwin S., ed. *Respect Black: The Writings and Speeches of Henry McNeal Turner.* New York: Arno Press/New York Times, 1971.
Robert, Dana L. *Christian Mission: How Christianity Became a World Religion.* Malden, MA: Wiley-Blackwell, 2009.
Roberts, J. Deotis. "Black Consciousness in Theological Perspective." In *The Black Experience in Religion*, edited by C. Eric Lincoln, 99–110. Garden City, NY: Anchor Books, 1974.
———. "Black Theological Ethics: A Bibliographical Essay." *The Journal of Religious Ethics* 3, no. 1 (1975): 69–109.
———. "Moral Suasion as Nonviolent Direct Action: The Legacy of William Stuart Nelson." *The Journal of Religious Thought* 35, no. 2 (Fall–Winter 1978–1979): 29–43.
———. *Black Theology in Dialogue.* Philadelphia: Westminster Press, 1987.
Robertson, John M. *Christianity and Mythology.* London: Watts, 1910.
Robinson, John A. T. *Honest to God.* Philadelphia: Westminster Press, 1963.
Rodriquez, Junius P. "Introduction: Slavery in Human History." In *The Historical Encyclopedia of World Slavery*, Vol. 1., edited by Junius P. Rodriquez, xiii–xxiii. Santa Barbara, CA: ABC-CLIO, 1997.
Russell, Norman. *The Doctrine of Deification in the Greek Patristic Tradition.* New York: Oxford University Press, 2004.
Salibi, Kamal S. *Who Was Jesus?: Conspiracy in Jerusalem.* London: Tauris Parke Paperbacks, 2007.
Sanders, Cheryl. "Christian Ethics and Theology in Womanist Perspective." *Journal of Feminist Studies in Religion* 59, no. 2 (1989): 83–112.
Sanders, E. P. *The Historical Figure of Jesus.* New York: Penguin Publishing Group, 1994.
Schweitzer, Albert, and William Montgomery (Trans.). *The Quest of the Historical Jesus: A Critical Study of Its Progress from Reimarus to Wrede.* New York: Macmillan, 1968.
Schweitzer, Don. *Contemporary Christologies.* Minneapolis: Fortress Press, 2010.
Sigal, Gerald. *The Resurrection Fantasy: Reinventing Jesus.* Bloomington, IN: Xlibris, 2012.
Sim, David C. "Jews, Gentiles, and Ethnic Identity in Matthew." In *Christians Shaping Identity from the Roman Empire to Byzantium*, edited by Geoffrey Dunn and Wendy Mayer. Leiden: Brill, 2015.
Simba, Malik. *Black Marxism and American Constitutionalism.* Dubuque, IA: Kendall Hunt Publishing Co., 2016.
Skinner, Tom. *How Black Is the Gospel?* New York: J. B. Lippincott, 1970.
Snowden, Frank M. *Blacks in Antiquity; Ethiopians in the Greco-Roman Experience.* Cambridge, MA: Belknap Press of Harvard University Press, 1970.
———. *Before Color Prejudice: The Ancient View of Blacks.* Cambridge, MA: Harvard University Press, 1983.
Stenger, Victor J. *God: The Failed Hypothesis: How Science Shows That God Does Not Exist.* Amherst, NY: Prometheus Books, 2008.
Stone, Howard W., and James O. Duke. *How to Think Theologically.* Minneapolis: Fortress Press, 1996.
Strauss, David Friedrich. *The Life of Jesus, Critically Examined.* Philadelphia: Fortress Press, 1973.
Swain, Carol M. *The New White Nationalism in America: Its Challenge to Integration.* New York: Cambridge University Press, 2002.
Taiwo, Olufemi. "Exorcising Hegel's Ghost: Africa's Challenge to Philosophy." *African Studies Quarterly* 1, no. 4 (1998): 3–16.
Temme, Jon M. "Jesus as Trailblazer: The Christology of Martin Luther King, Jr." *The Journal of Religious Thought* 42, no. 1 (April 1985): 75–80.

Terreblanche, Sampie. *Western Empires, Christianity and the Inequalities between the West and the Rest 1500–2010*. Johannesburg: Penguin Books, 2014.
Thomas, Rhondda Robinson. *Claiming Exodus: A Cultural History of Afro-Atlantic Identity, 1774–1903*. Waco, TX: Baylor University Press, 2012.
Thompson, Lloyd A. "Rome and Race." The University Lectures, 1981, University of Ibadan. Ibadan: University of Ibadan, 1987.
———. *Romans and Blacks*. New York: Routledge, 2015.
Thompson, Thomas L. *The Messiah Myth: The Near Eastern Roots of Jesus and David*. New York: Basic Books, 2009.
Thurman, Howard. "The Significance of Jesus I: Jesus the Man of Insight." Edited by Howard Thurman and Walter E. Fluker. September 12, 1937. The Papers of Howard Washington Thurman. Columbia: University of South Carolina Press, 2009.
———. "Review of J. Deotis Roberts's *Liberation and Reconciliation: A Black Theology*." *Religious Education* 66, no. 6 (1971): 464–66.
———. *With Head and Heart*. New York: Harcourt Brace & Company, 1979.
———. *Jesus and the Disinherited*. Boston: Beacon Press, 1996.
Tibebu, Teshale. *Hegel and the Third World: The Making of Eurocentrism in World History*. Syracuse, NY: Syracuse University Press, 2011.
Tillich, Paul. *Biblical Religion and the Search for Ultimate Reality*. Chicago: University of Chicago Press, 1955.
Timbie, Janet A. "Coptic Christianity." In *The Blackwell Companion to Eastern Christianity*, edited by Ken Parry, 94–116. Malden, MA: Wiley-Blackwell, 2010.
Trebilco, Paul. *The Early Christians in Ephesus from Paul to Ignatius*. Grand Rapids, MI: Wm. B. Eerdmans Publishing, 2007.
Tuckett, Christopher Mark. *Christology and the New Testament: Jesus and His Earliest Followers*. Louisville, KY: Westminster John Knox Press, 2001.
Turner, Henry McNeal. "God Is a Negro (1898)." In *Respect Black: The Writings and Speeches of Henry McNeal Turner*, edited by S. Edwin Redkey, 176–77. New York: Arno Press/New York Times, 1971.
Vermes, Geza. *Jesus the Jew: A Historian's Reading of the Gospels*. Minneapolis: Fortress Press, 1981.
———. *The Resurrection: History and Myth*. New York: Doubleday, 2008.
———. *Christian Beginnings: From Nazareth to Nicaea*. New Haven, CT: Yale University Press, 2014.
Vinzent, Markus. *Marcion and the Dating of the Synoptic Gospels*. Walpole: Peeters, 2014.
Wachal, Robert S. "The Capitalization of Black and Native American." *American Speech* 75, no. 4 (2000): 364–65.
Walker, Aswad. "Princes Shall Come Out of Egypt: A Theological Comparison of Marcus Garvey and Reverend Albert B. Cleage Jr." *Journal of Black Studies* 39, no. 2 (November 2008): 194–251.
Ware, Frederick L. *Methodologies of Black Theology*. Eugene, OR: Wipf and Stock, 2012.
Warnock, Raphael G. *The Divided Mind of the Black Church: Theology, Piety, and Public Witness*. New York: NYU Press, 2014.
Washington, Joseph R., Jr. *The Politics of God*. Boston: Beacon Press, 1969.
Wells, George Albert. *Did Jesus Exist?* Amherst, NY: Prometheus Books, 1992.
West, Justin C. "Mysticism and Liberation: An Exploration into the Relationship between Howard Thurman's Spirituality and Black Theology." *Black Theology* 11, no. 1 (2013): 31–57.
Wet, Chris L. de. *Preaching Bondage: John Chrysostom and the Discourse of Slavery in Early Christianity*. Oakland: University of California Press, 2015.
White, L. Michael. *From Jesus to Christianity*. San Francisco: Harper, 2004.
———. *Scripting Jesus: The Gospels in Rewrite*. New York: HarperOne, 2010.
Williams, Eric C. *Capitalism and Slavery*. Chapel Hill: University of North Carolina Press, 1994.
Williams, Preston N. "James Cone and the Problem of a Black Ethic." *Harvard Theological Review* 65, no. 4 (October 1972): 487–88.

Williams, Robert C. "(Review) Amos Jones Jr. *Paul's Message of Freedom: What Does It Mean to the Black Church?*" *Horizons* 12, no. 2 (1985): 376.

Wilmore, Gayraud S. "The Case for a New Black Church Style." In *The Black Church in America*, edited by H. M. Nelsen and R. Yokley, 323–35. New York: Basic Books, 1971.

———. "Black Messiah: Revising the Color Symbolism of Western Christology." *Journal of the Interdenominational Theological Center* 2, no. 1 (1974): 8–18.

———. "Black Power, Black People, Theological Renewal." In *Black Theology*, edited by James H. Cone and Gayraud Wilmore, 125–40. Ossining, NY: Orbis Books, 1993.

Wilson, Frank T. "Critical Evaluation of the Theme—The Black Revolution: Is There a Black Theology?" *The Journal of Religious Thought* 26, no. 2 (1969): 5–9.

Wilson, Robert Smith. *Marcion*. New York: AMS Press, 1980.

Wimbush, Vincent L. *The Bible and African Americans: A Brief History*. Minneapolis: Fortress Press, 2003.

Witvliet, Theo. *The Way of the Black Messiah*. Oak Park, IL: Meyer Stone & Co., 1987.

Wright, Jeremiah A., Jr. *A Sankofa Moment*. Dallas: St. Paul Press, 2010.

Wright, Jeremiah A., Jr., and Colleen Birchett. *Africans Who Shaped Our Faith*. Chicago: Urban Ministries Inc., 1995.

Wright, Leon Edward. "'Black Theology' or Black Experience?" *The Journal of Religious Thought* 26, no. 2 (1969): 46–56.

———. "Paul Revisited: From Cult to Cosmos." *The Journal of Religious Thought* 32, no. 1 (1975): 110–22.

Wright, N. T. *Who Was Jesus?* Grand Rapids, MI: William B. Eerdmans Publishing Co., 2001.

Wuthnow, Robert. *America and the Challenges of Religious Diversity*. Princeton, NJ: Princeton University Press, 2007.

Yamauchi, Edwin M. *Africa and Africans in Antiquity*. East Lansing: Michigan State University Press, 2001.

Yancy, George, ed. *Christology and Whiteness: What Would Jesus Do?* New York: Routledge, 2012.

Young, Josiah U. "Who Belongs to Christ?" In *Christology and Whiteness*, edited by George Yancy, 128–35. New York: Routledge, 2012.

Zambrana, Rocío. "Hegel, History, and Race." In *The Oxford Handbook of Philosophy and Race*, edited by Naomi Zack, 251–60. New York: Oxford University Press, 2017.

Index

Altizer, Thomas, 171, 172
Anderson, Victor, 139–140
Ashanin, Charles B., 35, 54n20

Baker, Thomas Nelson, 162, 187n17
Banner, William A., 8n13, 35, 54n17, 54n20
Bible, 62, 71–72, 74, 80n32–80n33, 94, 97, 97–98, 101, 102, 108, 113n50, 114n58, 114n60, 125, 130, 131, 149n41, 150n54, 150n58, 151n64, 177, 189n51, 190n64, 190n68; and Marcion of Sinope, 18, 25n29; Book of John, 16, 89; Corinthians, 140; Galatians, 68, 79n16, 140, 151n70; justification of oppression (particularly slavery), 13, 14, 51, 88; and Luke, 90, 140, 145n4; and Matthew, 71, 114n63–114n64, 145n4, 150n56, 150n61; New Testament, 15, 16, 17, 23n1, 25n20, 25n27–25n29; Old Testament, 4, 16, 17, 18, 19, 97, 98, 99, 100, 103, 107, 130; and Paul, 18, 68, 79n16, 79n18, 90, 102, 106, 130, 134, 140, 151n68, 190n69; secular re-evaluation, 6; the Gospels, 12, 16–17, 24n11, 25n27, 72, 108, 149n50, 150n52, 150n54–150n55, 150n57–150n58, 177, 189n43, 189n48, 189n58, 190n64
Black Christology, 1, 2, 3, 5, 6, 9–10, 10, 11, 12, 12–13, 14, 15, 18, 20, 22, 23, 70, 71, 75, 84, 87, 89, 91, 92, 94, 109, 112n18, 115, 116, 117–118, 119, 126, 127, 127–128, 129, 131, 132, 134, 136, 136–137, 137–138, 141, 142, 143, 144, 145, 145n5, 173, 177, 181, 185, 186; and authentic Jesus, 10
Black Liberation Theology, 1, 2, 7n3, 8n7, 14, 23, 57n50, 173

Black nationalism, 29, 52, 79n11, 89
Black Theology, 1, 2, 3, 6, 11, 12, 14, 18, 23, 23n2, 27–28, 59; and Black Power, 65, 79n11, 166; definition of, 31, 38, 65; in contrast to white theology, 11, 14, 29, 30, 32–33, 34, 36
Blackness, 37–38, 41, 43, 44, 45, 46; as theological concept, 10, 35
Bowen, J. W. E., 169
Bruce, F. F., 132, 149n48
Brunner, Emil, 91, 112n32, 112n35
Bultmann, Rudolf, 90–91, 112n33, 113n51–113n52

Cannon, Katie, 8n13, 125
Chabot, Sean, 30, 53n7
Camacho, Daniel José, 1, 7n2
Christianity, 9–10, 11, 11–12, 13, 14; and Africa, 111n9, 113n40, 123; and Roman imperialism, 72; as Racist Theology, 3, 42, 43, 44; and slavery, 3, 43, 65, 68, 117, 121, 123, 124–125, 125, 126, 130, 134, 140, 143, 144; historical formation of, 12, 129; in contrast to religion of Jesus, 21–22, 66; key Presumptions of, 5; and notion of Christologies, 116, 119, 120, 123, 126, 135, 143
Christology, 9; and Whiteness, 6, 11, 24n6, 29, 32–33, 34, 37, 38, 41, 42; and George Yancy, 33
Cleage, Albert, 53n2, 80n36, 84, 85, 86, 90, 92, 96, 97, 97–98, 98, 99, 99–100, 100, 100–101; and Black messiah-concept, 84, 87, 92, 93, 96, 97
Cone, James H., 1, 7n2, 12, 38, 45; and concept of ultimate reality, 44, 46, 46–49, 51–52, 60, 66, 88, 162; and Blackness, 24n14, 45

Index

Copeland, M. Shawn, 126, 141, 148n32, 151n73
Cox, Oliver C., 125, 148n27, 148n31

Davies, Everett F. S., 35, 54n20, 56n34
Douglass, Frederick, 43, 57n45, 73, 165, 180, 188n25–188n27; on authentic vs. inauthentic Christianity, 11, 14, 20, 22, 28, 33, 35
Du Bois, W. E. B., 39

Echols, Alice, 37, 55n27
Eichelberger, William L., 11, 11–12, 24n6, 112n25, 129, 129–130, 134, 135, 142
Ehrman, Bart, 25n20, 80n33, 122, 146n8, 147n22, 150n56

false universality, 60–61
Farmer, Sr., James Leonard, 64, 66, 70
Ferguson, Stephen C., vii, 7n4, 111n15

Gallagher, Buell, 34, 54n18
Gomes, Peter, 72, 74, 80n27, 104, 114n63, 151n64, 151n68, 189n42

Hagerty, Barbara Bradley, 1, 7n3
Harding, Vincent, 30, 53n2, 53n4, 53n8, 57n54, 79n11–79n12
Hart, William David, 133, 150n52
Hill, Charles Leander, 139, 141–142
Homolka, Walter, 121, 125, 147n17, 150n55

Jackson, John G., 133, 150n51
Jesus, 9; and Jewish identity, 18, 19, 22, 71, 85, 102, 105; as Black Messiah, 86, 94, 104, 107, 108; as historical person, 145, 174; death and resurrection of, 89, 90, 93, 107
Johnson, Jr., Joseph A., 10, 23n2, 24n7, 24n18, 29, 30, 32, 53n1, 53n6, 54n12, 66, 112n25, 117, 125, 146n7, 148n37
Jones, Major J., 10, 14, 23n1, 24n4, 24n17, 145, 153, 173, 186, 187n1, 187n2, 187n7; on Black God-concept, 161, 163
Jones, William R., 8n7, 24n13, 53n1, 164, 188n23

The Journal of Religious Thought, 35, 39, 53n9, 54n18, 54n20, 55n21, 55n22, 56n30

Kelsey, George D., 8n13, 31, 35, 36, 53n10, 55n25, 90, 136, 156, 157, 187n9
King, Martin Luther, Jr., 2, 39, 136, 137, 151n64, 187n1

Lee, Carleton L., 170
Lüdemann, Gerd, 80n33, 90, 91, 93, 112n29, 112n34

Marcion, 18
Mays, Benjamin, 29, 53n10, 62, 78n2, 117–137
McIntyre, Monie, 124
McKinney, Richard I., 31, 35, 52, 53n10, 59, 62, 135; and universality of Christianity, 61, 62, 72, 76; critique of "Black theology," 31, 52, 60, 73, 110, 135
monotheism, 19, 46–47
Morrison, Roy D., 53n1, 146n13, 178, 186, 189n63, 190n77

Nelson, William Stuart, 54n17, 55n21, 56n31, 56n34; and philosophy of non-violence, 39

Obama, Barack, 1, 7n1

Payne, Daniel, 38, 39, 56n30
philosophy of race, 2–3, 10, 14, 49
philosophy of religion, 9, 10, 23, 186; and African American experience, 4, 79n16, 151n70, 157; and faith, 167; and philosophical assessment of theological claims, 3, 169
Pinn, Anthony, 50, 57n52, 131, 134, 140, 149n46
Prater, Eugene G., 39, 56n30
presumptive context, 59, 117, 132

Ransom, Reverdy C., 92, 112n36
Roberts, J. Deotis, 36, 60
Robinson, John A. T., 46, 57n47

Sim, David C., 105
suffering, 50–51, 86, 107, 108, 109, 134; oppression and exploitation, 88, 124, 125, 127, 128, 144; redemptive, 14, 86–87, 89

theism, 18, 57n50, 166
Temme, Jon M., 137–138
Thomas, Linda, 1
Thompson, Thomas L., 108, 114n73
Thurman, Howard, 12, 15, 16, 24n11, 30, 31, 42, 64, 66, 102; on difference between Christianity and the religion of Jesus, 21–22, 66; on Jesus' racial identity, 22, 23, 64, 84, 90, 93, 110; *Jesus and the Disinherited* (1949), 24n11, 25n23, 30, 53n7
Turner, Henry M., 110n3, 154

Walker, David, 38, 39

Washington, Joseph, 4, 8n10
Williams, Eric, 124
Williams, Preston N., 51, 57n53
Williams, Robert C., 68
Wilmore, Gayraud, 24n12, 41, 53n2, 57n54, 86, 119, 135
Wilson, Frank T., 28, 31, 40, 42, 53n3, 53n10, 55n22, 57n42
Woodbey, George Washington, 92, 112n37
Wright, Jeremiah, 1, 7n1
Wright, Leon E., 31, 41, 42, 46, 53n10, 76, 77

Yancy, George, 33, 54n13–54n15, 57n39, 57n52, 111n11–111n12, 115, 145n1
Young, Josiah U., 130, 140, 149n45, 151n70

About the Author

Dr. John H. McClendon III is professor in the Department of Philosophy at Michigan State University. His areas of interests include African American philosophers and philosophical traditions; African philosophy, Marxism, philosophy of sports, and the African American experience; and philosophy of religion and African Americans. He is the author of the following books: *African American Philosophers and Philosophy: An Introduction to the History, Concepts and Contemporary Issues* (2019, coauthored with Dr. Stephen C. Ferguson II); *Philosophy of Religion and the African American Experience: Conversations with My Christian Friends* (2017); *Beyond the White Shadow: Philosophy, Sports, and the African American Experience* (2012, coauthored with Dr. Stephen C. Ferguson II); and *C. L. R. James's Notes on Dialectics: Left-Hegelianism or Marxism-Leninism* (2005).

www.ingramcontent.com/pod-product-compliance
Lightning Source LLC
Chambersburg PA
CBHW050905300426
44111CB00010B/1383